COOKING FOR LIFE

D0095798

COOKING FOR LIFE

❖ ❖

Ayurvedic Recipes

for

Good Food and Good Health

LINDA BANCHEK

Harmony Books

New York

Published by Harmony Books, a division of Crown Publishers, Inc., 201 East 50th Street, New York, New York 10022. Member of the Crown Publishing Group.

Random House, Inc. New York, Toronto, London, Sydney, Auckland

Originally published by Orchids and Herbs Press in 1989 as *The Ayurveda Cookbook: Cooking for Life*.

HARMONY and colophon are trademarks of Crown Publishers, Inc.

Manufactured in the United States of America

Book design by Debbie Glasserman

Library of Congress Cataloging-in-Publication Data
Banchek, Linda.
[Ayurveda cookbook]
Cooking for life: Ayurvedic recipes for good food and good health/Linda Banchek;
—American ed.
"Originally published as
The Ayurveda cookbook: cooking for life, © 1989"
1. Vegetarianism.   2. Vegetarian cookery.   3. Medicine, Ayurvedic.
I. Title.
RM236.B33   1992
641.5'636—dc20   91-33337
CIP

ISBN 0-517-88011-3

10 9 8 7 6 5 4 3 2 1

First Harmony Book Edition

CONTENTS

This timeless "science of life" offers more than good cooking and good food. It brings practical knowledge to today's cooks and everyone who enjoys eating and living well. This chapter updates Ayurveda for contemporary health-conscious Americans who either follow a vegetarian diet or simply want to maintain good health, and shows how you can be the best cook, an Ayurvedic cook, including ideas for setting up your own Ayurvedic kitchen: proper food preparation, storage, utensils, and equipment. Discover your own body type and what it means for you.

✦❖✦

What are Vata, Pitta, and Kapha and how do you cook for people with different dietary needs? Menu planning and cooking tips, ingredients charts, and other information are presented, including sample dinner menus with recipes and a set of main meal recipes especially good for each of the different constitutions.

This chapter presents some universal Ayurvedic cooking principles and useful information about foods good for everyone to eat.

Ayurvedic menu planning offers variety and balance, reflects the seasons, and relies especially on common sense in food selection. In this chapter you'll learn how to design your own recipes using foods that naturally combine well together, how to plan well-balanced, delicious meals, and more.

Suggestions for entertaining with an international flavor and sample menus guide you in planning your own festivities. The menus and recipes include elaborate dishes in the Indian style of cooking, a springtime menu from the French cuisine, a northern Italian dinner, and an American picnic.

This chapter helps you follow a sensible diet, not fads, to lose weight, offers general suggestions for light meals, and gives an eating program with nourishing recipes for new mothers.

✦❖✦

❖❖

Appendixes 275

Glossary 295

Acknowledgments 297

Index 299

❖❖

FOREWORD

By Richard Averbach, M.D.,
and Stuart Rothenberg, M.D.

This cookbook is unique in its field. In addition to providing delicious recipes, it introduces a new body of knowledge about nutrition, knowledge that is among the most time-tested on earth. Its insights into nutrition are based on Ayurveda, the world's most comprehensive tradition of natural medicine.

Ayurveda means "the science of life." Recognized by the World Health Organization, it even today serves as the primary health-care system for the majority of the populations of India and surrounding nations.

When and how did Ayurveda begin? Historians are uncertain, but within the Ayurvedic tradition itself it is held that there was never a time in human history when Ayurveda did not exist. The Ayurvedic textbooks say that the knowledge of Ayurveda is timeless and eternal, inherent in the structure of Nature, designed to point mankind in the direction of living life more in accord with natural law.

Yet due to the long passage of time, especially during recent centuries when India was under foreign domination, much of the fundamental knowledge of Ayurveda became distorted or even lost. Perhaps it is for this reason that Ayurveda has not been well known in the West until recent years. During the past several decades, however, a remarkable resurgence of this knowledge has taken place. Most notably, a comprehensive restoration of Ayurvedic knowledge, in keeping with the ancient classical texts, has taken place under the inspiration of Maharishi Mahesh Yogi, founder of the Transcendental Meditation program, working with leading Ayurvedic experts and scholars. This modern reformulation of Ayurveda, authentic and at the same time compatible with modern medical care, is called Maharishi Ayur-Ved.

Today, worldwide interest in Maharishi Ayur-Ved is growing both within the medical profession and among the general population. This is because Ayurveda offers potential solutions to some of the most problematic issues that face modern health care. Thousands of physicians in the U.S. and Europe have already received training in Maharishi Ayur-Ved and are incorporating its approaches into their practices. In the U.S., tens of thousands of patients have received Ayurvedic medical treatment. Major research findings have been reported, and research continues to be done, under the auspices of such leading institutions as the National Institutes of Health, Massachusetts Institute of Technology, and the Stanford Research Institute. In addition, Maharishi Ayur-Ved has received the focused attention of the news media, with hundreds of items appearing in leading newspapers and on television and radio. Several best-selling books on Maharishi Ayur-Ved have also appeared in recent years.

The most striking contribution that Maharishi Ayur-Ved offers to our modern knowledge of health is its unique perspective on the human body. Our current scientific perspective—the "modern medical model"—looks at the body as a collection of various material parts. These include our cells, tissues, and organs such as the heart, kidney, liver, and brain. But Ayurveda points out that underlying and orchestrating this physical structure of the body is a much more fundamental level of nature that we can call "intelligence." By intelligence, Ayurveda does not mean intellectual aptitude such as is measured by intelligence tests, but the basic fabric of Nature's functioning that guides, directs, and controls all of the myriad biological functions going on at any given moment in each of the more than 50 trillion cells comprising the human physiology. Ayurveda holds that the intelligence that governs our bodies—called "biological intelligence"—is the same intelligence that orchestrates the universe.

Perhaps a very simple analogy will make this concept of biological intelligence clearer. Consider a rose in your garden. The rose has many aspects—the tender and colorful petals, the hard stem, the sharp thorn, and so on—but underlying all of these diverse values of the rose is one unified level, which we call the sap, without which the rose would cease to exist. Cut the rose, and separate it from its source, and shortly it dies; if the rose is ailing, it is through this basic level of the sap that the knowledgeable gardener tries to nourish each and every aspect of the rose. In this same way, Ayurveda aims its strategies of prevention and treatment at the most basic level of human functioning —that of biological intelligence—focusing its attention on strengthening and balancing the physiology from within.

Viewing the human body from this new angle, we can never again see it in the same way. Taking the human body out of the perspective of being a solid, particulate, static, fragmented "frozen sculpture"— outside of or separated from Nature—this new framework instead sees the body as part of the continuum of Nature. Rather than being a sophisticated machine, the body is actually a continually self-regenerating, dynamic field of intelligence and energy, in constant interchange with the rest of the universe. While we have been brought up to think of our bodies as composites of matter that have somehow learned to think, Ayurveda wakes us up to the deeper reality that the human physiology is actually, at its basis, intelligence that has learned to express itself through matter.

Surprisingly, this view of the human body derived from Ayurveda is very much in keeping with today's leading edge of scientific thought. Modern physics, in its quantum field theories, tells us that matter is, in fact, nothing other than energy. Ultimately matter is simply the expression of various "modes of vibration" of abstract, nonmaterial quantum fields. Ayurveda agrees that matter derives from nonmaterial fields of energy; it further describes these fields as expressions of one underlying field of intelligence. Many leading physicists now feel that there is one basic "unified field" of intelligence at the foundation of all forms and phenomena in Nature. This most advanced level of human knowledge is very much in harmony with the ancient Ayurvedic view of the human body—even more so than the "material medical model" we have become accustomed to.

What does all this have to do with food and with the delightful sensory experience of cooking and eating? Quite a lot, actually—because, through the view of Ayurveda, food, like the body, is basically composed of patterns of intelligence. Eating, aside from being one of our most enjoyable experiences, is also one of the most intimate interactions we have with our environment, with nature itself. Through eating we extract from Nature the intelligence that is contained in food, and use this intelligence to maintain and build our bodies.

❖❖

According to Ayurveda, what is most important in eating is that the patterns of intelligence in the food and those in the body should *match*. If they do, the food will be most nourishing to the body—most supportive and balancing.

This brings us to one of the greatest insights and most fascinating areas dealt with in Ayurveda—our unique biologic individuality. Each of us has his or her own particular makeup, own psychophysiological or mind-body constitution. For short, we can call this our unique "body type." Everyone is an individual, with a distinct appearance and personality, and individual tastes and preferences. This biologic individuality includes not just different tastes, but different requirements for foods. For some people, certain foods will be in harmony with their body type and thereby promote balance—while for other people those same foods may be inconsistent with their body type and thereby create imbalance.

The body type is the sum total of all the patterns of intelligence that structure the body. But how do we understand what is a "pattern of intelligence"? To answer this, Ayurveda uses a framework and vocabulary that is new to modern science but that is in no way inconsistent with it. In fact, the Ayurvedic conception enriches and supports our modern knowledge of nutrition.

Ayurveda describes all the various patterns of intelligence in the human body in terms of the combinations of three basic modes of intelligence, or fundamental qualities, which it calls the three "doshas." The three doshas are a major theme and keystone of this book's approach to food and eating, so it will be worthwhile knowing something about them before proceeding into the material in the book.

Ayurveda describes the doshas as metabolic or mind-body fundamental qualities that regulate and govern the flow of biological intelligence in the body. The doshas straddle the gap between intelligence and matter, between consciousness and physiology. When the doshas are balanced, the whole mind-body system functions normally. There is maximum vitality, energy, and stability, as well as good immunity and resistance to disease. The goal of eating is to create balance of the doshas—which means to create balance throughout the mind-body system.

The three doshas are called Vata, Pitta, and Kapha. Because they have no precise English equivalents, it is easiest to use the original Sanskrit names for the doshas. But we can get a handle on what the doshas represent by looking at how Ayurveda describes their qualities and functions.

Our bodies are in a continuum with Nature, and so the doshas reflect properties of nature within us. In the body, Vata dosha represents and controls all movement. It has qualities similar to moving air. Vata is light, quick, mobile, rough, dry, and cold.

Pitta dosha controls digestion and metabolism. Pitta has qualities that resemble fire; it is hot, sharp, acidic, and slightly oily.

Kapha dosha governs the physical structure of the body, and also fluid balance. In quality, Kapha is said to resemble water and earth, being heavy, stable, slow, oily, and cold.

It is important to realize that any living organism must have all three doshas in order to maintain life. In our body, we must have Vata to maintain physiological movement such as normal respiration, passage of food through the digestive tract, movement of electrical and chemical impulses through our nervous system, and so on. At the same time, Pitta must be present to govern and regulate all of our metabolic processes, including absorption of nutrients throughout the digestive tract, and all of the sophisticated and enzymatic processes that carefully maintain homeostasis. Kapha must also be present, because Kapha maintains the solidity and integration of the physical structure, which would otherwise break down under the influence of the physical forces that our body faces each day, including the activities of the other two doshas.

When a doctor trained in Ayurveda looks at you, he or she sees signs of the three doshas everywhere. He cannot see the doshas themselves —they are invisible—but the signs of their activity are everywhere present. We have called them metabolic principles because they govern all of the physical processes in the body, without being quite physical themselves. Yet, the doshas are concrete enough to be influenced, increased or decreased, balanced or imbalanced, by the numerous activities, foods, thoughts, and emotions that we experience throughout the day. When an Ayurvedic doctor wants to reestablish balance on the level of the intelligence of your physiology, his first focus is to recreate balance on the level of Vata, Pitta, and Kapha.

The way you approach any aspect of your health depends a lot on how you see the situation in the first place. Up until now, you haven't considered diet in terms of balance or imbalance of Vata, Pitta, or Kapha. But now, with this new shift of emphasis, you can add a new level of knowledge that, when integrated with the modern principles of basic nutrition, can nourish and balance your system in a more fundamental way.

To use this book most effectively, you need to have some idea of your Ayurvedic body type. There are ten classical Ayurvedic body types, representing different possible combinations of the three doshas. To discover your own body type, see the Body-Type Quiz on pages 4–8.

We've said that the key to balanced eating according to Ayurveda is that the food should be supportive of your body type. The advantage of the framework of Vata, Pitta, and Kapha is that it allows us to understand the influence of every food we eat (and, in fact, every influence that we face in daily life) on the functioning of the physiology. By saying that a food has the influence of increasing Vata, for example, Ayurveda is describing the particular qualities of intelligence inherent in that food. Its approach matches the qualities of the intelligence of the food (by knowing their influence on the doshas) with the unique qualities of intelligence contained in the individual physiology (by knowing the body type), as the basis for determining the best diet for promoting and maintaining health.

Knowing that food has an intelligence value and that different foods have different qualities of intelligence doesn't mean that eating should become an intellectual headache. On the contrary, Ayurveda points us in the opposite direction—encouraging us to put our attention on the natural cues coming from the food and from within our own bodies. The knowledge of the doshas is designed to help us get more in touch with our own inner impulses for balance, and to match those impulses with the foods that will satisfy the body's needs.

How does this happen? Ayurveda says that one of the most important ways we have of interpreting the intelligence value of food is through its taste. This becomes clearer when we look at how animals in nature select food. Animals in the wild, given ample food resources, do not suffer from nutritional deficiencies and do not become obese. (The only animals who are known to become obese are domesticated pets.) How do animals select a balanced diet? They do so through sensory cues from the food, especially through taste and smell (these two are related) and other physical qualities such as dryness, oiliness, etc. Certainly animals in the wild do not eat according to intellectual conceptions such as "recommended daily allowances," yet they eat so as to create balance. Apparently nature mediates all their nutritional requirements (including "recommended daily allowances" of nutrients) through natural cues such as taste, smell, and other sensory qualities.

As physicians, we have found it noteworthy that in spite of extensive research in various areas of nutritional science, little attention has been given to the role that sensory cues such as taste may play in determining the nutritional qualities of diet. However, traditional Ayurveda holds that when our taste buds greet a bite of food, a wealth of information is conveyed to the doshas. Our taste buds are actually exquisitely sensitive detectors of the qualities contained in every food. For example, recent research on taste receptors in the tongue has shown that if we take something with a bitter taste and dilute it, our taste buds can still detect bitterness in a dilution of one part in two million. This remarkable precision and sensitivity of our sense of taste conveys to our mind-body system much of the knowledge it needs to maintain proper nutrition.

In all, Ayurveda describes six tastes: sweet, sour, salty, and bitter—the four which we are used to thinking of—along with two others, pungent and astringent. Pungent is the taste of any hot spice such as ginger or chili peppers, while the astringent taste is associated with the mealy and somewhat dry quality found in fruits such as pomegranates or in kidney beans. Ayurveda explains that because the six tastes reflect the basic composite intelligence value of food, for a diet to be fully balanced, it must contain a sampling of each of the six tastes. In this book, you will find that beginning to use all six tastes in cooking and structuring a balanced diet will not only be enjoyable, but will add zest and fulfillment to your eating experience.

Beyond the content of the food itself, there is one final area that Ayurveda considers to be crucial to nutrition—digestion. Ayurveda points out that proper digestion is one of the pillars of perfect health; poor digestion is considered a major factor in the production of imbalances and disease. To realize why, remember that every cell in your body is being re-created each day from the foods you are eating. It is only if the food is being used well, through proper digestion, that cells will be built well and the body will gain maximum nourishment. On the other hand, Ayurveda points out that if the food is used poorly, then imbalances are created and the disease process has already begun. For this reason, you will find that *Cooking for Life* offers not only recipes for preparation of Ayurvedically balanced and nutritious meals, but also advice on how to maintain and strengthen digestion so the physiology can fully utilize all of the nutrients and intelligence contained in the food.

Through Maharishi Ayur-Ved and this book, Linda Banchek offers to you the reader an opportunity for an exciting new adventure—an adventure in which we hope eating can become not only a more stimulating and satisfying experience, but also a pathway to perfect health.

PREFACE

Someone once said that irony is the point at which opposites meet and become one. Sometimes in researching and testing the food for this book, irony became so tangible as to appear as a separate ingredient in a recipe that reads: "Take a pinch or more of irony and sauté until transparent." The experience has given me insight into what it means for East to meet West. It was especially apparent during one research session when Dr. H. S. Kasture, a renowned Ayurvedic physician and professor (with mostly Indian food preferences), sat in a room on the plains of the American Midwest, and using a most ancient system of food analysis, gave a rating to something that never appeared in the Vedic literature—a scrumptious, typically American chocolate custard pie.

On that day, after Dr. Kasture and two members of the Ayurveda research team had spent the morning intensely tasting and rating herbal teas, spices, and various fruits (after that much use, the taste buds usually lie back and refuse to register even one more sensation), and just as we were ready to quit, our cooks and research assistants arrived with the noontime meal for more tasting and evaluation. On the menu: an Italian dinner, an American picnic, and some favorite desserts, including the wonderful chocolate pie. Everything looked and smelled so good that without hesitation we all began evaluating again with gusto!

That is how the research for this book was conducted. The cooks gave Dr. Kasture and his colleague, Dr. Subhedar, servings of prepared foods and raw ingredients as well, and our Ayurveda experts would declare the specific qualities and effects these have on particular constitutions. They then recommended special considerations and menu alterations. In moments of doubt they consulted the appropriate Vedic texts, primarily the *Charaka Samhita.*

Sometimes they were asked to rate such things unfamiliar to Indian tastes as parsley, French tarragon, thyme, or sage. When these were presented, the doctors' contemporary talents appeared. After a few rapid exchanges in Hindi and an occasional reference to a Sanskrit text, they would declare the qualities, tastes, and effects of each herb. I recorded this unusual application of the science of Ayurveda in an analysis of hundreds of ingredients and some popular recipes found in the contemporary Western vegetarian diet. And that is what has been collected in this book. Understanding the effects of food qualities, their tastes and properties, is to some degree a subjective science, and many new ingredients that have appeared in the last several thousand years were not around to be included in the ancient texts. Much of the information about food and culinary recommendations in *Cooking for Life* is the result of research I conducted with Drs. Kasture and Subhedar. They based their judgments on the work by Maharishi Mahesh Yogi, founder of the Transcendental Meditation Technique, who over the past ten years has reformulated Ayurveda in accord with classical ancient texts and has taken Ayurveda from a science that had come to be practiced over time in an incomplete form to a complete body of knowledge useful for us nowadays.

In this precise reformulation, Maharishi was aided by the most re-spected Ayurvedic physicians of India, whom he personally selected as the most authoritative custodians of Ayurvedic knowledge. These phy-sicians include Dr. Brihaspati Dev Triguna, former president of the All-India Ayurveda Congress and the world's foremost expert on pulse diagnosis; Dr. Balaraj Maharishi, the foremost expert on medicinal plants; and Dr. V. M. Dwivedi, the foremost expert on *rasayanas,* preparations for promoting longevity. Drs. Kasture and Subhedar are both students of Dr. Dwivedi.

The sources for this reformulation are the six encyclopedic Sanskrit texts of Ayurveda, other minor Ayurvedic treatises, and the oral tradi-tion of knowledge passed down through the ages from master to student. Under Maharishi's guidance, Drs. Triguna, Balaraj, and Dwivedi were able to integrate this extensive knowledge, including the many diverse chapters on nutrition and cooking, into a science of life that is simple and practical for any individual in any culture. Because this was authenticated Ayurveda was found to be complete and had restored the purity of the classical Vedic sciences, these physicians called it *Maharishi Ayur-Ved.*

Although food and cooking are important parts of Ayurveda, they constitute only one of the twenty approaches of Maharishi Ayur-Ved. These twenty approaches are described in Appendix 1.

This cookbook is going to be different from any other cookbook you've used. Oh, the foods, cooking styles, and recipes will seem familiar. Apple pie is, after all, apple pie. What makes this cookbook unique? When you use these timeless Ayurvedic principles described here you will know just what effect your cooking is having on those who eat . . . not in so many calories, grams of protein, and other intangibles, because each of us accumulates fat, burns calories, and digests protein in our own personal way. Instead, *Cooking for Life,* tells clearly and simply what you can expect when you eat, where you eat, depending on how and what you eat. That means when you serve your best apple pie to those you love, you'll know what it's really doing to nourish each of them. That's part of what Ayurvedic cooking is about.

The goal of Ayurveda as a health science is the development of extreme longevity and higher states of consciousness, a state in life known as enlightenment. Enlightenment is a normal human state in which a person lives his or her full potential in this state. In this state, the person feels mentally calm and alert, able to act most creatively and thus fully appreciate and experience life.

Ayurveda places great importance on making the most of our food and the way it is prepared because the quality of the diet plays an important role in the refined functioning of a person's mind and body. Such refinement is the basis for enlightenment.

This cookbook discusses the influences food has on us in two ways: according to how the taste and qualities of the ingredients affect the three *doshas* or metabolic principles, and also the three *gunas* in Sanskrit known as *sattva, rajas,* and *tamas.* The gunas describe the influence of food and other factors on the mind. Sattvic foods are pure or essentially superior and good for everyone to eat. Those foods that activate the mind and body are rajasic. But tamasic foods create inertia and make the mind dull and lethargic. The recipes in the book do not include or encourage the use of tamasic ingredients such as wine, meat, seafood, onions, garlic, mushrooms, eggs, or peanuts. The Ayurvedic texts describe the effects of these tamasic foods. Some of them may even have medicinal value. But as the title indicates, *Cooking for Life* emphasizes using the best and freshest ingredients that promote a full and healthy life. So, ingredients that do not nourish us to a robust, long life are not included in the recipes.

Finally, it is with sincere gratitude and a deep regard that I acknowledge my indebtness to Dr. Haridas Shridar Kasture and Dr. Pramod Dattatrya Subhedar, for putting into practice their firm belief that Ayurveda is a necessary part of modern life—Eastern and Western, and that the basic principles of this traditional science can be lived by everyone. And I would especially like to thank Maharishi Mahesh Yogi, who guides these and other leading Ayurvedic physicians to reformulate this uniquely essential knowledge of life, thus making it useful for us today.

COOKING FOR LIFE

❖✦❖

Chapter 1

ABOUT AYURVEDA, IN THE AYURVEDIC KITCHEN

About Ayurveda

USING TIMELESS KNOWLEDGE TODAY

Ayurveda (ah-yr-VAY-d-uh) is derived from the ancient Sanskrit: *ayu,* "life," and *veda,* "knowledge." As a science, Ayurveda includes all of life: the mind, the body, behavior, and the environment. Although it has been practiced in India for more than 5,000 years, Ayurvedic concepts are as practical for us today as in ages past. By following simple, time-tested Ayurvedic principles in cooking and eating, both good health and a comfortable sense of well-being naturally result.

AYURVEDIC FOOD

Ayurvedic food is not exotic or unusual—unless you want it to be. It simply consists of any delicious food, properly cooked, with full knowledge of its effects on the health and satisfaction of the eater. Even though Ayurveda has such a long Indian history that does not mean you should only eat Indian food to be healthy. For Americans who follow a vegetarian diet or are aiming in that direction, Ayurveda includes nearly all the kinds of foods we usually enjoy in our contemporary American vegetarian cuisine. Becoming an Ayurvedic cook might only be a matter of adjusting some of your favorite recipes by increasing or decreasing certain seasonings and other ingredients to suit your individual needs at particular times of the year. Ayurveda works well everywhere. No matter the country, the same basic principles of cooking for life apply.

❖✦❖

I

ENJOYMENT AND HEALTH

By following Ayurvedic principles when cooking and eating, you'll become more aware of subtle nuances in the tastes and textures of what you are eating. With more attention to these finer aspects of your food, you grow in enjoyment of the whole process of eating.

Good food
purifies the physiology,
gives strength and energy,
promotes health and clear thinking,
maintains life.

—THE UPANISHADS

When you begin following these time-tested Ayurvedic dietary practices the idea of grabbing a bite to eat somehow loses its appeal. Every meal becomes an occasion for celebration and enjoyment. The first principle of the science of life is *enjoyment*.

BALANCE AND THE DOSHAS

Recognizing the vital connection between a balanced diet and perfect health, Ayurveda provides a thorough understanding of nutrition useful for all constitutional types. Our bodies are made of the same elements found everywhere in nature: air and space, fire, water, and earth. According to Ayurveda, each person is naturally an identifiable constitutional type called VATA, PITTA, or KAPHA, or sometimes a combination of two or all three. Vata (pronounced VAHT-uh) is most like the movement of air and space, Pitta (PIT-uh) like the transforming energy of water and fire, and Kapha (KAHF-uh) has the structure of earth and water. These qualities or metabolic principles are called *doshas*. By maintaining balance of the three doshas, we enjoy good health. When a balance of Vata, Pitta, or Kapha is disturbed, illness results.

TO MAINTAIN BALANCE

The dietary key to maintaining good constitutional balance is to eat more of the foods that pacify a dominant dosha and less of foods that aggravate it. This does not mean eliminating all foods with the certain qualities or tastes that don't appear on your list of dosha-specific foods; that would be done only on the advice of a physician trained in Maharishi Ayur-Ved (see Appendix 4). For instance, the salty taste increases both Pitta and Kapha doshas. To keep these doshas in balance Pitta and Kapha types would generally reduce salt somewhat. But a reduced-salt diet is *not* a salt-free diet. Some small amount of the salty taste is necessary at each main meal for Pitta and Kapha, but not very much, and certainly not as much as is healthy for a Vata type.

VATA CHARACTERISTICS	PITTA CHARACTERISTICS	KAPHA CHARACTERISTICS
• light, thinner build • performs activity quickly • tendency to dry skin • irregular hunger and digestion, tendency toward constipation • quick to grasp new information, also quick to forget • tendency to worry • often light and interrupted sleep • aversion to cold weather	• moderate build • performs activity with medium speed • tendency toward red complexion and hair, moles and freckles • sharp hunger and digestion, can't skip meals, prefers cold food and drink • medium time to grasp new information • tendency toward irritability and temper • enterprising and sharp character, good speakers • aversion to hot weather	• solid, heavier build • slow, methodical activity • smooth, oily skin, hair is plentiful, tends to be darker • slow digestion and mild hunger • slow to grasp new information, slow to forget • tranquil, steady nature, slow to become excited or irritated • sleep is heavy and long • greater strength and endurance

What Is Your Body Type?

Right now you might want to identify your body type or constitution according to Ayurveda. This simple chart gives a general idea of the three body types. By answering the questions in the Body-Type Quiz that follows, you can get an even clearer idea of your own constitutional needs.

❖❖

Everyone is naturally made up of the three fundamental qualities. It is likely that two or, more rarely, three of them will predominate in your constitution. Even in a combination one of the elements dominates, and it is mentioned first in identifying your type. For instance, a Pitta-Vata type is somewhat more Pitta and less Vata than a Vata-Pitta type. The dietary considerations for those with dual or combined doshas are mainly seasonal ones. We'll discuss these combinations and seasonal cooking in more detail when we talk about menu planning in Chapter 5.

Body-Type Quiz

The following quiz is divided into three sections. For the first 20 questions, which apply to Vata dosha, read each statement and mark, from 0 to 6, whether it applies to you.

0 = Doesn't apply to me
3 = Applies to me somewhat (or some of the time)
6 = Applies to me mostly (or nearly all of the time)

At the end of the section, write down your total Vata score. For example, if you mark a 6 for the first question, a 3 for the second, and a 2 for the third, your total up to that point would be 6 + 3 + 2 = 11. Total the entire section in this way, and you arrive at your final Vata score. Proceed to the 20 questions for Pitta and those for Kapha.

When you are finished, you will have three separate scores. Comparing these will determine your body type.

For fairly objective physical traits, your choice will usually be obvious. For mental traits and behavior, which are more subjective, you should answer according to how you have felt and acted most of your life. Of course, if you answer with respect to your current state, the quiz may reflect your imbalances rather than your constitution.

SECTION I—VATA

	DOES NOT APPLY		APPLIES SOMETIMES		APPLIES MOST
1. I perform activity very quickly.	1 ▪ 2 ▪ 3 ▪ 4 ▪ 5 ▪ 6				
2. I am not good at memorizing things and then remembering them later.	1 ▪ 2 ▪ 3 ▪ 4 ▪ 5 ▪ 6				
3. I am enthusiastic and vivacious by nature.	1 ▪ 2 ▪ 3 ▪ 4 ▪ 5 ▪ 6				
4. I have a thin physique—I don't gain weight very easily.	1 ▪ 2 ▪ 3 ▪ 4 ▪ 5 ▪ 6				
5. I have always learned new things very quickly.	1 ▪ 2 ▪ 3 ▪ 4 ▪ 5 ▪ 6				
6. My characteristic gait while walking is light and quick.	1 ▪ 2 ▪ 3 ▪ 4 ▪ 5 ▪ 6				
7. I tend to have difficulty making decisions.	1 ▪ 2 ▪ 3 ▪ 4 ▪ 5 ▪ 6				
8. I tend to develop gas or become constipated easily.	1 ▪ 2 ▪ 3 ▪ 4 ▪ 5 ▪ 6				
9. I tend to have cold hands and feet.	1 ▪ 2 ▪ 3 ▪ 4 ▪ 5 ▪ 6				
10. I become anxious or worried frequently.	1 ▪ 2 ▪ 3 ▪ 4 ▪ 5 ▪ 6				
11. I don't tolerate cold weather as well as most people.	1 ▪ 2 ▪ 3 ▪ 4 ▪ 5 ▪ 6				
12. I speak quickly and my friends think that I'm talkative.	1 ▪ 2 ▪ 3 ▪ 4 ▪ 5 ▪ 6				
13. My moods change easily and I am somewhat emotional by nature.	1 ▪ 2 ▪ 3 ▪ 4 ▪ 5 ▪ 6				
14. I often have difficulty in falling asleep or having a sound night's sleep.	1 ▪ 2 ▪ 3 ▪ 4 ▪ 5 ▪ 6				
15. My skin tends to be very dry, especially in the winter.	1 ▪ 2 ▪ 3 ▪ 4 ▪ 5 ▪ 6				
16. My mind is very active, sometimes restless, but also very imaginative.	1 ▪ 2 ▪ 3 ▪ 4 ▪ 5 ▪ 6				
17. My movements are quick and active; my energy tends to come in bursts.	1 ▪ 2 ▪ 3 ▪ 4 ▪ 5 ▪ 6				

18. I am easily excitable.   1 ▪ 2 ▪ 3 ▪ 4 ▪ 5 ▪ 6

19. Left on my own, my eating and sleeping habits tend to be irregular.   1 ▪ 2 ▪ 3 ▪ 4 ▪ 5 ▪ 6

20. I learn quickly, but I also forget quickly.   1 ▪ 2 ▪ 3 ▪ 4 ▪ 5 ▪ 6

VATA SCORE ☐

SECTION 2—PITTA

	DOES NOT APPLY	APPLIES SOMETIMES	APPLIES MOST

1. I consider myself to be very efficient.   1 ▪ 2 ▪ 3 ▪ 4 ▪ 5 ▪ 6

2. In my activities, I tend to be extremely precise and orderly.   1 ▪ 2 ▪ 3 ▪ 4 ▪ 5 ▪ 6

3. I am strong-minded and have a somewhat forceful manner.   1 ▪ 2 ▪ 3 ▪ 4 ▪ 5 ▪ 6

4. I feel uncomfortable or become easily fatigued in hot weather—more so than most other people.   1 ▪ 2 ▪ 3 ▪ 4 ▪ 5 ▪ 6

5. I tend to perspire easily.   1 ▪ 2 ▪ 3 ▪ 4 ▪ 5 ▪ 6

6. Even though I might not always show it, I become irritable or angry quite easily.   1 ▪ 2 ▪ 3 ▪ 4 ▪ 5 ▪ 6

7. If I skip a meal or a meal is delayed, I become uncomfortable.   1 ▪ 2 ▪ 3 ▪ 4 ▪ 5 ▪ 6

8. One or more of the following characteristics describes my hair: early graying or balding thin, fine, straight hair blond, red, or sandy-colored hair.   1 ▪ 2 ▪ 3 ▪ 4 ▪ 5 ▪ 6

9. I have a strong appetite; if I want to, I can eat quite a large quantity.   1 ▪ 2 ▪ 3 ▪ 4 ▪ 5 ▪ 6

10. Many people consider me stubborn.   1 ▪ 2 ▪ 3 ▪ 4 ▪ 5 ▪ 6

11. I am very regular in my bowel habits—it would be more common for me to have loose stools than to be constipated.   1 ▪ 2 ▪ 3 ▪ 4 ▪ 5 ▪ 6

12. I become impatient very easily.   1 ▪ 2 ▪ 3 ▪ 4 ▪ 5 ▪ 6

13. I tend to be a perfectionist about details.   1 ▪ 2 ▪ 3 ▪ 4 ▪ 5 ▪ 6

14. I get angry quite easily, but then quickly forget about it.   1 ▪ 2 ▪ 3 ▪ 4 ▪ 5 ▪ 6

15. I am very fond of cold foods like ice cream and also ice-cold drinks.   1 ▪ 2 ▪ 3 ▪ 4 ▪ 5 ▪ 6

16. I am more likely to feel that a room is too hot than too cold.   1 ▪ 2 ▪ 3 ▪ 4 ▪ 5 ▪ 6

17. I don't tolerate foods that are very hot and spicy.   1 ▪ 2 ▪ 3 ▪ 4 ▪ 5 ▪ 6

18. I am not as tolerant of disagreement as I should be.   1 ▪ 2 ▪ 3 ▪ 4 ▪ 5 ▪ 6

19. I enjoy challenges and when I want something I am very determined in my efforts to get it.   1 ▪ 2 ▪ 3 ▪ 4 ▪ 5 ▪ 6

20. I tend to be quite critical of others and also of myself.   1 ▪ 2 ▪ 3 ▪ 4 ▪ 5 ▪ 6

PITTA SCORE ☐

SECTION 3—KAPHA

	DOES NOT APPLY	APPLIES SOMETIMES	APPLIES MOST
1. My natural tendency is to do things in a slow and relaxed fashion.	1 ▪ 2 ▪	3 ▪ 4 ▪	5 ▪ 6
2. I gain weight more easily than most people and lose it more slowly.	1 ▪ 2 ▪	3 ▪ 4 ▪	5 ▪ 6
3. I have a placid and calm disposition—I'm not easily ruffled.	1 ▪ 2 ▪	3 ▪ 4 ▪	5 ▪ 6
4. I can skip meals easily without any significant discomfort.	1 ▪ 2 ▪	3 ▪ 4 ▪	5 ▪ 6
5. I have a tendency toward excess mucus, phlegm, chronic congestion, asthma, or sinus problems.	1 ▪ 2 ▪	3 ▪ 4 ▪	5 ▪ 6
6. I must get at least eight hours of sleep in order to be comfortable the next day.	1 ▪ 2 ▪	3 ▪ 4 ▪	5 ▪ 6

7. I sleep very deeply.   1 ▪ 2 ▪ 3 ▪ 4 ▪ 5 ▪ 6

8. I am calm by nature and not easily angered.   1 ▪ 2 ▪ 3 ▪ 4 ▪ 5 ▪ 6

9. I don't learn as quickly as some people, but I have excellent retention and a long memory.   1 ▪ 2 ▪ 3 ▪ 4 ▪ 5 ▪ 6

10. I have a tendency toward becoming plump—I store extra fat easily.   1 ▪ 2 ▪ 3 ▪ 4 ▪ 5 ▪ 6

11. Weather that is cool and damp bothers me.   1 ▪ 2 ▪ 3 ▪ 4 ▪ 5 ▪ 6

12. My hair is thick, dark, and wavy.   1 ▪ 2 ▪ 3 ▪ 4 ▪ 5 ▪ 6

13. I have smooth, soft skin with a somewhat pale complexion.   1 ▪ 2 ▪ 3 ▪ 4 ▪ 5 ▪ 6

14. I have a large, solid body build.   1 ▪ 2 ▪ 3 ▪ 4 ▪ 5 ▪ 6

15. The following words describe me well: serene, sweet-natured, affectionate, and forgiving.   1 ▪ 2 ▪ 3 ▪ 4 ▪ 5 ▪ 6

16. I have slow digestion, which makes me feel heavy after eating.   1 ▪ 2 ▪ 3 ▪ 4 ▪ 5 ▪ 6

17. I have very good stamina and physical endurance as well as a steady level of energy.   1 ▪ 2 ▪ 3 ▪ 4 ▪ 5 ▪ 6

18. I generally walk with a slow, measured gait.   1 ▪ 2 ▪ 3 ▪ 4 ▪ 5 ▪ 6

19. I have a tendency toward oversleeping, grogginess upon awakening, and am generally slow to get going in the morning.   1 ▪ 2 ▪ 3 ▪ 4 ▪ 5 ▪ 6

20. I am a slow eater and am slow and methodical in my actions.   1 ▪ 2 ▪ 3 ▪ 4 ▪ 5 ▪ 6

KAPHA SCORE [   ]

Final Score: Vata _____ Pitta _____ Kapha _____

❖❖❖

DETERMINING YOUR BODY TYPE

Although there are only three doshas, Ayurveda combines them in ten possible ways to arrive at ten different body types.

Single-Dosha Types:
Vata
Pitta
Kapha

If one dosha is much higher than the others, you are a single-dosha type. Most indicative is a score where the primary dosha is twice as high as the second (for example, Vata–90, Pitta–45, Kapha–35), but smaller margins also count. A true single-dosha type displays the traits of Vata, Pitta, or Kapha very prominently. Your next-highest dosha will still show some influence in your natural tendencies, but to a much lesser degree.

Two-Dosha Types:
Vata-Pitta or Pitta-Vata
Pitta-Kapha or Kapha-Pitta
Kapha-Vata or Vata-Kapha

If no dosha is extremely dominant, you are a two-dosha type. This means that you display qualities of your two leading doshas, either side by side or in alternation. The higher one comes first in your body type, but both count.

Most people are two-dosha types. In some, the first dosha is very strong—they have scores like Vata–70 Pitta–90 Kapha–46, which would qualify as pure Pitta except for the prominence of another dosha, Vata. In other cases, where the difference is smaller, the first dosha still predominates, but the second will be almost equal. Your score might be Vata–85, Pitta–80, Kapha–40, which is a Vata-Pitta type, even though these two doshas are very close.

Finally, some people have scores in which one dosha stands out but the other two are exactly tied (for example, V–69, P–86, K–69). They are still likely to be a two-dosha type, but a written test did not pick up the second dosha—this person is either a Pitta-Vata or a Pitta-Kapha. If your score is like this, pay attention to the first dosha as your dominant one, and with time the second will become more clear.

Three-Dosha Type: Vata-Pitta-Kapha

If your three scores are nearly equal (for example, Vata–88, Pitta–75, Kapha–82), you are a three-dosha type. This type is considered rare,

IO   COOKING FOR LIFE

however. Check your answers again carefully, or have a friend help
you take the test again to verify your responses. Then reread the descriptions of Vata, Pitta, and Kapha that appeared earlier.

If you find yourself unable to give clear-cut answers on many points,
your body type may be obscured by a Vata imbalance. Vata often
creates confusion. It is the "leader of the doshas" and can mimic Pitta
and Kapha. You may be thin-framed but also overweight; prone to
worry but also irritable; or you may have insomnia for a stretch of
time followed by oversleeping. Vata imbalance is likely to cause such
changeableness.

Fortunately, body types are generally not ambiguous. As you gain
more understanding of the Ayurvedic system, you will be able to see
which answers were due to Vata imbalance and which to your true
nature. If you remain confused, consultation with a physician trained
in Maharishi Ayur-Ved.

SIMILARITIES AND DIFFERENCES AND THE UNIVERSE

There is a principle in Ayurveda known as *Samanya* (similarities) and
Vishesha (opposites). It explains how the body interacts with the world
around it and how the contents of the entire universe affect the body.
Ayurveda sees the human body as a miniature of the universe. Anything, any element or law of nature, found in the universe can be found
in a human body. This broad point of view is the basis for planning
an individual's diet to maintain a balance between the inner workings
of the body and changes in the environment.

Briefly, the rule is that any substance taken from outside of the body
that is similar to something within the body will cause that within
the body to increase. Likewise, anything taken from outside the body
that is different from something within the body will cause that within
the body to decrease. This is why the tastes and qualities of foods
most like one's body type increase that type. Like increases like.
So the oily and cold, heavy, wet, smooth, and sweet things that are
like the fundamental quality of Kapha found anywhere in the environment increase the element of Kapha in your body. Hot, salty,
spicy, light, dry food increases active, fiery Pitta because they are
most like the universal fundamental quality of Pitta. And all cold,
dry, windy, light, bitter things increase Vata within the body and
outside.

*Everything found in the universe
is found in the human body.
We take items from the universe,
maintain them for a while,
then release them.*

—DR. H. S. KASTURE

AYURVEDIC COOKING AND EATING

Whether discussing cooking or eating, Ayurvedic dieticians and physicians emphasize nourishment and enjoyment. They are less concerned with the relatively "new" concepts of caloric content, vitamins, minerals, fats, proteins, and carbohydrates than they are with proper digestion and the particular balance of food tastes and qualities that each person enjoys at each meal. This concept of the subtle effect of food taste and quality on nutrition, as well as enjoyment while eating and a good appetite, is the heart of Ayurvedic nutrition. When you follow a properly designed Ayurvedic diet all those nutrients currently listed as necessary for good health are naturally available.

Ayurveda takes into account the effects of everything on an individual and gives advice about what and how to eat in order to stay healthy and avoid future illnesses. For most people who follow Ayurveda, cooking and eating will not necessitate any major dietary changes, but an adjustment of some eating habits may naturally occur as you become more aware of how tastes and textures, and even the different times of day and changing weather conditions, make noticeable differences in your appetite and state of health.

GOOD DIGESTION AND GOOD HEALTH

Unless you are able to properly digest and assimilate what you eat, any nutritional information printed on food packages showing the amounts of protein, fats, and so forth per average serving is of little use to you. In Ayurveda, the main concern is that your digestive power, or *agni* (UHG-nee), is working properly. If it is not, then eating even the freshest and most highly nutritious foods will be of uncertain use to you because they cannot be well assimilated by the body.

A strong appetite is a healthy sign of a strong, well-functioning agni. But no matter how refined the food, how careful the preparation, and how beautiful the setting for dining, if digestion is not efficient nutrition will be poor. If the eater takes care of nutrition at its source—that is, by maintaining agni, the digestive fire—then good health naturally results.

Maintain your digestive power and eat.
Food is like fuel to the fire.

—DR. P. D. SUBHEDAR

Ayurvedic Eating: A Refined Pleasure

Ayurveda holds a far more subtle understanding of the sensory aspects of eating than most of us are accustomed to. As you read this book some food qualities or tastes such as salty and oily are obvious, but other descriptions are more refined. Until you become more experienced in identifying these, the Charts of Ingredients (pages 283–290) might be helpful.

Food Tastes and Qualities

Properly balanced meals incorporate a variety of tastes and food qualities into every main meal. Of the many tastes and qualities that food ingredients can have, the six major ones organized by Ayurveda are: SWEET, SALTY, SOUR, PUNGENT, ASTRINGENT, and BITTER tastes and LIGHT, HEAVY, DRY, OILY, HOT, and COLD qualities. In Ayurveda every taste and quality has a specific and known effect on the balance of the doshas and the digestion. The chapters in this book devoted to diet for the particular body types of Vata, Pitta, or Kapha list the best foods for balancing each individual's diet. And as a general reference the Charts of Ingredients list according to tastes, quality, and effects on each body type many commonly eaten fruits, vegetables, spices, herbs, beverages, grains, and other foods for a healthy diet.

THE BASIC FOOD TASTES
Sweet • Salty • Sour • Pungent • Astringent • Bitter

FLAVOR AND TASTE

First, it is important to note the difference in meaning between "flavor" and "taste." The concept of taste in Ayurveda is a general way to classify food groups according to their effects during the digestive process. Many flavors may be included in each taste. The distinct flavor of a food within the taste category makes it unique. *Flavor* is what makes eating so interesting. For example, there are many foods with a pungent or spicy taste, but they do not all have a hot or spicy flavor. Black pepper, basil, and saffron are described as pungent-tasting. Each one's flavor is very different from the other. And the spicy or pungent effect of that taste is not necessarily on the tongue or palate. Saffron is a heating herb whose taste effect is a kind of secondary reaction in the stomach rather than in the mouth. On the palate it has a rather bland, sweet flavor. But eating foods made with saffron makes you feel warm inside, especially if you have a Pitta constitution.

EXAMPLES OF THE SIX BASIC TASTES

SWEET

When we think of a sweet taste, sugar or honey comes to mind. But the sweet taste is not just sugar. Many foods such as rice, wheat, most fruits, some nuts, butter, milk, a few herbs and spices, and many vegetables have what Ayurveda considers a sweet taste. By briefly scanning the Charts of Ingredients it is possible to find a variety of sweet foods, many in combination with other tastes, that may surprise you. These are just a few: artichokes, beets, cucumbers, oranges, persimmons, and squash. The sweet taste may be produced in the mouth or the stomach.

SALTY

If you want to add the salty taste to the diet you can use table salt or condiments such as soy sauce, olives, and pickles. Many processed foods are quite salty. It is best to read the labels on packaged foods to find out how much salt, sugar, and other ingredients are being added to the product before packaging. This is especially true for breakfast cereals, which contain much more than just wheat, oats, or other grains.

SOUR

Some of the obvious foods with a sour taste are yogurt, cheese, grapefruit, and dill pickles. Some others are tomatoes, rosehips, green apples, rye bread, and peanuts. The sour taste in foods is experienced as sour in the mouth and during digestion. Sour dairy products take five or six hours to fully digest and should be eaten at the main meal of the day rather than in the evening or too close to bedtime.

PUNGENT

Chili peppers and radishes are pungent. So are peppermint, cinnamon, black pepper, ginger, parsley, sage, basil, and thyme. Some pungent tastes are easy to identify at first bite. Others have their spicy, or heating, effect later in digestion. For most people, using a small amount of pungent spices is plenty for them. This is especially true in the heat of summer and for Pitta types.

ASTRINGENT

The astringent taste dries body fluids and gives a puckery feeling in the mouth. Vinegar is astringent. So are beans, lentils, chocolate, turmeric, rosemary, celery leaves, peas, apples, barley, corn, and olive oil. If this taste is not immediately noticeable at first, it has its effect later in the digestive process.

BITTER

The bitter taste is obvious with the first bite. It only varies in strength. Horseradish leaves and dandelion greens are two healthful, bitter, and tonic herbs of spring. Chocolate, honey, walnuts, lettuce, and Swiss chard provide some bitterness to the diet as well.

FOOD TASTES

	VATA	PITTA	KAPHA
Sweet	↓	↓	↑
Sour	↓	↑	↑
Salty	↓	↑	↑
Pungent	↑	↑	↓
Bitter	↑	↓	↓
Astringent	↑	↓	↓

(↑) increases or aggravates and (↓) decreases or calms.

THE QUALITIES OF INGREDIENTS

In determining the quality of cooking ingredients, Ayurveda considers their internal effects as well as their textures, serving temperatures, or other obvious sensory characteristics. For instance, the qualities of hot or cold do not necessarily mean temperature in degrees of Fahrenheit, but their internal heating or cooling effects during digestion. So when we read that a steaming bowl of rice is cold, it is not cold to the touch but inside the digestive system. Just as saffron is not hot until it arrives in the stomach, a food feels hot only in the mouth, such as a radish, or hot both in the mouth and stomach, like pungent chili peppers.

It's not necessary to remember where the quality occurs; just know that these qualities—hot, cold, heavy, light, dry, and oily—may have their effect at more subtle levels of digestion. So when a particular food is listed here with a quality not immediately apparent, you'll know that it refers to its subtle Ayurvedic effect. A few additional, secondary qualities, such as smooth, sharp, and so forth, are mentioned in the Charts of Ingredients.

THE BASIC FOOD QUALITIES
Light • Heavy • Dry • Oily • Hot • Cold

❖❖

Examples of the Six Basic Qualities

LIGHT

Cereals, rice cakes, apples, celery, spinach, and other greens are light, as are some ingredients that have been heated by boiling or quick-frying in a very small amount of oil. Any ingredient with a light quality takes less time to digest. This makes it a food of choice for Kapha types and those people who want to lose weight.

HEAVY

Most high-protein food that is nourishing for all body tissues has a heavy quality. Those who do not need to reduce weight, including most Pitta and Vata types, should include heavy foods more than light ones in their diets. Some heavy foods are milk, sweet potatoes, peaches, avocados, cucumbers, sugar, breads and wheat products, nuts, meat, tofu, and beans. The heavy quality may not be apparent until after eating, as a secondary part of digestion.

DRY

Many grains, spices, and vegetables are dry in quality. Broccoli, cabbage, eggplant, spinach, yams, barley, oats, cayenne and other peppers, nutmeg, ginger, and vinegar are dry. Dry and light qualities often seem to be found together. These are qualities good for Kapha types and those reducing weight.

> *Unctuous Food*
> *Provokes subtle digestive power*
> *Digests quickly*
> *Moves Vata downward*
> *Increases physical strength*
> *Improves the senses*
> *Brings out full brightness of complexion.*
>
> —THE *CHARAKA SAMHITA*

OILY

An oily quality is more than just an oily feel to the touch. It is unctuous—that is, internally lubricating. This is an important quality for those with dry skin—people with Vata in their constitutions—and an important dietary consideration for everyone in winter when the air is dry. Although cooking oils and ghee are obviously oily during eating, other foods provide the necessary unctuous quality later in digestion. Some of these are milk, nuts, coriander, lentils, asparagus, carrots, oats, and rice. Oily and heavy food qualities are often found together in combination in nutritious, body-building foods.

HOT

Hot food does not necessarily mean pungent, spicy food, or food right off the stove. The hot quality in food is usually found during the digestive process rather than by touch. Heat is important for proper digestion, and the foods that are hot in quality are best for Vata and Kapha types who have less internal heat for good digestion. Some hot foods are corn, beans and lentils, seafood, turmeric, fenugreek, mustard seeds, asafoetida (hing), cloves, yogurt, and carrots.

COLD

In the same way, foods with a cold quality are not necessarily cold to the touch but are often experienced as cold after eating them. Some obviously cold foods are ice cream, cheese and milk, grapes, and other juicy fruits. Other cold foods include sugar, rice, wheat, lentils, artichokes, cucumbers, and zucchini. The cold quality of food is frequently found in combination with the food's heaviness.

FOOD QUALITIES

	VATA	PITTA	KAPHA
Heavy	↓	↓	↑
Light	↑	↑	↓
Dry	↑	↑	↓
Oily	↓	↓	↑
Hot	↓	↑	↓
Cold	↑	↓	↑

(↑) increases or aggravates and (↓) decreases or calms.

THE BEST TASTE AND QUALITY COMBINATIONS

Let us consider how the different taste and qualities of the various ingredients combine to produce the best recipes. After long experience, Ayurveda concludes certain combinations of ingredients to be better than others. These might be thought of as having superior, good, or inferior results. Generally, recipes that contain ingredients that interact well together, that is in a good or superior way, are also delicious and leave one with a pleasant and satisfied feeling after eating. Mixtures of inferior combinations can often taste unpleasant or leave one with an uncomfortable feeling after eating. An example (perhaps extreme) of this inferior effect is a sauce made with roux or base of milk (sweet, heavy, cold) and wheat flour (sweet and heavy), then flavored with salty olives and soy sauce. The sweet, heavy milk and the salty taste just don't work well together. To make the example more extreme we could add to the sauce such dry, bitter greens as chard, lettuce, or horseradish. Very unpalatable.

In designing your own recipes, you do not have to reinvent culinary science. Most of the time-tested ways of successfully combining ingredients in our cuisine have already been discovered. That is why good recipes are passed from one generation of cooks to another. In using the chart How Ingredients Combine the main idea is to favor the superior and good combinations as much as possible and avoid the inferior ones. Look across the lines to see how each quality blends with the different tastes and also observe how the tastes in each column work together when a certain ingredient contains more than one quality.

How Ingredients Combine

QUALITY	TASTE		
	SUPERIOR	GOOD	INFERIOR
Heavy	Sweet	Astringent	Salty
Light	Bitter	Pungent	Sour
Dry	Astringent	Sour	Salty
Oily	Sweet	Pungent	Bitter
Hot	Salty	Sour	Pungent
Cold	Sweet	Astringent	Bitter

Designing Your Own Recipes

One of the delights in the art of cooking is creating your own recipes. Designing a successful Ayurvedic recipe not only involves knowing how the various ingredients affect each of the different body types, but how these ingredients combine or interact with one another in the cooking process. In this book, all of the recipes and menus have been developed and rated by experts in Ayurveda for their specific action on each body type. Many of them required only simple adjustments to well-known recipes, while others are new creations. Similarly, we'll first discuss some basics to help you *adapt* your favorite recipes and create your own balanced recipes and meals.

When creating a new recipe we first consider the action of each ingredient. We then consider how the parts, the ingredients, combine to make the whole recipe. A finished recipe that can stand on its own is one that has become more than the collection of all the parts. It is now a part or ingredient in the whole menu. Later, when planning complete menus, we will see how each finished recipe interacts with all the others in the menu to make a well-balanced meal. As complicated as this may sound, it is not really so difficult. We have already discussed the influences of many of the ingredients commonly used in American cooking and many are listed in the Charts of Ingredients (pages 283–290), which may serve as a starting point and general guide for the design and adaptation of your own recipes. Keep in mind that when most ingredients are combined in a recipe and heated, their result is sometimes changed with the cooking process and there are a few rules of thumb that can help you in this regard. For instance, boiling water, milk, and broths, and dry roasting or frying grains in a small amount of oil before cooking lightens the heavy qualities they may have, while frying foods, especially deep-frying, or using unsaturated oils makes even light foods heavier in quality.

When several recipes containing widely differing tastes and qualities are served at the same meal, there will be a rebalancing of the overall effect within the entire menu. We will discuss this menu-planning point a little later. With the addition of each dish featuring another group of tastes and qualities, the entire meal becomes more varied, with greater depth and richness, and thus more suitable for many different people to eat. So one recipe has its own part to play in the whole meal, but unless it contains some overpowering taste or quality, it is only one of the players and not the prima donna.

As you eat so shall you think.

—DR. P. D. SUBHEDAR

THE SUPERIOR SALAD

Many superior food combinations are already a standard part of the American cuisine. One is the familiar mixed green salad with lemon or vinaigrette dressing. Typically the tossed salad with a simple dressing contains astringent, bitter, pungent, sweet, light, oily, and dry properties that all work well together. You might think of them as friends who have good influences on one another. The mixed greens in a salad (more than pale iceberg lettuce, please) are light in quality, sweet, bitter, astringent, and a little pungent-tasting. By adding such fresh, light herbs as parsley (pungent, astringent, slightly bitter), basil (pungent), tarragon (pungent, bitter), or thyme (pungent, astringent, bitter), the variety of qualities and the depth of taste increases. And then, when all of these are tossed with an oil and fresh lemon juice or vinegar dressing, the salad is a further blending of dry, oily, and light qualities, with the astringency of the vinegar and the sweetness of the oil that work nicely together. In such a dressed green salad there are a total of six different superior combinations of tastes and qualities and three good, and no inferior ones.

Including a tossed salad in the dinner menu makes the whole meal more easily balanced. The salad's particular combination of bitter, pungent, and astringent tastes, frequently lacking in American main dishes, is not only a most beneficial one for Kapha types, but it is healthy for everyone to eat a salad as part of a complete meal. Vata types usually eat a small amount of leafy green salad since they don't need very much of these tastes in their diets and raw vegetables are difficult for them to digest.

Almost anything in the world can be good
if taken in the proper quantity—
in balance.

—DR. P. D. SUBHEDAR

DESIGNING A NEW RECIPE: AN EXAMPLE

As you can see, by using this concept of including the best combinations of tastes and qualities in your recipes, your meals need not be a haphazard result of taking everything from the refrigerator, some things from the shelf, and putting them together in hopes of making "creative" meals. Satisfaction for an Ayurvedic cook is in *knowing* the healthful benefits of everything you serve.

One way to design a new recipe is to begin by thinking of the kind of dish you want to make combining all superior and good tastes and qualities that appeal to you. This is how the recipe for the appetizer Golden Yummies came about. These small crackers spread with a thin layer of cashew butter, then topped with a brilliant gold, warm mixture of coconut, raisins, spices, and cashew butter make an excellent appetizer. Starting a meal with a sweet taste is thought by Ayurvedic experts to be especially appetizing. Successful appetizers, those that stimulate the digestive fires, will be sweettasting, rather pungent, oily, heavy, and colorful, or any combination of these. The most stimulating, appetizing colors are red, gold-orange, and yellow.

GOLDEN YUMMIES

The ingredients in Golden Yummies repeat these properties.

Ghee: sweet, oily, cold	Sugar: sweet, heavy, cold
Cayenne: pungent, dry, light	Raisins: sweet, heavy
Saffron: sweet, pungent, oily	Cream: sweet, oily,
Allspice: pungent, astringent	heavy, cold
Coconut: sweet, heavy, oily, cold	Cashew Butter: sweet,
	heavy, oily

By looking again at the How Ingredients Combine chart on page 18, we see that the heavy and oily qualities in the coconut, cashew butter, and cream combine in a superior way with sweet-tasting ghee, saffron, coconut, sugar, cream, raisins, and cashew butter. This is a larger-than-average number of ingredients in the superior range to expect when designing a recipe; even two or three superior combinations are fine. The pungent aspects of a good appetizer that help to heat the palate or the digestion are well represented in this recipe by cayenne, saffron, and allspice. Had bitter-tasting turmeric been used for color instead of the saffron, the recipe would have looked yellow in color but it would not have had as superior a taste or effect since the bitter taste is an inferior combination with the oily ghee and coconut and the coldness of the cream and sugar.

"Companion" Cooking

Another way of looking at combining foods and ingredients is to compare it to a popular gardening term, "companion gardening," in which certain plants are thought to grow better near other plants. In Avurvedic cooking if you know which elements like (and which do not like) to be with which others, recipe design is easy.

Cinnamon likes Chocolate.
Vanilla prefers warm, sweet liquids and cakes.
Milk and Cream do not like lemon, salt, or fish,
But Milk loves Butter, Ghee, and Nutmeg.
Nutmeg likes Spinach and Zucchini, too.
Ghee likes some spices better than others:
Cumin, Fenugreek, Hing, Coriander, and Turmeric,
to name a few.

Fine-Tuning and Final Testing

You may make a recipe the first time and after one taste you know it's perfect. At other times you and other food lovers who want to help (there always seem to be several around) may feel more of something and less of something else would make it work better. The real final test of any Ayurvedic recipe is if it tastes undeniably delicious and feels nourishing . . . then you know you've got a winner.

Good Digestion: Agni and the Three Doshas

Now that we know the basic tastes and qualities that make a balanced meal, we will consider the second most important requirement for proper nutrition: a good digestive fire, or agni.

Each of the three constitutional types has its own metabolic rate and its own degree of agni. Pitta individuals, like the element of fire, have the most agni, and so they have the best digestion. In fact, when they are hungry it is their digestive fire that makes them seem ravenous. If they have to wait too long to eat after their agni is fully blazing, Pitta types become noticeably impatient. And too much hot, dry, or pungent food can irritate fiery Pitta. Kapha types are slow and sometimes unsteady in digestion. Right in the middle of a meal Kapha's digestive fire can just seem to go out. And Vata types often need help igniting agni. They have irregular digestive fire. Good appetizers and a balance of tastes and qualities are necessary for Vata and Kapha types to fully enjoy eating.

> *When one sits to eat*
> *Food is the fuel*
> *Digestion is the fire*
>
> —DR. H. S. KASTURE

APPETIZERS

What makes a good appetizer? Something with zip . . . something a little pungent, or warm, sweet, and unctuous, or any combination of these. Serve just enough of an appetizer to spark digestion, not to satisfy it. An appetizer can be as simple as a sweet pickle or gherkin, or a small amount of warm rice and ghee (refined clarified butter), or a relish of chopped fresh ginger, lemon juice, and a little salt. Even a pinch of ground ginger placed under the tongue just before eating will start the digestive fire and bring enjoyment to the whole meal.

EATING EVERYTHING: A BALANCED DIET

A balanced diet for anyone without specific health problems means eating some amount of all the tastes, qualities, and categories (*gunas* [GOO-nahs], see Chapter 5, under "Planning Good Meals") daily—even some of those things that increase a dominant dosha. For instance, those people of dominant Kapha constitutions would not avoid all Kapha-increasing foods because many of these are considered body-builders and maintainers of strength. But Kapha metabolism is so efficient in turning body-building foods into weight that those following a Kapha-reducing diet do not need large amounts of heavy, sweet, high-protein, oily foods. A balanced Kapha diet would include small amounts of Kapha-increasing foods and much larger portions of Kapha-decreasing foods. In fact, balanced Kapha types naturally favor light, pungent, dry, astringent foods.

The same idea of proportional balance applies for Pitta and Vata types. In the charts on pages 15 and 17 you can see how different tastes and food qualities influence each body type either by increasing (↑) or decreasing (↓) it.

SATISFACTION: A SIGN OF A BALANCED DIET

One practical test of good Ayurvedic food comes with a welcome sense of comfort and well-being after eating. It is a feeling of being neither very full nor hungry. Feelings of dissatisfaction or indigestion after eating a main meal can come from lack of balance in the ingredients used, poor cooking techniques, eating too fast, or too much, or without paying attention while cooking or eating. Some people overeat as a habit, or they eat meals that have little satisfaction built into them. Some meals will automatically satisfy one person and not another. Satisfying meals depend on whether the predominant tastes and qualities in the meal are good for that person and if the meal has been prepared with the cook's full attention.

BREAKFAST: AN EXAMPLE OF SATISFACTION

In Ayurveda, breakfast is considered a light meal or nourishing snack to be eaten only if hungry because the digestive fires are not strong in the morning. It is never a main meal. A typical non-Ayurvedic breakfast may include cereal with milk, toast with butter, orange juice, tea or coffee. This is considered a light meal, and both Pitta and Vata can start the day this way—minus the orange juice. Ayurveda does not recommend drinking grapefruit, orange, or other sour juices at the same meal that milk is served. But, with the exception of tea and coffee, everything else on this menu increases Kapha. At first Kapha might feel "full," but since the food lacks balance in the tastes and qualities best for Kapha, it is not really satisfying. As a result, after a short time Kapha will want to snack. In the American tradition of the coffee break, Kapha might have a midmorning pastry and more coffee or tea. Again Kapha-increasing and not satisfying. And snacking so frequently weakens the power of agni for its real work at the main meal around noon. A good breakfast for Kapha is a warm or hot drink and something light and dry, such as rice cakes, a slice of corn bread with a little honey, or thin-sliced toast, eaten plain or spread with a little ghee or nut butter.

DIGESTION

Ayurveda encourages eating practices that maintain good digestive power. Indigestion is the result of eating too much heavy food that cannot be assimilated properly. Sometimes overeating is simply a habit of anticipating that we might have to miss a meal and so we overfill the stomach to avoid hunger later. Overeating causes discomfort, heartburn, gas, and weakens agni. Ayurveda says that whenever the agni is weak the food is left undigested or "uncooked by the digestive fires." It is not converted into its constituent nutrients. The product of improper digestion is a sticky substance called *ama* (AH-muh). Ayurveda has described it as a sticky substance that becomes deposited in the body, blocking the channels and causing disease. It is the source of many disorders.

Other causes of improper digestion are eating when angry or otherwise upset, eating heavy sour dairy foods late in the evening when agni is weaker, that is, too close to bedtime, thus slowing the digestive process before its conclusion, and frequent snacking or eating when the stomach is still digesting the previous meal. Waiting three to six hours between meals with no snacking, except perhaps to drink a glass of water, juice, tea, or milk in between, is considered ideal because the digestive fire has time to be rekindled.

Wisdom is knowing
the difference between the
habitual demands made by the mind
and the simple demands of the body.

—DR. H. S. KASTURE

❖❖❖

EAT THE RIGHT AMOUNT

A simple Ayurvedic rule: Always eat the proper quantity. The wisdom lies in knowing how much is enough. Filling the stomach two-thirds to three-fourths its capacity is the maximum for the best digestive activity. Too much food produces a feeling of fullness and heaviness or lethargy after eating. With too little food agni begins burning body tissues for fuel, thus causing loss of weight, either muscle tissue or fat. But if we eat just a little less than what makes us feel full, then agni will remain strong. An overburdened agni becomes weak and disordered and cannot perform adequately.

DIET AND THE ENVIRONMENT

Dietary considerations in Ayurveda are based on the time of day when eating, the weather or seasons, and even the climate where we live and where the food is grown.

The time of eating is important. Breakfast, if eaten at all, should be taken as a light, easily digested meal. The biggest meal of the day should be around noontime, that is, when agni is strongest in the environment. This is an example of the similarity between one's internal digestive fire and the external fire of the sun. Ayurveda holds that the digestive capacity is greatest around 12:00 or 12:30 P.M. When we eat food near that time the digestive enzymes are ready to work most efficiently. Invite guests to lunch for a spectacular feast that everyone can enjoy. A lighter evening meal is best eaten between 5:00 P.M. and 8:00 P.M. If a heavy meal is eaten in the evening, there is not enough time for it to fully digest before bedtime. Although a light meal only needs two or three hours to digest, it is good to allow five to six hours after eating a full meal for the stomach and agni to be ready before eating again.

The ancient Ayurvedic physicians noted
that conditions are best for proper digestion
while sunlight is greatest.

In the summer eat fewer heavy, high-protein foods than during the colder days of spring and winter. These foods are harder to digest and assimilate, and during the hot summer months one's internal agni is overpowered by the heat found in the environment. That's when everyone's digestion appreciates the seasonally available light, juicy fruits and vegetables nature provides.

THE BODY: THE ENVIRONMENT

Common sense dictates that you eat when you are hungry and not just when the clock says it is dinnertime. Sometimes you might really crave some taste or particular food that you know is contrary to your needs. But you want it! This is a good, healthy sign that a certain element is low or lacking in your body's chemistry. The longing for a certain taste or quality comes from the very cells of your body that have a need to be nourished in a specific way. The body hints at what it wants to eat. It is the mind that creates incorrect eating habits or ignores the body's simple messages. These appetites come from the body's innate desire for balance. Food selection is one way the body demonstrates its wisdom to maintain balance.

EAT WHAT YOU LIKE

Ayurveda's advice is to always eat well of fresh, deliciously prepared food that naturally pleases you. When you feel an urge to eat something that you know is not in your best interest, by all means enjoy a little of it. You don't have to deprive yourself, or wait until the weather changes, or the season, or until you've had a chance to consult a certain food chart.

Ayurveda is like a tender-hearted mother who never likes to say, "No." Instead she says, "Just taste a little."

In fact, the word "No" rarely is heard in authentic Ayurveda, because everything in creation that is not actually poisonous or dulling to your consciousness is good and useful at some time for someone. And except for a few things that really shouldn't be eaten at certain times—such as yogurt, cheese, and sour cream late at night, or such unhealthy combinations as milk cooked with salt, seafood, or meat, or equal parts of honey and ghee, foods cooked with honey, carbonated drinks with food, and tamasic foods (see page 233)—you should eat what pleases you. Eat just enough to satisfy your desire, then let it go.

❖❖❖

CLIMATE

The climate in which the food is grown and where you live also affects your diet when you follow the principle of similarities and differences. Foods grown in dry areas and deserts tend to have light qualities, while those grown in moist, warm areas have heavy qualities. To achieve balance when living in humid or moist climates, it is best to eat more of hot, dry, and light foods. And when living in dry places add many cooler and more oily, heavy foods to your diet.

COMMON SENSE: THE EMPTY BAG

Dr. H. S. Kasture, a renowned Ayurvedic physician and professor, tells a story of an Ayurvedic physician who takes his shopping bag and goes to the market to buy food for dinner. All the beautiful fresh foods are displayed there in abundance.

First the man begins filling his bag with lots of little pink-skinned potatoes. "Uh-oh, these will increase my Vata," he says, and puts them back.

He then selects some luscious, red tomatoes, but just as he fills his bag, he remembers that tomatoes increase Pitta. So he returns them.

At the fruit stand the man picks out an inviting pineapple, a bunch of bananas, and a few oranges. Then he thinks to himself, "All these fruits increase my Kapha. I'll have to put them back."

And so he walks home to dinner with an empty bag.

Be a good eater, listen to your natural desires, follow common sense, and eat from a full bag.

In the Ayurvedic Kitchen

AN AYURVEDIC KITCHEN

An Ayurvedic kitchen is not a mysterious, new kind of sacred cooking space with specially imported furnishings or unusual utensils and equipment. It is simply a clean, well-equipped food preparation area located away from the center of household traffic. An Ayurvedic kitchen is a quiet place where the colors of the walls and cabinets, the comfort of the flooring, the room size and ease of getting around, and even the view from a window all contribute to the cook's general sense of well-being. This feeling, in turn, is subtly reflected in the kind of food prepared there.

When working in a modern Ayurvedic kitchen creative cooking becomes a welcome, relaxing activity worthy of a true artist. Like any creative work space an Ayurvedic kitchen should be simple, well lighted and well ventilated, orderly, and easy to keep clean. It doesn't have to be especially large or elaborate, but it should be well organized with equipment and ingredients within easy reach.

When stepping into the Ayurvedic cook's kitchen the atmosphere should feel calm, pleasant, pure . . . and be filled with deliciously enticing smells. Rather than being the center of attention for family or guests, the food preparation area itself is ideally a center of calm where the cook can work undisturbed by outside distractions.

KITCHEN DYNAMICS

Ayurveda considers the effects of the environment on the food as key to a healthy diet. The quality of the kitchen environment, the cook's feelings and attention, and the ingredients all interact dynamically to create a meal. The food, the raw material for the coming feast, is not only affected by the way it is prepared and heated, but it acts as a kind of carrier of everything that goes on during the entire cooking-serving-eating process. This is why the kitchen atmosphere is so important. An efficient, peaceful kitchen environment enhances your most generous feelings and encourages you to use your full attention while preparing the meal. When cooking, if you feel you have all the time in the world, you calmly proceed at a pleasant pace, working in an orderly manner without interruptions, and you produce deeply satisfying meals. A bustling, noisy, distracting atmosphere creates an unsettledness in the cook and the food.

Traditionally, the kitchen is *only* for cooking, and is separated—at least by a partition or an island—from the dining area and from direct access to the outside entry of the house or apartment. It should not be used as a passageway from one room to another. To keep it fresh and clean. In the Vedic tradition, outdoor clothing and shoes are not worn in the kitchen. Whenever possible, only the cook and those involved in food preparation should be in the kitchen while cooking is going on. You might find it helpful to anticipate the needs of others by setting out a carafe of hot water, tea, juice, or fresh fruit in the dining area to keep from being unnecessarily disturbed.

THE COOK'S ATTENTION

The cook's thoughts, feelings, and physical well-being affect all parts of the meal and contribute to the making of a good cook's reputation. This is one of those age-old secrets of why some cooks receive rave notices no matter what they make. Or why some people prefer one cook's apple pie to any other's. Perhaps this is why "just like Mom used to make" describes better than anything all the loving attention that Mom put into her food even more than what kind of food she made.

We have already considered the peaceful effect the kitchen environment has on your undistracted attention, but the quality of the thoughts and feelings you have while working are equally important. For this reason you should neither cook (nor eat) when you are ill or feeling angry or upset. The quality of the cook's attention has at least as much to do with the success of a meal as the kind of work space, all of the ingredients, the table setting, and any utensils you use. To maintain your undivided attention avoid such distractions as listening to music, having long telephone conversations, playing the radio or television, chatting with visitors, or anything that keeps you from thinking about and being with the job at hand.

When cooking without distractions, you become more aware of the various parts of meal preparation, including appetizing color combinations, the proper balance of taste and qualities for each dish, as well as the needs of each of the people who will be eating. When you enjoy the intensely creative cooking experience in this way anything else will seem like an unwelcome distraction.

In the quiet of the kitchen just before starting to cook you survey everything that you'll use—all the fruits and vegetables, the spices and herbs, the oils, and grains, and how you plan to handle them to achieve the desired results. All during the cooking process your attention will naturally go beyond the kitchen as you think affectionately of those who will be nourished by what you prepare. Everyone benefits from fully using your undivided attention.

❖❖❖

FIRST, PREPARE THE COOK

Preparation of a good Ayurvedic meal involves more than just producing something to eat. Of course a good cook collects the assorted ingredients, washes, chops, stirs, fries, bakes, seasons them, and creates something delicious—the result of much more than the collection of raw ingredients. As an Ayurvedic cook, with the thoughtful preparation of every meal you offer a special gift to those who are to eat. But preparations for the real Ayurvedic meal begin, most important, with the preparation of the cook.

A fully prepared cook is satisfied in mind and body. Eat something just before you begin cooking a large meal and sit quietly for a few minutes. Meditate daily to nourish your mind and body. The practice of Transcendental Meditation (TM) is a part of Maharishi Ayur-Ved. A fundamental principle of life is that deep rest is the basis for dynamic activity. We get ready for the activity of cooking by transcending all activity for a few minutes in the morning and evening. By regularly practicing the TM program, a cook, or anyone, naturally feels calm and orderly while working. Even though there may be many dishes to prepare, lots of steps to follow in a recipe, or a feeling of pressure about the time, the sense of restful alertness gained from TM stays with you while you work, allows you to enjoy yourself and be more consciously aware of all that goes into a successful meal.

The quality of the cook's thoughts and feelings while working are carried by the food itself. By eating something like tea and toast, a sandwich, or a piece of fruit before beginning to cook, you can avoid tasting the food excessively and be less tempted to save some for yourself before serving it. These rather greedy thoughts are considered to affect the food, causing feelings of emptiness or dissatisfaction in those who eat it.

Food prepared by a loving,
settled, sattvic cook helps
create loving, settled, sattvic people.

—NANCY LONSDORF, M.D.
A MAHARISHI AYUR-VEDA PHYSICIAN

FRESH IS BEST

Ayurveda says, "Fresh is always best." Foods are delivered to us from all parts of the country, usually over long distances.* Although it would be wonderful, not all "fresh" foods are garden fresh or even locally grown. But finding and using the freshest ingredients, grown without pesticides and properly stored, should be an Ayurvedic cook's goal. The cook's real responsibility for the quality of the ingredients begins when they are brought into the kitchen. It's worthwhile to begin a little garden near your kitchen and grow the herbs and vegetables you like most to eat.

When you grow an Ayurvedic kitchen garden
you enjoy the best fresh produce
right at your doorstep.

Although Ayurveda strongly prefers using fresh ingredients, they may not always be available. When a canned or bottled ingredient makes up only a small part of a recipe and is served as a part of a meal full of freshly prepared food, it is fine to eat.

LEFTOVERS

Fresh ingredients freshly prepared are better for everyone than old leftovers. When the main meal is eaten at noon or a little after, as is best, certain leftovers can be stored in the refrigerator or a cool place and reheated in the evening, or, at the very latest, for breakfast. This includes rice and whole grain dishes not containing vegetables or dairy products, lentil dahls, Lassi, undressed salads, fruits cooked with sugar, and baked goods. There is simply not enough nutritional value left in the cooked food to make eating it worthwhile. Vegetables and unsweetened cooked fruits do not keep well as leftovers.

When preparing beans, grains, and dahls left from the previous meal, heat them very well by frying them in a little hot oil or ghee rather than boiling or baking them again.

* An item of food travels an average of 1,200 miles before arriving at your kitchen. *Harper's* Index, April 1991.

❖❖❖

Cook Plentifully

Even if you cook simply, always cook as plentifully as you can. There should be more than enough food prepared for everyone. Sitting down to eat with feelings of abundance and a welcome invitation to enjoy fully makes for happiness and satisfaction in everyone at the table. This is not a recommendation for extravagance or waste, however. In the Ayurvedic view, food is a blessing not to be wasted. Extra portions of cooked food should be given to a neighbor or friend in need, or offered as a special treat to someone you think would enjoy it. This does not mean your old leftovers that have had the life cooked out of them, but extra amounts of your freshly prepared food.

Food should not be wasted
Always cook more than enough.
And, if there is extra food,
send it to someone who needs it.
Send enough for the needy person and a guest.

—DR. P. D. SUBHEDAR

Cleanliness

Meal preparation includes cleaning, cutting and chopping, mixing and heating, and food storage. It is important to keep the work area clean. Washing the hands before beginning, after handling soiled things, and frequently while cooking are healthy habits. It is also important to regularly wash all parts of the kitchen surfaces with a mild bleach solution of about one teaspoon bleach per gallon of water. This is especially useful in preventing bacterial buildup on wooden cutting boards and spoons. The solution is so mild it does not affect food tastes.

In addition to washing fruits and vegetables before using them, whole spices, lentils, and grains, including nonenriched or imported rice, should also be sorted and cleansed. They can often hide little stones or twigs. Wash rice, beans, and grains in cool water, rinsing two or three times, or until the water runs clear.

HEATING

Cooking is a lot like performing chemistry experiments. All ingredients have chemical components. Heating them can change the food properties and cause chemical interactions that sometimes alter the effect of the original raw ingredients. By heating water, milk, and some other foods, heavy elements are made lighter and easier to digest. That's why it is better to drink boiled water and milk cooled to a comfortable temperature. Cold foods are heavy and congestive to the stomach, slowing digestion. Cooking such foods as cabbage and apples makes it easier for the stomach to convert them into useful nutrients than when they are served raw either by themselves or in salad.

Good cooking is not a matter of fast or slow time.
Just cook the food for as long
as needed until it's done.
No more no less.

—DR. H. S. KASTURE

COOKING METHODS

Of the most commonly used heating methods steaming, boiling, frying, grilling, and baking are best. Of these, steam is the very best way to preserve the most nutrients, especially those in vegetables, fruits, and whole grains. The nutrients that leave the vegetables during the steaming process are reserved in the steam. Turning the steamer off for a few minutes before uncovering enables many of the moisture-laden nutrients to return to the vegetables. Although microwave cookery had not yet been described thousands of years ago when the ancient texts of Ayurveda were written, modern Ayurvedic physicians do not recommend this means of cooking for anything other than occasional. They feel that the process unevenly heats the nutrients, making their nutritional effect unpredictable. In a single microwaved dish containing various ingredients, certain items can be well-done while others remain cold or partially raw, and the consistency or texture of the food sometimes unpleasantly surprises the palate.

Good, efficient cooking is not necessarily a matter of speed. But neither is Ayurvedic cooking a tedious, slow process with the cook spending a long time stirring the pot. The practical Ayurvedic cook just heats things for as long as they need to be cooked without making a mood of it by slowing the process down or rushing to get the meal done at the expense of the nourishing value of the food.

FASTER COOKING: A PRESSURE COOKER

If getting a meal cooked and served quickly is important, then try a pressure cooker. By using steam heat, pressure cooking is a fast, healthful way to cook a variety of foods simultaneously. An entire meal can be prepared in a few minutes in a pressure cooker. For a rice and mixed vegetable dinner simply layer rice on the bottom of the pan with a proper amount of water and add your choice of vegetables cut into pieces of equal size. Follow the manufacturer's directions for the correct length of time to cook rice. The seasonings can be adjusted before serving. This is a cooking method that holds appeal for busy professionals and families who don't have time to fuss but want to serve highly nutritious meals. Cooking a mixed meal in a pressure cooker also has the advantage of allowing the cook to season and sauce the different foods as they finish cooking according to each family member's needs.

OTHER TIME-SAVERS

Other timesaving main dish methods include grouped steaming and baking. To prepare a large amount of mixed vegetables and pasta in a hurry, use a very large bamboo steamer (available at most Oriental grocery stores) placed to fit over a 6- to 8-quart pot half full of salted, boiling water. Layer the steamer with thinly chopped vegetables, the heaviest laid on the bottom up to light leafy greens on top. Then cover and steam. Meanwhile, cook small pasta shells or vermicelli in the water underneath. Everything should be done in about 6 to 8 minutes.

If you have to go out for an hour or two before you are expected to bring forth a wonderful meal, then prepare tightly covered casseroles of vegetables and noodles in a sauce, baked potatoes, or seasoned potatoes and carrots in olive oil, and Perfect Lentil Soup (page 164) in a slow (300°F.) oven. Make a number of condiments beforehand.

FOOD STORAGE

In an Ayurvedic cook's kitchen the refrigerator is rarely filled to capacity. If you opened the freezer you might find ice cubes, ice cream, nuts, flours, grains, and extra spices in cold storage, but little else. Frozen foods, even milk, have altered molecular qualities and offer less or uncertain nutrition. Since we don't eat ice cream primarily for its nutritional value, freezing it hardly matters. But cooking up large batches of food and freezing them for later use is not nutritionally practical, even though it seems to save time. Either canned or frozen foods can be used as garnishes, or they may make up a small proportion of a dish. Eating frozen or canned ingredients might be all right once every week or two, but these foods should not make up the greater proportion of the diet, since, like leftovers, they contribute to the production of ama.

> *First, select fresh foods*
> *that are locally grown,*
> *and in season.*

FOOD STORAGE: HOW TO USE A REFRIGERATOR

Even the refrigerator in an Ayurvedic cook's kitchen is mostly empty of fresh produce or leftovers. For the most part, chill whatever vegetables and fruits are necessary for the next couple of meals, as well as those basic dairy products that keep for a few days. Refrigerators of today are cold, closed systems that encourage the slow deterioration of food. They would be more useful for storage if they had air exchange systems. Without ventilation, as one food spoils everything else follows or is affected by the spoilage. However, refrigerators are good for long-term storage of items that are kept in sealed containers, such as nuts, nut butters, pickles and other condiments, salad dressings, jams, jellies, and fruit preserves.

It is important—about every week or two—to empty the refrigerator of fresh produce and anything stored for long periods of time and wash the interior thoroughly with a mild bleach solution of a teaspoon of bleach to a gallon of water.

❖❖

STORING ROOT CROPS

The best way to store such root crops as potatoes, yams, parsnips, and sweet potatoes is in a cool, dark, ventilated cabinet. Replacing the doors on a built-in kitchen cabinet with a decorative lattice or screen would allow enough ventilation if it is located in a cool place. Otherwise, store small quantities of roots in the bottom drawer of the refrigerator. Use and replenish them frequently.

STORING FLOURS AND OTHER GRAINS

An exception to the concept of food storage for freshness is the Ayurvedic guideline for storing wheat and rice. Old wheat and rice, that is, rice and wheat that have been carefully stored for two to four years, have more nutrition available in them than new wheat or rice. But freshly ground flour is preferred and seems to hold the most flavor in baking. As a rule, use any ground flour within two months or less after purchase or milling. After that, flour deteriorates quickly. Just before using flour, sift it or stir it well to air it.

Store flour, whole grains, nuts, and other foods in tightly covered plastic, ceramic, glass, or stainless steel containers. The only disadvantage to glass for food storage is that it chips and breaks easily. To be sure of freshness you might want to refrigerate or freeze flours, nuts, and grains, especially in the summer.

EQUIPMENT AND UTENSILS

The best kitchen utensils and equipment are those tools the cook feels most comfortable using. Use cooking equipment that does not reduce or alter the active nutritional ingredients in the food. It is best to avoid cooking and storing food in metals that cause chemical reactions, such as copper, aluminum, plastic- or Teflon-coated pans, or pans with the enamel chipped. Copper pans are not recommended for cooking foods but can be used for boiling water. Copper-clad pan bottoms conduct heat very well and are good on stainless steel pans, but copper should never come into contact with food. Recommended materials for the casserole dishes, pots, and pans include stainless steel, well-seasoned carbon steel, cast iron, earthenware, ceramic, and glass. Care should be taken when using imported earthenware and ceramics because some of the glazes used contain high lead levels.

Either stainless steel or wooden spoons and utensils are best choices. Use a separate spoon for each dish being prepared. A single spoon used for all the cooking subtly transfers the flavors from one pot to another and muddles the individual tastes.

Eating Your Ayurvedic Meals at Work

Nothing matches a home-cooked meal. When you can't go home for your biggest meal of the day because you are eating at work or school, bring a hot lunch with you in wide-mouth thermoses and other sealed containers. In India many people go to work and school with stainless steel "tiffin carriers" that look like a column of stacked bowls containing freshly cooked vegetables, rice, soup, and fruit. Little jars or sealed containers of spices and condiments can be left at work or carried along with lunch.

Even better than bringing your main meal from home every day is a properly functioning school cafeteria or an Ayurvedic corporate kitchen that provides an array of well-cooked foods representing all the six tastes and six qualities to give those dining something healthful to choose from. An Ayurvedic dining room is a sensible company health benefit.

Cooking for a Mixed Group

Cooking for a group or family means providing a varied selection of tastes and qualities so everyone eating will feel satisfied. When cooking for only one or two people the menu can be restricted to a few dishes that you know meet your diner's constitutional needs. Say you're balancing Pitta dosha and your guest is Vata-Pitta and the season is summer. It's easy to make an all–Pitta-reducing meal. With a larger group of people who run the gamut of dietary needs, at least two distinctly different entrées should be served as well as a variety of condiments and side dishes containing all the different tastes. At that point it is up to those dining to select what is best for them to eat.

The cook simply offers the meal as attractively as possible. You also give your best attention to each dish as you prepare it. Your thoughts about those whom you are lovingly cooking for ultimately affect them as they eat.

When judging the consistency of a dish before serving it, aim for it to be most easily digestible and balancing for the specific type of person who will be eating it. Thick soups, dahls, and even some milk-based sauces and drinks are not easy for Vata and Kapha types to digest. It is better to dilute them and adjust the seasonings accordingly. Most people with Pitta constitutions can easily digest thick foods or just about anything else. If you are serving a group of people with varied dietary needs—as most large groups are—always prepare the more easily digestible versions of a recipe and provide a varied selection of tastes and qualities so there's something for everyone to enjoy. The foods and cooking principles discussed in Chapter 5 may help you prepare meals for large groups of people.

The Moment of Judgment

There comes a point in the preparation of a meal when the cook needs to make a judgment about the overall tastes and consistencies of each dish. In tasting the food, take a small amount out of the pan with a separate spoon and taste it. It is not necessary or desirable to taste the food frequently during cooking. Taste a dish only when it seems to be finished or there is a question about its effect. With experience and growing attention to the food preparation process the tasting of the food before serving becomes a rare necessity.

Adjusting Seasonings

Tasting for a balance of seasonings, or adjusting the seasonings, means sampling the most liquid part of the dish and making changes as necessary. Take a small spoonful and, as it passes over the tongue to the throat, notice which of the six tastes are most outstanding or where the sensation of taste occurs. If you've cooked something spicy the predominant sensation will be in the back of the throat. When a dish is rich in flavors the tastes will enliven many parts of the palate. One well-prepared entrée can deliciously satisfy the six essential taste requirements for a balanced meal, and it will be a memorable experience for everyone eating it. Moroccan Delight (pages 175–177) is such a recipe.

JUST BEFORE SERVING

And finally, the cook looks at the many finished dishes and takes a kind of mental inventory to see that all of the tastes, qualities, and categories are represented. At this point some last-minute adjustments can be made by adding condiments, pickles, or perhaps a quickly prepared warm side dish to balance the meal further and increase the variety. Add a little more of the bitter taste with a bouquet of shortened celery sticks with the leaves left on or some sour coolness with a bowl of lime and lemon wedges. If bitter, pungent, and astringent tastes are underrepresented (a common lack in American cooking), make a small bowl of wilted lettuce by quickly sautéing chopped lettuce with minced ginger for 30 seconds in a little hot oil. When you are satisfied that the menu offers enough balanced choices, serve the dinner with pride and be ready to accept all the justified compliments you'll receive.

Every kitchen should be filled
with appetizing smells.
Then when the guests arrive
they can't help but say,
"Everything smells great."
Without any other appetizers
they are ready to eat.

—DR. P. D. SUBHEDAR

ANY QUESTIONS?

Although we've discussed many general ideas to get you started practicing this traditional but new "science of life," including identifying your body type, how to eat, and what it means to be an Ayurvedic cook, you may have some other questions. Questions and Answers About Ayurveda (pages 277–281) may have the answers. The questions in the Appendix are commonly asked food questions that Dr. Kasture and Richard Averbach, M.D., a Maharishi Ayur-Ved physician, answered when they were teaching an Ayurvedic diet course at Maharishi International University. If you have other specific questions about your health and diet, please consult a competent Ayurvedic physician. A list can be found on pages 291–292.

Chapter 2

COOKING FOR VATA, PITTA, AND KAPHA

For Vata

WHAT IS VATA?

As we've seen, everyone is naturally one of the three primary types: Vata, Pitta, Kapha, or perhaps a combination of these three. Vata is most like air and space. It is dry, cold, windy, and light. Your nature is most like Vata if many of the characteristics in this list best describe you.

VATA CHARACTERISTICS

BALANCED	OUT OF BALANCE
Vivacious	Restless
Joyful, serene	Nervous, or flighty
Alert, quick learner	Forgetful, distractable
Confident	Anxious, worried
Light but sound sleep	Difficulty sleeping
Moves lightly, gracefully	Body stiff and slow
Smooth skin, regular bowels	Dry skin, constipated

THE BEST DIET FOR VATA

Following a Vata-balancing diet is one way Ayurveda suggests to maintain good health. If your Vata is aggravated, follow a good Vata-reducing diet and visit an Ayurveda physician, too, for other recommendations.

Vata types and any combinations that include the element of Vata, such as Vata-Kapha, Vata-Pitta, and Vata-Pitta-Kapha, should follow a Vata-balancing diet during the winter and very early spring and whenever the cold, dry, windy weather that most disturbs Vata types prevails in your locale. Those with a completely Vata nature should follow a Vata-balancing diet all year round. If you also have Pitta or Kapha as part of your constitution, then emphasize the foods in those particular diets during their seasons. We'll talk more about modifying your basic diet with the change of the seasons later on. If a physician trained in Maharishi Ayur-Ved has given you a specific diet to balance your doshas, follow that diet.

GENERAL VATA DIET

FAVOR

- Warm, delicious food and drink
- Tastes: sweet, sour, and salty
- Qualities: Heavy, hot, and oily
- Small to moderate amounts of food
- Eat frequently—every four to five hours
- Enjoy rich foods

REDUCE

- Cold food
- Chilled drinks
- Weight-reducing food
- Tastes: bitter, astringent, pungent
- Qualities: cold, dry, light
- Very heavy and infrequent meals

TASTES AND QUALITIES BEST FOR VATA

Certain food tastes and qualities are better for Vata types than others. For a balanced meal serve all six tastes and six qualities but eat most of those foods that reduce Vata.

BEST FOOD TASTES FOR VATA
Sweet • Sour • Salty

SEASONAL CONSIDERATIONS FOR VATA

Warm, sweet, sour, salty, slightly pungent foods with heavy, oily, hot qualities that build the body's tissues, muscles, and bones and increase strength are the best ones for people with Vata constitutions. Vata, most like the element of wind or air, is bothered in windy, dry, or cold weather. During such weather when agni, that fiery element, is neither very active in the environment nor in Vata's digestive system, people with this constitution find it difficult to feel warm inside or to digest food effectively. They should particularly reduce raw or undercooked vegetables, light snacks, cold drinks, and carbonated beverages.

BEST FOOD QUALITIES FOR VATA
Heavy • Hot • Oily

Light, dry (or drying), and cold foods are difficult for Vata to digest and only aggravate the excessive lightness and dryness of Vata's constitution. If these heavy and oily qualities prove to be too difficult to digest or you are a Vata type who gains weight from eating rich foods, try following a light Vata diet as described on pages 262–263.

MENU PLANNING FOR VATA

The most useful menus for Vata begin with several selections that are delicious and stimulating to the appetite, and then continue with one or two substantial main dishes featuring heavy, oily qualities served during the middle of the meal. Soups provide a warm, appetizing start to a meal for everyone—especially Vata types. They should be served frequently, even at every main meal, during Vata season. A steaming bowl of bouillon or a tasty, thin vegetable soup appears as a regular feature in Vata's menu plan, even in the summer. Good, nourishing soups are not necessarily thick or heavy, but they should be delicious and richly flavored.

If a thick soup is to be served as the first course, it should be preceded by a good, stimulating appetizer; otherwise, it would be better to include it as the main part of a light meal with bread and a salad. Serving a thick soup as an appetizer to Vata has a good chance of shutting down the digestive fire and putting an early end to Vata's interest in the meal. It is easy to make Vata Broth (see pages 147–148) or a mixed vegetable soup by selecting three or four vegetables from the Vata-balancing diet list, adding them with a few herbs or spices to boiling water, and simmering for an hour before serving.

BALANCE FOR VATA

So, if you follow a Vata-balancing diet by eating many substantial, warm, rich, nourishing foods, good things naturally will happen. You'll thrive and not feel hungry right after eating, your digestion will work efficiently, your skin and hair will look healthy, and your physical stamina will remain more constant. As long as you eat in a balanced way at lunch and dinner, without between-meal snacking, you will maintain good digestive power with the ability to use all your food's nutrients.

It is especially after eating meals made up of undercooked or light, dry foods that Vata types remain hungry and feel dissatisfied and uncomfortable. The rice cakes that satisfy Kapha are too light for Vata. And vegetables that are briefly steamed but still crunchy are fine for Pitta but are difficult for Vata to digest. Sautéing any vegetables in a little oil makes them more digestible for Vata types.

SATISFACTION AND BALANCE

It is an important point to remember in planning an Ayurveda menu to include all six tastes and six qualities in both lunch and dinner. A healthy meal for Vata will consist of mostly sweet, salty, sour, heavy, oily, and hot ingredients. But each menu also includes a few bitter, astringent, pungent, light, dry, and cold ingredients, no matter what your specific body requires. To achieve balance just eat a bite or two of those tastes or qualities that increase Vata, but for the main part of the meal eat the foods that are best for your own balance. Eating in a balanced way brings feelings of satisfaction.

FOR A VATA-BALANCING DIET

FAVOR

General:	increased quantity of food, oily (unctuous), warm food and drinks, heavy, heating food; sweet, sour, and salty tastes
Dairy:	all dairy products
Sweeteners:	any sugar, honey, molasses
Oils:	all oils, especially ghee and sesame
Grains:	rice, wheat, oats
Beans:	mung, masoor, tofu
Fruits:	grapes, cherries, peaches, melons, avocado, coconut, banana, orange, pineapple, plums, berries, mango, papaya, olives, lemon, lime
Vegetables:	beets, carrots, asparagus, cucumber, sweet potato, artichoke, radishes, turnips
Spices:	asafoetida (hing), basil, black pepper, caraway, cardamom, cinnamon, clove, cumin, garlic, ginger, mustard, poppy seeds, salt
Nuts:	any except walnuts
Beverages:	tepid water, fruit and vegetable juice, warm milk, herbal teas
Meat:	chicken, turkey, seafood (for non-vegetarians)

REDUCE

General:	light diet, dry foods, cold food and drinks; pungent, bitter, and astringent tastes
Grains:	large amounts of barley, corn, millet, buckwheat, rye
Fruits:	apple, cranberries, unripe fruit
Vegetables:	peas, green leafy vegetables, broccoli, cabbage, cauliflower, zucchini, potato, or raw vegetables, most sprouted legumes/ seeds/beans, tomatoes, peppers
Spices:	allspice, coriander, nutmeg, turmeric, oregano
Nuts:	walnuts
Beans:	all beans except soy (tofu), mung, masoor, and Urad lentils
Beverages:	iced drinks, carbonated drinks, thick milkshakes, coffee, black tea
Meat:	beef (for non-vegetarians)

COOKING AND EATING TIPS FOR VATA

- Heat food thoroughly and serve it promptly.
- Eat warm, well-cooked food.
- Drink tepid or warm liquids during and at the end of the meal, layering solid food with liquid.
- Always eat bread spread with ghee, butter, or nut butters—never dry.
- Cook all vegetables until soft.
- Serve all soups—including lentil and bean soups—in a very liquid consistency.
- Prepare cooked cereals and grains with milk rather than water whenever possible.
- Serve tossed green salads without thick, raw vegetables.
- Do not serve dried-out or leftover cooked food.
- Serve soft, ripe fruit.
- Steam or soak dried fruits in water before eating.
- Do not eat while standing up, driving, talking on the phone, or watching television.

SPICES:

asafoetida (hing), caraway, cardamom, cinnamon, cloves, cumin, salt, ginger, licorice root powder, mustard seeds, Vata Churna,* pepper

HERBS:

basil, dill, fennel, parsley, saffron, savory, tarragon

GRAINS & OTHER STAPLES:

rice, wheat flours, couscous, pasta, lentils, mung beans, ghee and cooking oils, sugar, raw honey, molasses, dates, raisins, figs, coconut, sweet potatoes, nuts and nut butters

* A Maharishi Ayur-Ved product that can be ordered by mail. See Appendix 5, page 293.

IN VATA'S PANTRY

Above are some commonly used, less perishable foods for Vata-balanced cooking. These items can be kept on hand year-round and used as needed every day. You may need to shop at a good natural foods store for some items.

ABOUT THE RECIPES

Although the recipes and sample menu in this chapter are especially good for maintaining Vata in balance, many of these recipes can be prepared for a meal to serve to people with different dietary needs. Sometimes a recipe that is good for one body type is also beneficial for others. When using Ayurvedic menu-planning principles it is difficult (and artificial) to try to create recipes exclusively for one constitution, because so much in life is good for everyone. At a meal offering a variety of dishes, each person would simply select the amount from each that is best. Because some of these recipes are useful for more than the Vata constitution, they may be good, sometimes with minor changes, for balancing Pitta or Kapha doshas, too. All the recipes with recommendations for the different constitutions are in Chapter 4.

MAIN POINTS IN AYURVEDIC MENU PLANNING

- Present all six tastes and six qualities.
- Order of the meal: Begin with an appetizer as soon as food is ready.
- Alternate heavy and light foods throughout the meal.
- Use color, texture, and delicious flavors to stimulate the eye and palate.

ABOUT THE VATA MENU

As with any healthy meal, the menu for a well-balanced Vata meal contains all six tastes and six qualities, but a Vata-balancing menu will feature a greater number of foods with salty, sour, sweet tastes and heavy, oily (unctuous), hot qualities than Vata-increasing foods that are light, bitter, astringent, or dry. The best Vata menus start with a good appetizer, continue with a substantial entrée and bread, and end with a rich, mouthwatering dessert.

The following sample menu would make a rather elaborate meal if everything on the menu were served. If the heavy, sweet desserts seem too filling, a simple sweet fruit salad or a couple of cookies could conclude the meal. This menu is an example of a Vata-reducing meal, not an absolute plan to follow. The predominant tastes and qualities of each selection are noted. Some of the dishes on this menu may benefit Pitta or Kapha types as well, but our main interest here is cooking for Vata.

A Sample Vata Menu

RELISH TRAY
Pickles • Olives • Cheeses • Dips • Sauces • Spreads
(Sweet, Sour, Pungent, Salty)

GINGER CARROT SOUP
(Pungent, Sweet, Oily, Salty, Hot)

ASPARAGUS SALAD WITH RASPBERRY VINAIGRETTE
(Sweet, Bitter, Slightly Sour and Astringent, Cold)

RICH STUFFED PEPPERS *
(Sweet, Salty, Slightly Bitter, Astringent, Pungent, Heavy, Oily)
OR
ZUCCHINI AND TOMATO FRY
(Sweet, Sour, Slightly Bitter and Pungent, Oily)

SQUASH ROLLS WITH BUTTER
(Sweet, Slightly Salty, Oily)

CREAMY RICE PUDDING
(Sweet, Heavy)
AND/OR
CHOCOLATE CUSTARD PIE
(Sweet, Heavy)

* Recipe follows and also appears in Chapter 4, Ayurvedic Recipes (pages 181–182).

❖✦❖

Why is this such an outstanding menu for Vata? Good appetizers are essential for sparking Vata's digestion, so this meal begins with two very different appetizers. The relish tray, frequently appearing at dinner parties, contains sweet pickles, salty olives, crackers and chips, cheeses, dips, and spreads. It is of particular interest since it presents quite a variety of sweet, sour, salty, and pungent little appetizers that invite Vata to nibble just enough to spark digestion but not to dull the appetite. Recipes for some dips and spreads, as well as the other dishes on the menu, are in Chapter 4.

The second appetizer on the menu, Ginger Carrot Soup, keeps Vata's digestion active and provides a fine lead into the heavier parts of the meal. This soup is very warming and sweet—a little too pungent for Pitta's comfort, but just right for both Vata and Kapha.

Even if you were dining out you could order from the dinner menu to suit your needs. But always ask for warm water to drink rather than iced drinks. Choose a hot soup, not a green salad, to begin the meal, and conclude with a warm dessert such as fruit pie, not ice cream or cheesecake.

Some salads are better for Vata than others. Instead of the typical tossed green salad with its light qualities, bitter, and astringent tastes usually found on a dinner menu, Vata enjoys a heavier, sweeter, oily salad with the astringent and bitter tastes present but not dominating. Asparagus, a choice vegetable for Vata because it contains oily, sweet, and heavy properties, dressed with Raspberry Vinaigrette makes a delicious and colorful salad nourishing for Vata. The Raspberry Vinaigrette also adds a small amount of necessary astringency and dryness to the menu as a whole.

DESIGNING A VATA-BALANCING RECIPE

Just what are we looking for in an excellent Vata-balancing recipe? When analyzing any recipe we consider the list of ingredients, the cooking method(s), and finally, by tasting the finished product, we experience how well all the cooked ingredients work together. You can find more about Ayurvedic recipe design in Chapter 1.

Let's take a moment to examine a recipe from Vata's menu. Rich Stuffed Peppers are good in every way for Vata. The following recipe makes a mostly sweet-tasting entrée that is heavy and oily in quality—a satisfying combination for Vata to enjoy.

RICH STUFFED PEPPERS
Serves 4–6

3 large green peppers, halved and blanched
½ cup ghee or unsalted butter
¾ cup chopped celery stalks and leaves
2 small zucchini, cubed
¼ cup chopped parsley
½ cup chopped sweet red pepper
¼ cup coarsely chopped pecans or cashews
4 cups soft bread cubes
½ teaspoon salt
1 teaspoon crushed sage
½ teaspoon thyme
¼ to ½ teaspoon coarsely ground black pepper
1 large tomato, peeled and cut in 6 wedges

1. To blanch the peppers, bring 2 quarts of water to a boil. Meanwhile, halve the peppers and remove the seeds and membrane. Drop them into boiling water and allow them to boil for 3 minutes. Remove the soft peppers from the pot, place them in a colander, and immediately run them under cold water. Drain the pepper halves, hollow sides down, on a towel until you are ready to stuff them.

2. Preheat the oven to 350°F.

3. For the stuffing, heat the ghee in a large frying pan or deep pot. Add the vegetables and sauté, stirring frequently, for about 20 minutes, or until they are soft. Add the chopped nuts, then the bread cubes and seasonings. Toss well and heat through. Mound the stuffing into the pepper halves and place them in a lightly oiled 7 × 11-inch baking pan or other deep casserole, with the tomato wedges around the edges. Bake, uncovered, for 10 minutes.

NOTE: Instead of tomato wedges a simple tomato sauce can be served along with the peppers.

The sweet-tasting peppers are first well cooked by blanching, then again by baking. Both the sweet taste and the well-cooked vegetable are important in Vata's diet. This recipe's rich variety comes from the stuffing. It has a fine blend of the six tastes that help bring balance to the recipe and the whole meal.

When designing an Ayurvedically balanced recipe, every single ingredient doesn't have to be Vata-decreasing. But the majority should be ones that help balance Vata. If there is a question about how a certain ingredient affects Vata, please see the Charts of Ingredients beginning on page 283. For instance, the ghee, sweet pepper, pecans, salt, pepper, tomato wedges, and bread cubes (made from wheat bread) all reduce Vata and make up most of the recipe. The others are present to a minor extent to give Vata a small experience of the bitter, astringent, and pungent tastes. These minor players include parsley, thyme, sage, and some celery leaves.

Perhaps you're wondering why, if all six tastes are represented in this recipe, we think it is best for Vata and not Pitta and Kapha as well. After all, everyone needs all six tastes in a balanced meal. Actually, this is a good recipe for reducing Pitta as well as Vata. They share a need for sweet, heavy, and oily foods. It's more a matter of emphasis in tastes. Pitta would only eat one tomato wedge to experience the sour taste and might increase the amount of bitter and astringent-tasting celery and parsley, if desired.

The answer for Kapha types is found in the qualities. Stuff the green peppers with herbed or Roasted and Spiced Barley with Vegetables (pages 78–79) for Kapha and those watching their weight, instead of using heavy, oily, and sweet wheat bread stuffing. The dry, light qualities of this pungent recipe are more beneficial to Kapha. It's an example of why we look at both the tastes and qualities of the ingredients when designing a recipe.

More About the Vata Menu

The other entrée choice on the menu, Zucchini and Tomato Fry, is a recipe that at first glance may appear to increase Vata because people with Vata imbalances usually eat very little zucchini. The objection to serving zucchini, compared with other squashes that are all good for Vata, is that the skin's bitter taste aggravates Vata. But peeling the zucchini before cooking it will make it have about the same effect on Vata as other squashes.

Likewise, the tomato's sweet-and-sour tastes are good for reducing Vata, but the tomato skin is particularly difficult for Vata to digest. So scald tomatoes under hot water for a minute or two and peel them before using. By combining the particular spices in this recipe and frying everything in ghee, the Zucchini and Tomato Fry enriches the depth of this Vata menu by adding more sweet, sour, slightly bitter, and pungent tastes and a welcome oily quality. Bread, hot biscuits, or dinner rolls regularly appear on a Vata menu. The best breads are made from whole grain wheat, rye, or oat flours rather than light and dry corn bread. The Squash Rolls in this menu are not only sweet and heavy, a common characteristic of most wheat-based breads, but with the addition of the cooked squash, the rolls have a particularly moist, tender, heavy, delightful consistency for nourishing Vata.

Either of the desserts on this menu is rich and nourishing for Vata. Creamy Rice Pudding represents a hallmark for Vata cookery. The rice is cooked so well that the individual grains almost disappear. This makes the pudding particularly digestible and satisfying for Vata. Rice pudding is always served warm to aid in digestion.

Being able, in fact encouraged, to eat rich desserts is one of the nicest things about following Vata's diet. If they are too cold in quality and temperature, Vata has trouble digesting them. Because it is primarily sweet and heavy, the Chocolate Custard Pie on the menu can be enjoyed by Vata at will, particularly if it is not served ice-cold.

OTHER RECIPES ESPECIALLY FOR VATA

When planning other menus, try any of these recipes appropriate for a Vata diet. They can be found in Chapter 4.

BEVERAGES
Bed and Breakfast Drink
Date Shake
Fragrantly Spiced Lassi
Plain Refreshing Lassi
Saffron Milk Tea
Three-in-One Supreme
Watermelon-Strawberry Punch

APPETIZERS
Cheese Crackers
Ginger Pickle
Golden Panir Cubes
Golden Yummies

SALADS
Beet Ginger Salad
Carrot Raisin Salad
Macedonia di Fruita
Splendid Layers Salad
Tossed Green Salad

DRESSINGS, SAUCES, DIPS, AND MARINADES
Avocado Cheese Sauce and Dip
Basic Cheese Sauce
Cream Tahini Sauce
Deanna's Vinaigrette
Ginger Soy Gravy
Gold Sauce
Herbed Vinaigrette
Pitta Churna Salad Dressing and Marinade (or use Vata Churna)
Red Sauce
Scrumptious Sesame-Orange Sauce
Simple Vinaigrette Dressing

OTHER BASICS
Everyday Granola
Ghee
Panir and Ricotta Soft Cheese

BREADS
French Bread
Light Corn Bread
Little Flat Breads
Puris and Chapatis
Squash Rolls

SOUPS
Perfect Lentil Soup
Potage Printanier
Sweet Potato Soup
Thermos Flask Soup
Vegetable Soup with Fresh Herbs

MAIN DISHES
Artichokes Stuffed with Herbed Cheese
Curried Vegetables and Panir
Fried Spiced Potatoes
Green Beans in Tomato Sauce (Fagioloni in Umido Volponi)
Moroccan Delight with Couscous
Oven-Baked French Fries
Pasta and Green Sauce
Petis Pois Braisé Laitue (Peas Braised with Lettuce)
Saffron Rice
Simple Rice Pilaf
Stuffed Shells with Artichoke Cream Sauce
Sweet Summer Curry
Tofu Nut Burgers
Vegetable Whole Grain Sauté

SIDE DISHES (AS PART OF A MAIN MEAL)
Green and Gold Baked Squash
Layered Vegetable Loaf
Savory Wild Rice Casserole
Simply Baked Carrots

DESSERTS
Almond Custard Fresh Fruit Pie
American Apple Pie
Apple Dumplings with Vanilla Sauce
Fresh Ginger Cookies
Fruit Shortcake
Italian Hazelnut Cookies
Jam Diagonals
Kaffa's Dream
Lemon Scones
Lemony Date Bars
Marble Crumb Cake with Vanilla Sauce and English Cream
Oatmeal Raisin Cookies
Old-Fashioned Orange Tea Cake
R&S Couscous
Rich Quick Chocolate Mousse
Strawberry Yogurt Pie

Super Chocolate Brownies
Swedish Chocolate Cream Pie
Sweet Chocolate Cake with Cherry Sauce
Sweet Fruit and Spice Tea Bread
Sweet Potato–Apple Pie
White Figs in Apricot Cream Sauce

For Pitta

WHAT IS PITTA?

Of the three basic constitutions Pitta is most like fire, that is, hot, dry, and light. Your nature is most like Pitta if many of the characteristics in this list best describe you.

PITTA CHARACTERISTICS

BALANCED	OUT OF BALANCE
Enterprising, idealistic	Pressures self and others
Energetic, organized	Too time-conscious, excited
Often charismatic leader	Task-oriented, overly critical
Lively, friendly, warm	Irritable, quick-tempered
Curious, broad interests	Activity overload
Radiant, warm skin, freckles	Blemishes, gray hair, hair loss
Good appetite and digestion	Ulcers, stomach upsets

THE BEST DIET FOR PITTA

Throughout the year but especially in hot weather, Pitta follows a cooling, sweet, and nourishing diet. If you have a strong desire for Pitta-increasing foods, enjoy them in the winter, and then only in moderation. If you feel that Pitta is increased, follow a good Pitta-balancing diet and visit an Ayurveda physician, too, for other recommendations.

Those people with such combined doshas as Pitta-Kapha or Kapha-Pitta should follow the Pitta-balancing diet in summer and into the fall while the weather remains hot and the Kapha-balancing diet during the cold part of spring and in damp, cold weather. Those with Vata-Pitta and Pitta-Vata imbalances usually follow a Pitta-decreasing diet in summer and Vata during the rest of the year. We'll talk more about modifying your basic diet with the change of the seasons later on. If you are primarily Pitta in nature, then the simplest thing to do is follow the Pitta-balancing diet year round.

Of course, if a physician trained in Maharishi Ayur-Ved has given you a specific diet to balance your doshas, follow that diet.

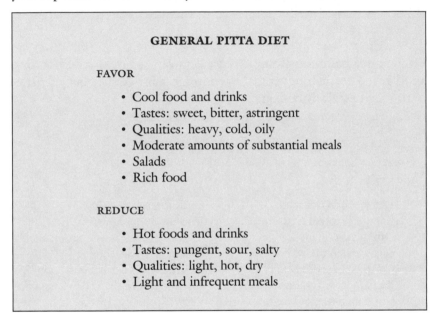

GENERAL PITTA DIET

FAVOR

- Cool food and drinks
- Tastes: sweet, bitter, astringent
- Qualities: heavy, cold, oily
- Moderate amounts of substantial meals
- Salads
- Rich food

REDUCE

- Hot foods and drinks
- Tastes: pungent, sour, salty
- Qualities: light, hot, dry
- Light and infrequent meals

TASTES AND QUALITIES BEST FOR PITTA

A properly balanced meal for everyone—including Pitta—contains foods with all of the six tastes and six food qualities, but people following a Pitta-pacifying diet prepare most of their meals with an emphasis on ingredients that reduce or help balance Pitta.

BEST FOOD TASTES FOR PITTA
Sweet • Bitter • Astringent

Seasonal Considerations for Pitta

People with outstanding Pitta characteristics are naturally warm, even in winter. They are most like a lovely, hot summer day, so menus for Pitta types during summer and into early autumn include a greater proportion of moist and cooling foods, less heavy-to-digest protein, and lots of sweetness. A Pitta-balancing diet is abundant in seasonally fresh fruits and vegetables. Almost all of the fruits and vegetables available during the hot months help to pacify Pitta as do mixed green salads that naturally contain the bitter and astringent tastes useful in keeping Pitta happy.

Care should be taken not to eat salads, fruits, and light foods exclusively in the summer. Foods with heavier, oily qualities need to be included in all main meals, too. Eating only light or dry food aggravates Pitta. Typically, Pitta has a strong appetite requiring substantial, satisfying meals that include such wheat products as pasta, breads, and rolls as well as other foods with heavy qualities—rice, artichokes, potatoes, and tofu are a few standards. Especially good news for those on a Pitta-balancing diet is that they do not need to skip sweet desserts. Since sugar and other naturally sweet foods pacify Pitta, desserts are an important part of each main meal. Starting a meal with some sweet-tasting food is especially pleasing to Pitta.

BEST FOOD QUALITIES FOR PITTA
Heavy • Oily • Cold

Other Seasonal Menu Changes

Drinking lots of water and cooling fruit beverages, particularly sweet fruit juices, is most refreshing for Pitta in the summer. For those following a Pitta-reducing diet in the winter and early spring, fresh sweet fruits and cooling vegetables are still important, but also more of the warm soups and higher-protein entrées we associate with cold winter days can appear on the menu.

There is no need for watermelon in the winter.
Your body needs watery food in the summer.
Nature grows foods
according to the correct season for you.
We must think more about Nature
when we plan our meals.

—DR. P. D. SUBHEDAR

MENU PLANNING FOR PITTA

The first consideration in planning a meal for Pitta is that it look beautiful. Those with a Pitta nature respond strongly to visual cues. So colorful, elegant presentation does as much to stimulate Pitta's appetite and bring enjoyment to the meal as warm, pungent appetizers do for Vata and Kapha. In fact, special appetizers aren't as necessary for Pitta as is a menu that features salads and a substantial main dish or two containing more bitter and astringent tastes, various sweet, pungent, sour, and bitter condiments, and ending with a delectable dessert, all beautifully presented.

SATISFACTION FOR PITTA

Feeling satisfaction after meals comes not only from what you eat but how and when you eat. Unlike Vata and Kapha, those with the Pitta constitution rarely need to stimulate agni. Their digestive fires are ready whenever the food is. But maintaining the good digestion of those following a Pitta-balancing diet depends on eating at regular times, eating when hungry, and as far as possible, not postponing meals. Pitta types not only become irritable when they get overly hungry, they tend to eat too much too quickly without enjoying the food or giving their digestions the opportunity to work well. This results in feelings of dissatisfaction or discomfort after eating.

FOR A PITTA-BALANCING DIET

FAVOR

General: cool foods and drinks, liquids, heavy, oily foods; sweet, bitter, and astringent tastes
Dairy: milk, butter, cream, panir (soft cheese), ricotta
Sweeteners: all sweeteners except honey and molasses
Oils: ghee, sunflower, coconut, olive
Grains: wheat, rice, oats, millet
Fruits: grapes, cherries, melons, avocado, coconut, orange (sweet), plums (sweet), lime, apple, peach, dried fruit
Vegetables: asparagus, cucumber, cabbage, potato, sweet potato, green leafy vegetables, broccoli, cauliflower, celery, sprouts, squash, green beans, parsnips
Beans: all beans, lentils, tofu
Spices: anise, black pepper and ginger—in small quantities, cardamom, cinnamon, coriander, dill, fennel, licorice root, nutmeg
Nuts: blanched almonds, walnuts, cashews
Beverages: cool water in large quantities, sweet fruit juices, mint teas, warm or cool milk, milkshakes, fruit smoothies
Meat: chicken, turkey, egg whites

REDUCE

General: hot foods and drinks, light, dry food; pungent, sour, and salty tastes
Dairy: yogurt, cheese, sour cream, cultured buttermilk
Sweeteners: honey and molasses
Oils: almond, sesame, corn, safflower
Grains: corn, rye, large amounts of millet, oats, or barley
Fruits: grapefruit, olives, papaya, persimmon, banana, orange (sour), pineapple (sour), plums (sour), unripe strawberry
Vegetables: hot peppers, tomato, carrots, spinach, beets, onions
Spices: allspice, asafoetida (hing), basil, cayenne, cloves, cumin, fenugreek, garlic, mustard, salt, pepper, saffron
Nuts: peanuts, almonds (unblanched)
Beverages: hot drinks, lemonade or sour drinks, herbal teas, buttermilk, Lassi, large amounts of coffee or black tea
Meat: red meat, seafood, egg yolks

COOKING AND EATING TIPS FOR PITTA

- Eat cool, rather substantial or heavy, rich-tasting soups, appetizers, and main dishes served in moderate portions.
- Light foods such as tossed salads or dishes of millet and barley should make up less than one-third of a meal.
- Serve mostly warm to cool foods rather than steaming hot ones.
- Use varieties of sweet fruits in mixed casseroles with vegetables, rice, and other grains.
- When following new recipes, reduce the salt by one-half.
- Substitute 2 tablespoons yogurt for each whole egg in baking recipes and increase the leavening slightly.
- Sip tepid or slightly chilled drinks with a meal, not iced ones.
- Serve a salad of leafy greens frequently.
- Rarely cook with tomatoes, cheese, yogurt, sour cream, or pungent spices.
- Instead of pungent or frankly fiery spices, use ground licorice root, cinnamon, coriander, nutmeg, fennel, and fresh cooling herbs.
- Do not serve leftovers from the day before.
- Do not prepare food or eat when upset, angry, or agitated.
- Sit down to eat in a settled, undisturbed atmosphere.
- End a meal with a sweet dessert or fresh sweet fruit.

SPICES:

anise seeds, cardamom, cinnamon, coriander, licorice root, mace, nutmeg, poppy seeds, paprika, turmeric, Pitta Churna*

HERBS:

dill, fennel, parsley, savory, tarragon

GRAINS & OTHER STAPLES:

ghee, rice, wheat flour, pasta, lentils, sugar, dried fruits, walnuts, cashews, blanched almonds, nut butters, olive, sunflower or safflower oils, potatoes, sweet potatoes, yams

* A Maharishi Ayur-Ved product that can be ordered by mail. See Appendix 5, page 293.

IN PITTA'S PANTRY

Opposite are some less perishable foods frequently used when cooking for Pitta types or in the hot weather of Pitta season. These staple items can be kept in stock all the time and replenished as needed.

ABOUT THE RECIPES

Although the recipes and sample menu in this chapter are especially recommended for maintaining Pitta in balance, some of these recipes can be prepared for a meal to serve to people with different dietary needs. Many times a recipe that is good for one body type is also good for others because each of the three types have some needs in common. When using Ayurvedic menu-planning principles, it is nearly impossible to create recipes useful for just a single constitution because so much in life is good for everyone. Good Ayurvedic menus, like life itself, cannot be so strictly limited that their enjoyment is lost. Abundance and variety invite diners to enjoy the meal. At a dinner offering a variety of dishes, each person would simply select the amount from each that is best for him or her. Because some of these recipes are useful for more than the Pitta constitution, they may be good—sometimes with minor changes—for balancing Vata or Kapha doshas as well. All the recipes with recommendations for the different constitutions are in Chapter 4. But let's look at a sample menu for Pitta.

A Sample Pitta Menu

POMEGRANATE JUICE WITH MINT LEAF GARNISH
(Sweet, Astringent, Sour, Slightly Pungent, Cold)

CREAMY SUMMER GARDEN SOUP *
(Sweet, Bitter, Astringent, Heavy, Oily, Cold)

MOROCCAN DELIGHT
(All Tastes, Heavy, Oily)

* Recipe follows and also appears in Chapter 4, Ayurvedic Recipes (page 159).

SPLENDID LAYERS SALAD
(Sweet, Bitter, Astringent, Oily, Heavy)
OR
COLESLAW WITH CARAWAY DRESSING
(Sweet, Sour, Salty, Bitter, Dry, Astringent)

LITTLE FLAT BREADS
(Sweet, Slightly Bitter and Salty, Heavy)

PINEAPPLE ICE
(Sweet, Cold)

OATMEAL RAISIN COOKIES
(Sweet, Slightly Salty, Heavy)

ABOUT THE PITTA MENU

Although the sample menu in this chapter is especially good for those who want to balance Pitta dosha, it features all six tastes and food qualities with an emphasis on sweet, astringent, bitter tastes and the heavy, oily, and cold qualities that best suit Pitta diets. (All recipes in this menu are in Chapter 4.)

This sample menu for Pitta begins with a small glass of slightly chilled pomegranate juice. Pitta enjoys a light appetizer, and the sweet, astringent, yet sour and mildly pungent tastes in pomegranate juice refresh and stimulate the palate and Pitta's appetite. Bottled pomegranate juice is usually available at natural food stores. If you don't have it, you can also use apple juice. The first two items on Pitta's menu are liquid. Those with Pitta constitutions use more liquid in their diet than others. Cooling liquids are especially beneficial. The juice and soup that comes right after it are good beginners to the meal. Served cold, the Creamy Summer Garden Soup with the consistency of a good vichyssoise is rich in feeling, cold, and refreshing to eat in the summer. (In the winter and the cold days of spring you might prefer to eat it warm.) In a moment we'll look at the Creamy Summer Garden Soup recipe as an example of good Ayurvedic recipe design for Pitta.

The main dish on this menu, Moroccan Delight, is rich in colors, flavors, substance, and varied textures that are all most appealing to Pitta. All six tastes are represented, and the heavy and oily qualities help to satisfy Pitta's strong appetite. Moroccan Delight (the delight happens as you savor the subtle blend of flavors) makes a festive dinner entrée for parties because the heavy, oily, sweet properties are especially beneficial for those with Vata dosha or the combination of Vata-Pitta and Pitta-Vata. Of course it's fine to serve a tossed salad of mixed greens at this meal, or at any meal for Pitta, since the bitter and astringent tastes in greens benefit Pitta. In this menu we have Splendid Layers Salad, a dense salad of various colorful raw vegetables layered with sprinklings of Pitta Churna Salad Dressing. Its cold and heavy qualities combine well for Pitta types since the heavier vegetables provide enough substance for Pitta's healthy appetite. Be sure to cut everything into easy-to-eat, bite-size pieces during preparation. Each vegetable might be cut in a different shape to add visual interest as well.

If the Splendid Layers Salad seems too much to serve at this meal you can substitute a simple Coleslaw with a Caraway Dressing. The coleslaw salad, a basic "cold" salad for Pitta that can even be eaten in winter when cabbage is at its best, changes the effect of the menu slightly because it is adding more sour taste to the meal. But the entire menu is rather light in the sour taste since Pitta needs very little of it. Coleslaw with Caraway Dressing does not increase Pitta when it is served as part of a balanced meal. It's not a salad for a light meal or to be eaten by itself. But Splendid Layers Salad is so filling and sweet, bitter, and astringent that it can be served with bread and butter and a light dessert to Pitta for a light meal, especially in summer.

Any kind of bread could be included in this menu, but Little Flat Breads, similar to Naan and other eastern breads, accompany Moroccan Delight nicely. Pitta should usually have bread with every main meal. Wheat, barley, millet, chick-pea, and oat flours make the best breads for Pitta. The hot, dry qualities of cornmeal and the sour taste of rye increase Pitta dosha.

For dessert either cooling, sweet Pineapple Ice or sweet, heavy Oatmeal Raisin Cookies can be served. Or offer both of them. Pineapple Ice, a perfect dessert for Pitta especially on a hot day, is easy to make and similar to authentic Italian ices. Sweet, ripe pineapple is especially calming to Pitta. After such a large meal a heavier dessert probably would not be appreciated, but if you wanted to make any sweet heavy dessert the menu would still be balanced. Pitta thrives on sweetness.

A PITTA-BALANCING RECIPE

Creamy Summer Garden soup, a rich jade-green, sweet, bitter, and oily cold soup, starts with Pitta Broth as its base. This soup is thoroughly Pitta-reducing and delightful for those following a Pitta diet anytime, but especially in the heat of summer.

CREAMY SUMMER GARDEN SOUP
Serves 6

4 cups chopped Swiss chard, loosely packed
2 small zucchini, thinly sliced
1 cup chopped bok choy or Napa cabbage leaves
1 cup chopped beet greens
1 small parsnip, peeled and sliced
5 cups Pitta Broth (recipe follows)
1 very ripe avocado, mashed
1 cup heavy cream (½ pint)
1 teaspoon minced fresh French tarragon or ½ teaspoon dried
½ teaspoon ground white pepper
6 or 7 mint leaves, chopped
½ cup shredded raw beets or thinly sliced red radish
8 to 10 sprigs fresh fennel, dill, or small mint leaves

1. Steam the vegetables for 12 minutes, or until the zucchini is very soft. Or cook the vegetables in a pressure cooker for 4 minutes. Cool slightly and puree in a food processor or blender until creamy.

2. Heat the Pitta Broth in a large heavy pot and add the vegetable puree. Simmer and stir until well blended. Use a hand mixer in a small bowl or a food processor with a steel blade to blend the mashed avocado with half of the cream. Slowly add the rest of the cream, blending until smooth and creamy. Add the tarragon, the pepper, and the mint. Stir vigorously into the vegetable soup. Serve warm with a shredded beet garnish, or cover, cool for an hour, then chill for at least 3 hours before serving.

3. Serve in a large decorative glass bowl with a shredded beet or sliced radish and fresh herb garnish. Or garnish each bowl individually as you serve it.

NOTE: When this soup is heated and thickened with cornstarch or flour it becomes a Creamy Summer Sauce, delectable when poured over steamed vegetables or vegetable pastry turnovers.

Pitta Broth
Makes 2 quarts

2 quarts water
1 teaspoon salt
1 cup chopped broccoli
1 cup chopped green beans
1 cup peeled and diced potatoes
1 cup chopped celery or lovage leaves
½ teaspoon white or black pepper
2 tablespoons Pitta Churna
         or
   2 teaspoons ground coriander,
   ½ teaspoon crushed anise seed,
   3 or 4 crushed green cardamom pods or
   other Pitta-reducing spices, to taste
1 tablespoon ghee (optional)

In a large pot of boiling salted water, put the vegetables, the pepper, and the spices. Turn to low, cover, and simmer for 15 minutes. Stir in the ghee if you are making an oily broth. Then turn off the heat and let the pot sit undisturbed for 30 minutes. Use a colander to strain out the vegetables and use the broth. The vegetables can be pureed and used in a creamy soup, or they can be eaten with a little butter.

NOTE: Pitta Broth makes a refreshing drink and summer appetizer when served chilled with a celery stick and a garnish of fresh fennel or dill. Strain the warm broth through a coffee filter for extra clarity.

When designing a soup recipe for Pitta, you can hardly go wrong to start with almost all Pitta-reducing vegetables. Pitta Broth, a combination of Pitta-reducing vegetables, herbs, and spices, is a basic soup stock. The flavor of the broth will vary depending on the combination of ingredients you use. When making this broth, choose at least three different Pitta-reducing vegetables, herbs, and spices. Use 3 or 4 cups of mixed vegetables. The best ones for reducing Pitta taste bitter and astringent. Pitta Broth is useful as a gravy base or for the beginning of a vegetable cream sauce, other soups, or simply as a refreshing summer beverage.

The vegetables in the Creamy Garden Soup will vary with the seasons. You can just as easily make a Creamy Winter Soup for pacifying Pitta by substituting romaine lettuce leaves for the Swiss chard, which is usually available from late spring until fall; also use celery leaves instead of beet leaves if they aren't in season, and in winter a sweet or white potato, additional parsnips, or a turnip, jicama, rutabaga, or other heavy, cold root vegetable.

The idea is to use about 6 or 7 cups of mixed vegetables that are primarily bitter, astringent, and slightly sweet-tasting. A beautiful and interesting soup can be made using varieties of lettuce, kale, and collard greens. The tastes and colors change slightly with the varying ingredients, but the delicately smooth consistency is maintained by the cream and avocado.

You can pick freely from a huge array of vegetables when making this soup, but there are fewer spices to choose from. Pitta is limited in the herb and spice department. It is good to consult the Charts of Ingredients (pages 283–290) before randomly adding a lot of spices. An exception is black pepper and its first cousin, white pepper. Even though it is pungent-tasting, the pepper in this recipe is fine for Pitta because it is used very moderately, and Pitta is not really aggravated by small amounts of black or white pepper. The same can be said for cooking with small amounts of pungent-tasting ginger and cumin. It might be tempting to pep this soup up with some pungent picante sauce or sour yogurt. The first choice would be better for Kapha and the sour yogurt for Vata. Pitta's recipes rarely need pepping up; just a rich depth of sweet, bitter, and astringent tastes satisfy. Fresh mint, tarragon, fennel, and dill—green herbs that soothe Pitta—are better choices than pungent oregano, basil, sage, or thyme. Even though these herbs are used in small amounts, they are first-class herbs for their combined effect of cooling and reducing Pitta.

OTHER RECIPES ESPECIALLY GOOD FOR PITTA

When planning other menus, try any of these recipes appropriate for a Pitta-balancing diet. They can be found in Chapter 4.

BEVERAGES
Bed and Breakfast Drink
Chilled Pitta Broth
Date Shake
Fragrantly Spiced Lassi
Pineapple Mint Tea
Plain Refreshing Lassi
Rose Petal Milkshake
Sweet Fruit Smoothies
Three-in-One Supreme
Watermelon-Strawberry Punch

APPETIZERS
Cheese Crackers
Golden Panir Cubes
Golden Yummies
Pineapple Ginger-Cream Spread

SALADS
Asparagus Salad with Raspberry Vinaigrette
Macedonia di Fruita
Tossed Green Salad

DRESSINGS, SAUCES, DIPS, AND MARINADES
Avocado Cheese Sauce and Dip
Basic Cheese Sauce
Cream Tahini Sauce
Deanna's Vinaigrette
Ginger Soy Gravy
Gold Sauce
Herbed Vinaigrette
Scrumptious Sesame-Orange Sauce
Simple Vinaigrette Dressing

OTHER BASICS
Everyday Granola
Ghee
Panir and Ricotta Soft Cheese

BREADS
French Bread
Puris and Chapatis
Squash Rolls

SOUPS
Perfect Lentil Soup
Potage Printanier
Sweet Potato Soup
Thermos Flask Soup
Vegetable Soup with Fresh Herbs

MAIN DISHES
Couscous
Green Beans in Tomato Sauce (Fagioloni in Umido Volponi)
Layered Vegetable Loaf
Oven-Baked French Fries
Pasta and Green Sauce
Petis Pois Braisé Laitue (Peas Braised with Lettuce)
Quick Vegetable Medley
Saffron Rice
Simple Rice Pilaf
Sweet Summer Curry
Tofu Nut Burgers
Vegetable Whole Grain Sauté

SIDE DISHES (AS PART OF A MAIN MEAL)
Fried Spiced Potatoes
Green and Gold Baked Squash

DESSERTS
Almond Custard Fresh Fruit Pie
American Apple Pie
Apple Dumplings with Vanilla Sauce
Apple Pie Filling Without Sugar
Chocolate Custard Pie
Creamy Rice Pudding
Fruit Shortcake
Italian Hazelnut Cookies

Jam Diagonals
Kaffa's Dream
Lemon Scones
Lemony Date Bars
Oatmeal Raisin Cookies
R&S Couscous
Rich Quick Chocolate Mousse
Strawberry Yogurt Pie
Super Chocolate Brownies
Sweet Chocolate Cake with Cherry Sauce
Sweet Fruit and Spice Tea Bread
Toasty Cinnamon Bar Cookies
White Figs in Apricot Cream Sauce

For Kapha

WHAT IS KAPHA?

Kapha is most like the earth after a spring rain. As a quality it is stable, cold, wet, smooth, soft, and heavy. Your nature is most like Kapha if many of the characteristics in this list best describe you.

KAPHA CHARACTERISTICS

BALANCED	OUT OF BALANCE
Tranquil, easygoing, loving	Depressed, bored, dull
Strong with good stamina	Listless, stubborn
Steady, methodical activity	Lethargic, body stiff
Large, well-built body	Overweight
Plentiful hair, smooth, oily skin	Very oily hair/skin
Careful learner, good memory	Disinterested
Sleeps soundly and long	Excessive sleeping
Slow, regular digestion	Poor appetite
	Frequent colds, sinusitis

THE BEST DIET FOR KAPHA

The best diet for Kapha is opposite to Kapha's heavy, slow nature. It contains large amounts of light, dry, hot foods with more pungent, bitter, and astringent tastes than sweet, sour, or salty ones. Kapha is naturally sweet enough. Much of the dietary advice for Kapha suits anyone trying to lose weight as well. A simple way Kapha types and those on weight-reducing programs can maintain their health is by following a Kapha-balancing diet. Visit a qualified physician trained in Maharishi Ayur-Ved for other useful weight-loss suggestions. It may happen that your constitution is a combination of Kapha with Vata or Kapha with Pitta, or even a mixture of Kapha-Pitta-Vata. In that case follow each suggested dosha-balancing diet during the proper season and a Kapha-balancing diet during the cold, wet, rainy weather of late winter and spring. Those with all-Kapha natures should follow a Kapha-balancing diet all year.

GENERAL KAPHA DIET

FAVOR

- Warm food and drinks
- Tastes—pungent, bitter, astringent
- Qualities—light, dry, hot
- Light meals
- Appetizers, salads, soups
- Rice cakes and crackers

REDUCE

- Cold food and drinks
- Rich desserts
- Heavy meals, too much food
- Tastes—sweet, sour, salty
- Qualities—cold, heavy, oily
- Snacking between meals

TASTES AND QUALITIES BEST FOR KAPHA

Here are the best food tastes and qualities for Kapha body types. All six tastes and six qualities are served in every balanced meal, but Kapha should eat foods that have most of those that help to maintain Kapha in balance.

BEST FOOD TASTES FOR KAPHA
Pungent • Astringent • Bitter

KAPHA'S SPECIAL NEEDS

Kapha appreciates warm, light, easily and quickly digested foods that are on the dry side. People with Kapha characteristics have strong, well-knit bodies that need fewer body-building foods than either Vata or Pitta types. For the sake of healthy growth and balance, do not completely eliminate foods with heavier qualities that build strength, but eat moderately of them. Kapha types need to develop and maintain a strong body. Such items as breads, pasta, rice, beans, and rich main dishes and desserts simply need to make up a smaller proportion of any day's menu. Since Kapha types tend to put on fat easily, reducing oily, fatty ingredients, for example, by substituting low-fat milk for whole milk or eating fried foods infrequently, is important for maintaining Kapha's balance.

BEST FOOD QUALITIES FOR KAPHA
Light • Hot • Dry

MENU PLANNING FOR KAPHA

Fortunately, menu planning for Kapha is not entirely a question of reducing and avoiding even though Kapha doesn't eat the heavy sweet dishes found on Vata's and Pitta's menu. Most herbs and spices benefit those reducing Kapha. The flavors in main dish casseroles, steamed vegetables, grain dishes, and tossed salads can be enhanced with the pungent tastes of hot peppers, ginger, fresh basil, thyme, tarragon, oregano, and other herbs that delight the palate.

Cooking for Kapha means having fun experimenting with many subtle flavor combinations popular in the contemporary American light gourmet cuisine. Earthy Kapha types enjoy sensory pleasures. The key to successful Kapha-balancing meals is to prepare varieties of small to medium-size portions of elegantly presented preparations filled with many hidden nuances of texture, fragrance, and flavor that delight the senses and palate.

When planning a Kapha-balancing menu, alternate light and heavy courses throughout the meal. Or if all the food is served at one time only prepare one heavy, substantial main dish to eat with salads and side dishes lighter in quality. Those following a Kapha-balancing diet would then select the amount they want to eat from each. Too much heavy food overburdens Kapha's slower digestion.

BALANCE

The most nutritious meals for everyone are full of interest and variety. They do not have to be particularly elaborate, but by using many different seasonings and a wide variety of ingredients that include something of all the six tastes and six qualities, it is easy to serve balanced meals every day. If most of a recipe is made up of weight-reducing or Kapha-decreasing ingredients such as barley, leafy greens, pungent herbs and spices, or lentils, then the addition of sweet red peppers, raisins and dates, or even a tomato—which by themselves increase Kapha—won't change the total Kapha-reducing effect of the dish. And this is a good way to add appetizing colors and some sweet or sour tastes to the meal without having them dominate.

Roasting, toasting, and baking make foods lighter and drier. These are the best cooking methods for Kapha-types. Wheat bread increases Kapha, but when it is dried from toasting it does not increase Kapha as much. Sweet, heavy potatoes increase Kapha; baked is the best way to cook potatoes for Kapha. Unsweetened crackers and popcorn are the best dry snacks for Kapha. They are light and dry. Besides, corn has a hot quality that is good for reducing Kapha.

Although a healthy meal emphasizes those tastes and qualities best suited for maintaining Kapha in balance, every meal should include

FOR A KAPHA-BALANCING DIET

FAVOR

General: lighter diet, dry foods, warm foods and drinks; pungent, bitter, and astringent tastes

Dairy: low-fat milk or moderate amounts of whole milk, dilute Lassi

Sweetener: honey

Grains: barley, corn, millet, buckwheat, rye

Fruits: apple, pomegranate, persimmon, papaya, watermelon

Vegetables: asparagus, eggplant, beets, broccoli, potato, cabbage, carrot, cauliflower, celery, green leafy vegetables, sprouts, radish, hot peppers, parsnips, squash

Spices: most spices (see Charts of Ingredients)

Nuts: walnuts, blanched almonds (small amounts)

Beans: most lentils

Beverages: warm water, most herbal teas, some fruit juices (in moderation), vegetable juices

Meat: chicken, turkey (for non-vegetarians)

REDUCE

General: large quantities of food; unctuous, heavy, cold food and drinks; sweet, sour, and salty tastes

Dairy: yogurt, cream, butter, sour cream, cheese, whole milk

Sweeteners: sugarcane products, molasses, corn syrup

Oils: all except small amounts of almond, corn, walnut, sunflower, or sesame oils, ghee

Grains: large quantities of wheat, rice, or oats

Fruits: grapes, melons, avocado, coconut, dried fruit, banana, orange, pineapple, plums, berries

Vegetables: tomato, cucumber, sweet potato

Beans: beans, tofu, and other soy products, Urad lentils

Spices: caraway, poppy seeds, salt

Nuts: all except walnuts, small amounts blanched almonds

Beverages: iced/cold drinks, cold milk, milkshakes, buttermilk, Lassi, sweet fruit juices

Meat: seafood, red meat

sweet, sour, salty tastes as well as some foods with oily, cold, and heavy qualities. Kapha can nibble at these but would avoid eating large amounts. The foods listed in the reduce or avoid part of the Kapha-balancing chart contain Kapha-increasing tastes and qualities.

BALANCE IN THE WHOLE MEAL

Although certain foods or recipes, when eaten by themselves, increase Kapha, their effect is somewhat neutralized when they are eaten moderately as a part of a balanced meal. Macedonia di Fruita, the fruit salad from the Italian menu in Chapter 5, is an example of balance within the whole meal. Whether served as a salad or dessert, this decorative display of sweet apples and oranges, melons, figs, grapes, dates, and other seasonal fruits nourishes all body types. Individually, each of these fruits increases Kapha. In fact, the entire salad increases Kapha because sweet fruit increases Kapha. Such a fruit salad is not something that people with Kapha constitutions would eat as a meal by itself or in a large amount, but when it is served as a part of a balanced meal—that is, with other Kapha-reducing dishes—Macedonia di Fruita benefits everyone, even Kapha types.

KAPHA'S AYURVEDIC MENU INCLUDES:

- a pungent, sweet appetizer,
- foods with all six tastes and qualities,
- varied colors, textures, and flavors stimulating the senses and palate,
- thoughtful order of presentation starting with a pungent appetizer,
- alternating light and heavy courses,
- ending with a light sweet.

SPARKING KAPHA'S DIGESTION

Kapha usually appreciates a pungent appetizer to start the meal. Grated fresh salted ginger with a spritz of lemon juice makes a simple condiment. Or even a pinch of powdered ginger under the tongue just before eating will spark Kapha's appetite. A steaming bowl of peppery soup, a teaspoon or two of rice and ghee, a sweet gherkin pickle, or a couple of sweet and pungent little condiments will help ignite the digestive fires and make a meal most useful for Kapha. Because agni is so variable in Kapha's digestion, pungent tastes should be interspersed throughout the meal. This is especially true when serving foods that are heavy and more difficult to digest.

Unlike Vata and Pitta, who enjoy very sweet appetizers or might even want to eat a light dessert at the beginning of the meal, Kapha's appetite will remain steady throughout a meal that begins with a pungent, somewhat sweet appetizer.

COOKING AND EATING TIPS FOR KAPHA

- Kapha appreciates light, dry, warm foods that are not too sweet, salty, or oily.
- Make some naturally heavy foods lighter and easier to digest by heating them. Bring water and milk to the boiling point, then allow to cool before drinking or cooking.
- Lighten rice and other grains by dry roasting or frying them in a small amount of oil until the grains begin to turn a light brown. Then cook as usual.
- When following new recipes, try reducing both salt and sugar by one-half the amount called for.
- Use corn and barley as grains and baking flours.
- Serve tepid water with meals, but drink nothing for one hour after eating.
- Eat such heavy foods as bananas, milk products, potatoes, and yams with a little honey, black pepper, ginger, or other pungent spices rather than by themselves.
- Avoid between-meal snacking to maintain a strong appetite.
- Serve a pungent or sweet appetizer before the main meal.
- Serve small to moderate portions of heavy or filling dishes.
- Eat a tossed salad of mixed leafy greens daily.
- Sit comfortably and eat in a settled atmosphere.

In Kapha's Pantry

For those with Kapha constitutions and others following weight-reducing diets it's important to maintain a year-round supply of a selection of nonperishable foods. To keep the freshest ingredients on hand buy staples, especially flours, herbs, and spices, in small quantities, store them carefully, and replenish as needed.

SPICES:

> allspice, anise seeds, asafoetida (hing), black pepper, cayenne pepper, celery seed, cinnamon, coriander, cloves, cumin, ginger, Kapha Churna,* nutmeg, mustard seeds, turmeric

HERBS:

> basil, dill, fennel, oregano, parsley, thyme, rosemary, sage, saffron, savory, tarragon

GRAINS & OTHER STAPLES:

> barley, barley flour, cornmeal, millet, rice, rice cakes, unsweetened crackers, honey, walnuts, lentils, ghee, corn oil, herbal teas, black tea, and coffee

* A Maharishi Ayur-Ved product that can be ordered by mail. See Appendix 5, page 293.

ABOUT THE KAPHA MENU

Menus for Kapha emphasize light, dry, hot food and a lot of pungent or spicy, bitter, and astringent tastes. They are consistently lower in salt, sugar, and other sweeteners as well as cold, heavy dairy products, cheese, wheat flour, breads, and pasta. But as we've seen elsewhere, every balanced menu should include all the six tastes and six qualities.

This sample menu for balancing Kapha includes more selections than you might normally prepare, except perhaps for a party or big buffet. But it will give you an idea of how to plan nourishing meals to cook for Kapha.

Although the sample menu is especially good for maintaining Kapha in balance, many of these recipes, with very minor alterations, can be used for people with different dietary needs. Or they may appear as smaller side dishes in a main meal. Many times a recipe good for balancing one body type is also good for one of the others. When using Ayurvedic menu-planning principles, it is difficult to create recipes exclusively for one constitution because so many foods are good for everyone. When you're planning a family meal that includes a variety of dishes, remember that each person will simply select the amount from each dish that is best for him or her. We'll talk more about diverse menu planning in Chapter 5. The recipes from this sample menu can be found in Chapter 4.

A Sample Kapha Menu

GOLDEN YUMMIES
(Sweet, Oily, Slightly Pungent)

VEGETABLE SOUP WITH FRESH HERBS
(Pungent, Light)

VEGETABLE WHOLE GRAIN SAUTÉ
(Sweet, Astringent, Light, Oily)
OR
ROASTED AND SPICED BARLEY WITH VEGETABLES *
(Pungent, Sweet, Astringent, Oily, Light)

TOSSED GREEN SALAD WITH VINAIGRETTE
(Pungent, Bitter, Astringent, Oily)

LIGHT CORN BREAD AND BUTTER
(Sweet, Salty, Hot, Light)

FRESH GINGER COOKIES
(Sweet, Pungent, Salty, Dry)

WHITE FIGS À LA KAPHA
(Sweet, Heavy)

* Recipe follows and also appears in Chapter 4, Ayurvedic Recipes (pages 182–183).

What is there about this menu that makes it so good for Kapha and for those watching their weight? It begins with a great appetizer, Golden Yummies, which is good for all doshas but ideal for Kapha. A beautiful golden yellow with a pleasing texture, one or two of these sweet, oily, pungent, and heating delights will spark Kapha's appetite. (There is more about how this recipe was designed in Chapter 1.)

The Vegetable Soup with Fresh Herbs is also a stimulating appetizer, and either the Golden Yummies or this soup could begin the meal. This light and pungent soup is excellent for reducing Kapha and stimulating the digestive fires at the same time. Its basis, Kapha Broth, is made with three or more Kapha-reducing, seasonally available vegetables, water, and a few Kapha-appropriate herbs of choice. Vegetable Soup with Fresh Herbs can be cooked with semolina pasta or rice to make it a little thicker for serving as part of a light meal. Or add cooked barley before serving to those following a very light diet.

The main dish choices on the menu, Vegetable Whole Grain Sauté or Roasted and Spiced Barley with Vegetables, help decrease Kapha. The simple-to-make Vegetable Whole Grain Sauté made with barley is a light, easily digested main dish that is also just right for Kapha but can be eaten by anyone as part of a balanced meal. This recipe adds sweet, astringent tastes and light and oily qualities to the menu. The use of sprouted Urad beans—whole black gram—adds a sweet, nutty flavor. These particular sprouts are very nourishing and somewhat weight-producing because Urad gram contains more oil and heaviness than other legumes. They are the best legumes for building tissues, muscles, and, if eaten in excess, fat. For those who want to include this dish in a weight-reducing diet, mung bean or brown lentil (muth) sprouts can be used instead of the heavier, more fattening Urad. Because of their light and dry qualities and astringency, lentil and bean sprouts, raw or sautéed, are better for Kapha than for either Vata or Pitta. Let's look at the other entrée, Roasted and Spiced Barley with Vegetables, in some detail as an example of recipe design for Kapha.

ROASTED AND SPICED BARLEY WITH VEGETABLES
Serves 6 to 8

3 tablespoons ghee
1/2 teaspoon cayenne
1 cup barley, rinsed and drained
1 1/2 teaspoons salt
3 1/2 cups hot water
1 cup bite-size broccoli florets
2 tablespoons olive oil

> *1 teaspoon minced fresh ginger*
> *or ½ teaspoon ground*
> *¼ cup sesame seeds*
> *¼ cup roasted pumpkin seeds*
> *1 sweet red pepper, cut in 1-inch squares*
> *1 cup washed and chopped Swiss chard*
> *(mixed ruby and white look best)*
> *½ cup washed and chopped beet greens*
> *2 teaspoons salt*
> *½ teaspoon coarsely ground pepper*

1. To prepare the barley, heat the ghee in a heavy iron skillet or a 2-quart pot over moderate heat. Stir in the cayenne. Lower the flame to simmer and after the cayenne is heated, about 1 minute, stir in the barley. Roast the barley by continuously stirring it until the grains are medium brown. Watch carefully not to burn it. Then sprinkle on the salt, add the hot water, and stir once or twice. Cover tightly and simmer for about 1 hour. It's all right if some liquid remains. Fluff up the barley with a fork, cover, and set aside while you prepare the vegetables. Or make the barley ahead of time and prepare the vegetables just before serving.

2. Steam the broccoli for 3 to 4 minutes and set it aside.

3. Heat the oil in a wok or a large heavy frying pan. Add the ginger and the sesame seeds. Fry over moderate heat until the seeds just start to pop. Add half the pumpkin seeds, stir, add the red peppers, and stir well. Stir in the chard and the beet greens. Add the steamed broccoli, the salt, and the pepper. Toss well and cover tightly. Turn off the heat and let the vegetables steam while you reheat the barley over medium heat, stirring until any remaining liquid is gone.

4. Fold in the remaining pumpkin seeds and spread the barley on a serving platter. Arrange the vegetables on the bed of barley and serve.

A KAPHA-BALANCING RECIPE

Why is Roasted and Spiced Barley with Vegetables such a good recipe for Kapha? The ingredients are nearly all Kapha-reducing, and the cooking methods—roasting, frying in small amounts of light oil, and steaming—are good ones for Kapha as well; the finished dish sparkles with appetizing colors and textures, and it tastes delicious.

Although everyone can eat some of this dish as part of a balanced meal, for Kapha it is a first choice as a main dish because the barley is essentially light in quality, easily digested, and not too filling. The outstanding tastes of this recipe are pungent, sweet, and salty. The most important ingredient in this recipe is the barley, and of equal interest is how we handle it. Light, dry, astringent barley is a low-fat, low-salt grain that Kapha can enjoy in almost any amount. It is too light in quality and astringent for Vata to eat regularly, and although its astringency is good for Pitta, the lightness is rather unsatisfying to Pitta's appetite. For those following a Kapha-Pitta diet barley is better than for someone with Pitta alone. And even better for the lightness, in this recipe we roast the barley in a pungent oil before boiling it. Heating changes the effect of many ingredients. We talked previously about how boiling milk and water lightens them and makes them easier to digest. Heating grains in just a little oil (or preferably, none at all if you watch them very carefully) removes some of their heavy quality. It is a good habit to regularly roast rice, bulgur, and other whole grains when cooking for Kapha.

In this recipe the roasted barley absorbs the spicy cayenne taste, carrying the pungency right through the whole dish. The amount used is not the mouth-burning and eye-watering type, but simply comfortable. It's important to know that even though Kapha can eat pungent food it is not healthy to overdo it.

The remaining ingredients, pumpkin and sesame seeds, and the variety of vegetables in this recipe are all good for reducing Kapha.

MORE ABOUT THE KAPHA MENU

A mainstay in any Kapha menu is a green leafy salad that includes several types of lettuce and other fresh greens. Tossed green salads are an especially good daily staple for Kapha because they not only add texture and color to a meal, they contribute some of the bitter, astringent, and pungent tastes we want in a balanced menu. A squeeze of lemon, lime, or orange juice, or a simple vinaigrette is enough to pleasantly dress Kapha's salad. For other Kapha menus choose any of the salad dressings in this book. They have been rated good for all body types.

The Light Corn Bread is a sweet, salty, hot, light bread that is good for both Kapha and those wanting to reduce weight. As with many other Kapha-reducing foods, corn bread is good to eat as part of a light evening meal. Cornmeal has a hot quality that is experienced after eating rather than in the mouth. This is good for Kapha. Spread the corn bread with a little raw honey rather than butter.

FRESH GINGER COOKIES

This cookie is one of those rare desserts that Kapha can eat in more than small amounts. They are sweet, pungent, salty, and astringent. Since they are made entirely with barley flour, one of Kapha's best grains, and contain a generous amount of pungent ginger, they are a good dessert to serve to weight watchers. The fresh ginger really makes these sparkle!

WHITE FIGS À LA KAPHA

Although other figs like black Mission or brown Turkey figs are nourishing, none is held in such esteem as Calmyrnas—known in Sanskrit as *anjier*. Also called white figs, they are closer to a pale blond color when dry. They are sold dried at most supermarkets and health food stores. The concentrated sugar in anjier and all dried fruits is Kapha-increasing, so eat them in moderation. Dried fruit digests better when it is steamed or simmered in a small amount of water to return some of the liquid to it.

Plump some Calmyrna figs in a vegetable steamer for 5 minutes and serve them warm. One or two figs and a few fresh ginger cookies make a satisfying dessert for Kapha.

OTHER RECIPES ESPECIALLY FOR KAPHA

When planning your own menus, try any of these recipes appropriate for a Kapha-balancing diet. They can be found in Chapter 4.

BEVERAGES
Bed and Breakfast Drink
Fragrantly Spiced Lassi
Indian Spiced Milk Tea
Plain Refreshing Lassi
Saffron Milk Tea
Three-in-One Supreme II

APPETIZERS
Cheese Crackers
Curried Herb Cheese Dip
Golden Panir Cubes
Pineapple Ginger-Cream Spread

SALADS
Confetti Rice Salad
Macedonia di Fruita
Tossed Green Salad

DRESSINGS, SAUCES, DIPS, AND MARINADES
Cream Tahini Sauce
Deanna's Vinaigrette
Ginger Soy Gravy
Gold Sauce
Herbed Vinaigrette
Pitta Churna Salad Dressing and Marinade
Raspberry Vinaigrette
Scrumptious Sesame-Orange Sauce
Simple Vinaigrette Dressing

OTHER BASICS
Ghee
Kapha Broth
Panir and Ricotta Soft Cheese
Sprouted Whole Beans and Seeds

BREADS
French Bread
Little Flat Breads
Puris and Chapatis
Squash Rolls

SOUPS
Ginger Carrot Soup
Potage Printanier

MAIN DISHES
Curried Vegetables and Panir
Green and Gold Baked Squash
Green Beans in Tomato Sauce (Fagioloni in Umido Volponi)
Layered Vegetable Loaf
Savory Wild Rice Casserole

SIDE DISHES (AS PART OF A MAIN MEAL)
Couscous
Fried Spiced Potatoes
Moroccan Delight
Petit Pois Braisé Laitue (Peas Braised with Lettuce)
Saffron Rice
Simple Rice Pilaf
Sweet Summer Curry

DESSERTS (IN MODERATION)
Apple Pie Filling Without Sugar
Fresh Ginger Cookies
Fruit Shortcake
Ginger Spice Cake with Lemon Sauce
Italian Hazelnut Cookies
Jam Diagonals
Lemon Scones
Lemony Date Bars
Marble Crumb Cake with Vanilla Sauce and English Cream
Simple Shortbread
Super Chocolate Brownies
Sweet Fruit and Spice Tea Bread
Toasty Cinnamon Bar Cookies
White Figs á la Kapha

✦✦

Chapter 3

SOMETHING FOR EVERYONE

EAT WHAT YOU LIKE

From what you've read thus far it may seem that Ayurvedic cooking is limited to the single person with very specific needs. But those who cook for families or groups needn't worry. One of Ayurveda's strengths is that not only is the effect of every ingredient known and predictable for each person, but a great many foods are good for everyone to eat, making it unnecessary to prepare separate meals for each member of the family with different doshas. That means many of our most commonly used ingredients overlap in their usefulness for balancing all three doshas. In this chapter we'll look at these foods.*

What's most important is to eat the foods you enjoy. It's good to remember that by eating too much of a limited variety of foods, even the universally good foods discussed in this chapter, Vata, Pitta, and Kapha are inclined to increase, become aggravated and unbalanced, and give you the experience of illness. Moderation is always the key to healthy eating. With that consideration aside, what can *all* of us enjoy?

WATER

Many people don't think of water as food. But water is essential to everyone's diet and good digestion. Noncarbonated spring water is fine to drink and tap water, too, in areas with good water quality. When there is a choice, a tepid or warm temperature for drinking water is best, especially in winter and on cool days. Although cool or tepid water is fine to drink in the summer or on hot days, many people who have changed from drinking ice water prefer comfortably warm water year round.

---

* All the recipes and food recommendations in this book are for the general population. People with diabetes or other medically restricted diets should follow their doctor's advice.

✦✦

*Ayurveda declares water to be
the first choice among all drinks.*

To heat water, bring it to a full boil and then let it cool to a comfortable drinking temperature. Boiled water is thought to be better for the body because of the molecular changes occurring in the heating process that make it lighter and easier to digest, especially for those people with Kapha constitutions or others who need lighter qualities in their diets. And Vata always appreciates drinking all liquids warm, including water.

Ice-cold water is not beneficial to the maintenance of a strong agni, even in the heat of summer when most iced drinks are served, although people with Pitta constitutions can drink refrigerated or chilled drinks during hot weather. For good digestion and lasting refreshment drinks made with lots of ice are not recommended, even for Pitta types. People with Pitta constitutions who have been following an Ayurvedic routine for some time say they are more comfortable in hot, humid weather if they drink warm water.

WATER WITH MEALS

Water is the best drink to serve at all meals. It should be sipped with the entire meal, that is, before eating, during the meal, between courses, when not chewing food, and after eating. You might think of it as layering the food with liquid. But remember, only fill the stomach two-thirds to three-fourths of its capacity, so that at the end of the meal one-third of the stomach contains food and one-third water. The rest should be left empty to allow for comfortable digestion.

JUICES OR TEAS: BEFORE AND AFTER EATING

Fruit juices and other drinks are best appreciated by themselves or with a light snack rather than as a part of the meal. Kapha types should drink fruit juices in moderation because of sweet fruit's high sugar content. A small glass of apple juice or pomegranate juice is a highly recommended appetizer to serve to everyone shortly before the meal begins. It should be served at room temperature or only very slightly chilled. Pomegranate juice is sold at most natural food stores.

Some people, especially in winter, may prefer to end a meal with a warm cup of herbal tea. Tea can be served 10 or 15 minutes after the meal is finished, rather than as an ongoing part of the meal. The Charts of Ingredients in the Appendix lists specific teas that have been tested for their effects on each constitutional type.

COFFEE AND BLACK TEA

Of the great variety of teas and coffees to choose from, black teas and limited amounts of coffee are all right for Kapha to drink, and to a much lesser extent, those with Pitta constitutions, if it feels comfortable. Whichever of the many different flavors of coffee or tea is your favorite, or whether it is decaffeinated or not, the effect is the same because a bitter, slightly pungent taste and dry quality dominates all of them. Black tea is somewhat astringent and drying as well. The combination of these tastes and qualities increases Vata and Pitta dosha slightly. Just like fruit juices, milk, and herbal teas, coffee and black tea are best for digestion when enjoyed outside of the main meal.

MORE ABOUT HERBAL TEAS

While investigating teas, the Ayurvedic research team sampled all the widely available herbal tea blends. Most of these were blends of certain organically grown, pesticide-free herbs and spices with a predominating rosehip/hibiscus base that decreased Vata and increased Pitta and Kapha.

One blend, considered most useful for its tonic or healthful effects, Emperor's Choice, is sweet, astringent, and a little bitter. Ginseng and other herbs make it a good tonic that increases the appetite but not weight. When served as an appetizer to the main meal or by itself, this blend is especially good for Kapha body types and those wishing to lose weight. Because of its appetizing qualities one would not end a meal with Emperor's Choice, however.

By using one or a combination of herbs or spices listed in the Charts of Ingredients, you can make your own simple herbal teas that appeal to your tastes and dietary needs. Or serve Ayurvedic teas especially formulated to benefit each specific body type during the changing seasons. If not available at your grocery or health food store, these teas and other products are available from Maharishi Ayur-Ved Products International Inc.*

*Ayurveda is dedicated to
all those who want to become
good eaters.*

—DR. H. S. KASTURE

MODERATION: A GOOD AYURVEDIC PRINCIPLE FOR EVERYONE

By now you know that certain foods and spices may increase or reduce the balance of Vata, Pitta, or Kapha in your physiology. But what if you're particularly fond of something that you know will aggravate your doshas—do you need to eliminate it altogether? Not necessarily; usually you just reduce the amount.

The Ayurvedic principle of moderation, applied to all foods, is the best to follow. For instance, you may wish to have a cup of chamomile tea and you notice on the Charts of Ingredients that this herb increases Vata, decreases Kapha, and has a neutral effect on Pitta when drunk in moderation. If you are a Vata type who loves chamomile tea, then once or twice a week enjoy a small amount of it. If it is a windy, cold day a Vata-decreasing tea would be a better choice. This is an example of moderation in Ayurveda. Drinking chamomile tea every day or several times a day may be excessive for Vata and even Pitta to some extent. The situation is the same for Vata types who are habituated to drinking coffee or black tea. Moderation gives the most comfort in the long run.

Similarly, fresh ginger tea is a marvelously refreshing and stimulating drink for both Vata and Kapha types, but even those with a Pitta constitution may sip ginger tea on a cool day or during the cold season if they want it. Generally, ginger tea is not one of Pitta's favorites. Pungent teas are entirely too stimulating for those with Pitta constitutions in warm or hot weather.

Remember, too, in Ayurvedic cooking just a pinch of some spice can change the effect of a recipe. It is not necessary to use great quantities of herbs and spices to achieve a balance of tastes. It's just a matter of using common sense when applying the information in the

* To order Maharishi Ayur-Ved Products call 1-800-ALL-VEDA.

ingredients charts and knowing your own comfort zone when trying to satisfy your appetite.

MILK: NATURE'S MOST PERFECT FOOD

Sweet-tasting, heavy, cold, and nourishing milk is nature's most perfect food. Of the several kinds of milk, cow's milk rates as the most nutritious for everyone to drink at every age. Milk is one of the superior, *sattvic* foods that should be a regular part of the diet. Ayurveda does not support the unfounded idea that milk is not for humans to drink. If someone has a milk intolerance, discuss it with an Ayurvedic physician. Whenever possible heat milk and serve it warm. Just bring it to a boil and allow to cool to a comfortable drinking temperature. As with water, this process of heating makes milk lighter and easier to digest. Bringing the milk to a frothy boil several times in succession with a pinch of grated gingerroot makes it more digestible. Although those with Pitta constitutions can drink milk cold, both Kapha and Vata appreciate the warmth. Because of the milk's cold and heavy qualities drinking it right from the refrigerator makes hard work for both Vata's and Kapha's agni.

The best additions to warm milk include ghee, sugar, honey, tea, or certain sweet or pungent spices. People concerned about high cholesterol or those watching their weight can substitute skim milk and might avoid adding ghee to their warm milk. Kapha types and children can drink warm milk best with a little ground ginger and raw honey in it. The ginger helps to heat and lighten the milk for greater digestibility as does the honey.

Whenever possible, buy nonhomogenized milk. Homogenizing milk not only thoroughly mixes the fat and lighter milk together, but the process changes the fat molecules, making them more difficult to digest. Using whipping cream that's been ultrahomogenized, a process that splits the fat into particles so tiny they can penetrate the cell walls before they can be digested, encourages the production of ama and fattiness.

MILK COMBINATIONS

Milk—whether whole, skim, half-and-half, or heavy cream—is so full of nutritious qualities it is considered a whole food, complete in itself, that digests best by itself. Milk is not a good beverage to accompany a meal. Other than such sweet or pungent foods as wheat, rice, sweet fruits, ginger, saffron, cayenne, honey, ghee, and some other sweet or pungent-tasting spices and herbs that combine well with milk, Ayurveda recommends that you enjoy drinking milk by itself. Sugar, honey, wheat cereal products, and other such sweet-tasting ingredients aid in the digestion of milk. Ayurveda especially recommends avoiding mixing salt or salty and sour foods with milk. Milk does not digest properly with either meat or seafood.

SOME MILK-BASED BEVERAGES

There are a few milk-based beverages you might like to try at different times of the day. Enjoy them for breakfast, before bed, or as an afternoon snack, rather than with a meal. Although somewhat cold and heavy for Kapha and Vata dieters, Fruit Smoothies are especially popular with those following a Pitta-reducing diet in summer. A tumbler of Fruit Smoothy made with a mixture of sweet fruits and a slice of buttered toast might make a satisfying light evening meal for Pitta when it's too hot to cook.

For an exceptionally satisfying and almost instantly Pitta-pacifying drink, try Rose Petal Milkshake made from Maharishi Ayur-Ved Rose Petal Conserve. Vata and Kapha can enjoy it warm in any season. Some other milk-based recipes you might enjoy are Bed and Breakfast Drink, Saffron Milk Tea, Sweet Fruit Smoothies, and Three-in-One Supreme. (Recipes in Chapter 4.)

BUTTERMILK AND LASSI

Drinking buttermilk has almost gone out of style in America. It once was a popular, healthful beverage when we were a more rural country. But we see food interests come and go, so perhaps the liking for buttermilk will return. Some people have never tasted it or developed a taste for it. The commercial buttermilk that you buy from your local grocery store is fine to drink. Both Lassi (LAH-see), unflavored yogurt thinned with water to a drinking consistency, and buttermilk benefit all three constitutions in the same way. They make especially refreshing warm weather drinks. They are especially good for the digestion at the end of the meal.

These sour, cold, and heavy beverages decrease Vata and are neutral for Pitta and Kapha when enjoyed moderately. They are best served alone as fine thirst quenchers on a hot day or at the end of a meal rather than the beginning. Lassi is traditionally drunk at the end of a meal as a digestive aid, rather than sipped during the meal. When drunk it is a nourishing food. Cold buttermilk, Lassi, or even large amounts of yogurt are not as healthful to drink in cold weather as in warm. This is especially true for Vata and Kapha types. A small amount of salt, sugar, or such spices as ground cumin or ginger add to the taste. It's good for Kapha types to add raw honey, warm water, and ground ginger to both Lassi and buttermilk.

CHEESE

Cottage cheese and most of the other kinds of soft cheese are good for Vata. Excessive amounts of any cheese, particularly semisoft and hard cheeses, are too sour and aggravating for Pitta and Kapha digestions. And even though cheese gives a sour taste that is good for reducing Vata, hard cheeses take so long to digest and assimilate that they contribute to the production of ama, an undigested substance that results from improperly digested food and leads to the development of disease. Large quantities of hard cheese are difficult for all three types to digest. But such fresh soft cheese as ricotta or panir can be eaten by everyone, even in moderation by Kapha types.

SOFT CHEESE: RICOTTA AND PANIR

You can buy soft cheese or easily make it yourself (see pages 145–146 for the recipe). Essentially, ricotta and panir are the same cheese, except the first one comes from Italy and the other from India. Panir is usually the firmer of the two. It is possible to buy ricotta at most general grocery and specialty food stores. Good ricotta is made without stabilizers, gelatin, and additives. Read the label. Or, better yet, make your own curds and whey.

CURDS AND WHEY

Making soft cheese produces curds and whey just as Little Miss Muffet may have done. In the simple home cheese-making process hot milk is separated with lemon juice or vinegar into curds, the thick cheesy part, and whey, the resulting clear, highly digestible, nutritious liquid. You cook with the curds as with other soft cheese. It's delicious when used with stuffings and dumplings. But what to do with the whey?

A gallon of whole milk may produce a couple of quarts of whey. For a rich, nutty flavor, and added nutrition, substitute whey for the water in preparing rice and other grains. Or use it as a soup base, for some or all of the liquid in baking breads and cookies, or add fresh chopped mint or other herbs or dosha-balancing spices to warm whey and serve it as a nutritious beverage. And because whey no longer has the same sweet taste of whole milk, salt can be used in cooking with it. You should always try to find a use for whey because it is too good to discard, although if you have too much to use in a day or two, pouring it on the compost pile is better than down the drain.

HONEY, MOLASSES, AND SUGAR

Honey, molasses, brown or white sugar, and raw sugar—including brands called Turbinado and Sucanat—are all sweeteners that everyone can use to some extent. Although the sweet taste is important for everyone to include in each meal, sweeteners should be limited in diets for the overweight. Rice, wheat, milk, and fruit are naturally sweet-tasting foods that can be enjoyed instead of sugar-sweetened foods. White or granulated sugar does not have the nutritional value of other sweeteners and when eaten in excess aggravates both Vata and Kapha doshas. Some people believe that the sugar, jaggery or gur, from India is a more ancient or traditional Ayurvedic sweetener. Made from raw cane or palm juice by the "open pan" method of preserving, jaggery has about a 30 percent moisture content and ferments quickly. Because it is unpasteurized, jaggery cannot be imported into the United States.

Raw cane sugar approximates the Indian version but it has a low moisture content and long shelf life. It is unbleached or otherwise chemically refined and it contains traces of molasses. Granulated, white cane sugar has all the molasses removed, and it is then bleached and washed white. Brown sugar is simply refined white sugar with caramel coloring and/or some of the molasses put back in after the refining process. Both molasses and honey contain heating properties, so eating large amounts increases Pitta dosha. For that reason honey is the sweetener of choice for adding heat to Kapha's diet. And it tastes good mixed in herbal teas. Honey seems to carry the different herbal properties of the flowers it was gathered from and for that reason may have subtly differing effects depending on its origin.

Ayurveda regards honey as an essential medicine and a food. Among other things it is good for the heart and the eyes. Unlike sugar, honey has a couple of culinary cautions. Honey should never be heated either in cooking, baking, or by adding it to boiling liquids. Heating it causes a chemical change that makes it bitter, and Ayurveda says heated honey produces ama. Always use raw honey rather than that heated by pasteurization. It can be safely added to liquids that have been heated then cooled to a warm temperature. If, over time, stored honey has become crystallized in the jar, warming it to pouring consistency in a pan of hot water from the tap is fine. Just don't boil it. Honey and ghee have an interesting relationship. Both are considered Sattvic foods. But mixing honey with equal amounts of ghee is said to result in skin problems. By mixing twice as much honey as ghee you can improve your digestive fire, or agni. Using more ghee than honey directly nourishes body tissues and, if eaten in large amounts, it increases weight.

WHOLE GRAINS

Except for a few notations about quantities for each body type, everyone can include the following grains in a well-balanced diet unless they've been advised otherwise.

RICE

Rice, an easily digested food for everyone's physical development, is sweet-tasting with cold, heavy qualities. Rice is such a versatile ingredient it should be a staple item in any kitchen. Two of the nicest things about cooking with rice are that it absorbs the flavors of liquids and spices prepared with it and complements almost any main dish in a meal.

BASMATI: THE QUEEN OF ALL RICE

The best rice should unfailingly result in attractively separate grains and never be sticky; it should display the longest grain possible and have a delicious, uniquely nutty flavor. The only rice that matches this description is basmati, the standard by which all other rices are measured, the queen of all rice.

According to Dr. Bill D. Webb, of the U.S. Department of Agriculture and foremost rice expert in the United States, there are two classes of basmati: authentic Punjabi basmati and all its imitators. In its raw state premium basmati appears as a very fine, polished, long, slender grain. But the unusual thing about this rice is that when cooked it elongates up to 200 percent of its original size. Basmati has the natural capacity to absorb more water than other long-grain rice. This ability to absorb water keeps it from becoming sticky. And it always has a distinctive flavor and aroma.

For some time the USDA has tried to grow basmati rice in different test sites, but they have not been able to reproduce the same unique flavor or the elongating properties of Indian basmati. Dr. Webb thinks it might be because the specific laws of nature in its growing environment—the Punjab of India—have yet to be found in the United States or elsewhere in the world.

OTHER RICES

Other long-grain rices grown from basmati seed might be classified as basmati II. One of these, called Texmati, is widely available in natural food stores. It is a cross between basmati and American long-grain rice. Although sometimes sold as basmati, it is considered simply a good long-grain rice. There are also California and Thailand basmati types available, but they do not have the authentic flavor and length when cooked. However, these are nutritious and less expensive substitutes. Processed instant-type rices are not acceptable substitutes, though.

Sweet rice is a very short-grain rice that can be found in oriental grocery stores. It makes an unforgettably rich pudding, but may not be to your taste for everyday fare. Wild rice, a tasty, dark, long grain that is not strictly speaking a true rice but a grass and thus a nutty-flavored substitute, is not as easy to digest as rice. Brown rice, or red rice as it is known in Ayurveda, is not regarded as digestible as Basmati although many people feel it is a healthful rice good for bodybuilding and general nutrition. Although not always considered as tasty as polished basmati, with its outer layer of bran intact it is richer in fiber and vitamins. In some countries brown rice and other of the more nutritious whole grains are fed to cows more often than to people.

RICE FOR KAPHA AND WEIGHT REDUCTION

Everyone can benefit from eating rice, but those with Kapha constitutions eat it less frequently than either Pitta or Vata, and they should dry roast or fry the washed rice in a little ghee or oil for a few minutes until the grains are transparent, then steam or boil it as usual. This gives the rice a lighter quality that Kapha types appreciate. People watching their weight should eat less rice because it builds all tissues, including fat. If you have a cool place where you can store a large sack of rice in a sealed container for one year, or more, you will have old rice, which Ayurveda holds in the highest for people low in Kapha.

WHEAT

Wheat, another sweet grain that enhances all aspects of nutrition, can generally be eaten by everyone except people with the intestinal disease known as celiac sprue. Wheat is rarely associated with allergies. Something growing with or on the wheat may cause reactions in some people. If someone thinks he or she has a wheat allergy or an allergy related to any of the foods mentioned here, he or she should consult a physician trained in Maharishi Ayur-Ved.

Wheat flours are most commonly used in the American diet for making a wide variety of breads, desserts, and pasta. Whole wheat and unbleached white flours are the most nutritious for everyday baking. Semolina wheat, known as durum, makes wonderful pastas and couscous. Dry wheat breakfast cereals—sometimes mixed with rice and oats—make good morning or evening light meals. Not as widely used, bulgur, a traditional Middle Eastern grain of cracked wheat berries, is available at natural food stores and many supermarkets. Kasha, the roasted kernels, or groats, is treated as a grain but is actually the fruit of the buckwheat plant. It is high in digestible protein and very good for building muscles, tissue, and, in excess, fat for Vata and Pitta. The process of toasting kasha lightens it, making it good for Kapha in moderation. Both spelt and a registered grain called Kamut are simple, nonhybrid ancestors of the wheat family that contain a lot of nutrition and bake a little differently than the wheat flour we get at the grocery store. Available at natural food stores, spelt and Kamut act in the three doshas in the same way as other kinds of wheat, increasing Kapha and decreasing Vata and Pitta.

BARLEY

Even though barley, whether unhulled or pearled and boiled, or used as a flour, is not as nutritious as other grains, it has a light, easily digested quality. Barley that has been very well cooked in a lot of water makes a kind of soupy porridge that is soothing for convalescents. Barley is so good for Kapha body types that it should be their grain of choice and eaten frequently. Barley has very little fat or sodium, making it an especially good rice substitute for those needing to lose weight. When served as a main dish or as the major part of the meal, barley is too light in quality to satisfy the needs of Pitta and Vata, as rice and wheat do. Some cooks find it is more versatile than wheat or rice. For all body types, barley is useful in preventing constipation. The water left from cooking whole barley has diuretic properties. It can also be used as a base in making vegetable soups.

Green peppers stuffed with herbed barley or a simple sauté of barley tossed with some favorite steamed vegetables are satisfying foods for weight watchers. Without changing the result, barley flour can replace up to one-third of the wheat flour in a recipe, making baked goods more edible for Kapha types. Using too much barley flour results in a strong bitter taste in breads and cakes. Whole barley is a good basic grain to prepare for those recovering from illness. Ayurveda considers barley a food for the prevention of illness when it is part of a well-balanced diet.

CORN AND MILLET

Whole corn and cornmeal used in baking are nourishing for everyone, especially those with Kapha constitutions. Its light, heating properties make it less appetizing for Pitta, especially in the summer. Corn bread or cornmeal mixed with other grains when making bread helps to reduce fat.

Millet is a sweet whole grain, a staple of African cookery, but served most frequently in America as birdseed. It's versatile enough to substitute for other grains when we want to add more variety to meals. Millet also makes an easily digested, warm breakfast cereal healthy for everyone.

LENTILS

Lentils, members of the legume family and also called pulses or gram, are available either polished and split (lentils) or whole (gram). They can be made into a soup with vegetables and herbs, or cooked alone into a thick broth known as dahl (sounds like "doll"). For nutritional balance dahl is usually served with rice. In a richly varied vegetarian diet lentils help to provide an easy way to maintain a proper intake of amino acids, essential minerals, and trace elements. Adding an astringent taste to a meal, they are especially recommended for Pitta and Kapha diets. The lentils listed in this book can be found in most natural food or Asian grocery stores. There are interesting and subtle differences in the flavors of each type, and it can be fun to experiment with them. Whole lentils require soaking for a couple of hours before cooking. If you are in a hurry, split lentils cook much faster than the whole gram. Brown lentils as well as yellow or green split peas are available at most grocery stores. They can be substituted in the recipes calling for lentils, but the consistency and flavor of pea soup remains identifiable and doesn't achieve the delicacy of lentil dahl. Lentil and bean dishes are best cooked with a pinch of hing in the boiling water; this aids in the later stages of digestion and reduces gas.

HOW TO COOK DELICIOUS DAHL

Simmering lentils on top of the stove in 5 to 7 parts salted water to 1 part lentils for 3 or 4 hours is the most common way of cooking them. A little salt and varied seasonings can turn a rather bland pot of boiled lentils into a tasty soup or dahl. One of the easiest seasonings to use in making an authentic Indian dahl is Maharishi Vata Churna. It is a special blend of spices that are most healthful for Vata types and everyone else in cold, windy weather. If you're in a hurry, Vata Churna already includes hing in it, so you won't have to add more to the boiling water. A speedy and altogether healthy Ayurvedic cooking suggestion is to prepare lentils, as well as rice or vegetables, in a pressure cooker. The lentils can be cooked into a soup prior to preparing the vegetables or other dishes for the meal, and then heated again just before serving.

If you're in too much of a hurry to stay and watch the pressure cooker but you have plenty of time, put the washed lentils, salt and seasonings, a teaspoon or so of ghee, and 6 or 7 cups of water in a deep casserole. Cover tightly. Place in the oven and turn to 300°F. Allow this soup to bake from 4 to 6 hours. If you're a little late getting to it, perhaps 7 or 8 hours, the dahl will look pretty thick. But by adding boiling water to make the consistency you want you'll have a delicious soup.

Sprouted whole gram, especially mung, Urad, and brown lentils, are delicious and full of protein when slightly sprouted and fried in oil or ghee. Soak about half a cup of whole gram in tepid water for about 24 hours or until the beans are soft and just sprouting a "tail." Then drain them and stir-fry in 2 teaspoons of oil for 2 to 3 minutes.

Reheat any lentil and bean dishes left over from the noon meal by frying them in hot oil. All lentils, beans, and unprocessed rice should be picked over carefully to remove any little stones, and then washed very well, usually in three changes of cool water, before cooking.

LEGUME CHOICES

There are many popular legumes either whole or split lentils to choose from for making dahl. A lentil is the whole gram (bean) that has been skinned and split in half. The whole legume, relative of the pea, looks like a small bean but it is referred to as a gram to distinguish it from such true beans as Great Northern, Pinto, Red, and others that are boiled into soups and stews. Most are available at Asian groceries or natural food stores. The following list describes the most popular readily available ones.

GREEN MUNG GRAM
These are the same little beans sprouted for use in Chinese cooking. When served as a very liquid soup, whole mung bean dahl is good for everyone. If a person has excellent digestion, that is, very active agni, a mung dahl of a more solid, thick consistency can be eaten. Prepared in this way, it is a good food to eat when feeling particularly ravenous.

MUNG LENTILS/SPLIT MUNG BEANS
Split mung lentils cook more quickly than the whole bean and do not cause gas when thoroughly cooked. When properly prepared, in its most digestible state, mung dahl should look very creamy.

CHANA LENTILS
Also called split chick-peas, Chana (KA-nah) lentils are light, rich-tasting, and easy to digest. This dahl is also a good food to eat in cases of diarrhea.

TOOR LENTILS
When bought at an Indian grocery store, these split pigeon peas appear a shiny, golden yellow. They are covered in oil for preservation. Before cooking, the oil must be thoroughly washed off under very hot water. Richly delicious, Toor dahl can be a regular part of everyone's diet; although it is heavy and nutritious, it may cause gas.

URAD GRAM
Whole Urad (OOR-ad) beans are sold as black lentils that look like very small black beans. They should not be confused with black turtle beans, which even though small are about twice as large as Urad beans. The inside of the bean is pure white and rather oily. Cooking Urad dahl takes about twice as long as any other, but it makes a rich, hearty, exceptionally nutritious soup. Sprouted and fried is the best way for Kapha types to eat them.

URAD LENTILS
These are the black urad beans that have been skinned and split in half and are creamy white in color. They are very good for everyone, especially for those with Vata and Pitta constitutions. White lentils act as a tonic and general body-builder. Eating too much Urad dahl, however, increases Kapha and fat. These lentils cook faster than the whole Urad beans, are just as nutritious, and benefit from the addition of turmeric for a richer color.

MASOOR LENTILS
The fastest-cooking of all lentils, bright coral-colored masoor also has somewhat less nutritional value than the others. But they only take about 15 minutes to make.

BROWN (MUTH) LENTILS
These are the flat, brown-colored lentils commonly found in supermarkets. They can be cooked into a stew or dahl like other lentils, or prepared as a hearty and unusual breakfast food, or a side dish at a

regular meal by frying just-sprouted muth lentils in a little oil or ghee with a choice of dosha-appropriate spices, then served with rice.

DRIED BEANS

Ayurveda gives a general guideline for eating dishes cooked with dried beans. Once a week is enough for anyone. Beans are nutritious body-builders and hard to digest at the same time. Most beans are all right for Kapha and Pitta, but they aggravate Vata. Although Pitta is increased somewhat by eating beans, the increase is not significant, except, of course, for spicy chili beans. Because of their heavy body-building nature, eating too many bean dishes increases Kapha. Soy-beans and soybean products, including tofu, are fine for Vata and Pitta types, but because of their cold, heavy, sometimes oily qualities, they increase Kapha. For Vata constitutions eating beans once a week is enough. For Kapha, eating a dish containing tofu once a week is plenty. And during Kapha season tofu should be significantly reduced in the menu of anyone subject to colds or bronchial problems and general feelings of sluggishness.

FRUITS

The best fresh fruits for daily consumption are apples, sweet oranges, and melons (in season)—especially that summertime favorite, water-melon. Dried dates, raisins, and figs are good for everyone. Ayurveda says they bring a feeling of fulfillment and satisfaction. Even though dried they are neither dry in quality nor too drying for Pitta to enjoy fully. Vata can soak dried fruits in hot water before eating them. The concentrated sweet taste in dried fruits increases Kapha.

GHEE AND OTHER OILS

All cooking oils have sweet and oily aspects that increase Kapha and decrease Vata and Pitta. Corn and sesame oils, if used exclusively, will increase Pitta. Ghee increases agni without increasing Pitta dosha. Both a *rasayana* and an auspicious food of the superior category, ghee is a superb first choice in cooking oils. Rasayanas (rah-SAI-uh-nahz) are foods that promote longevity. We'll say more about these at the end of the chapter. Ghee can be made from any kind of butter, but that from cow's milk is the best. For medicinal purposes, Ayurveda uses a specially refined ghee that has been heated and filtered many times. Simply refined ghee, well filtered once, is used for cooking. When properly made, ghee needs no refrigeration since there are no milk solids left in it to spoil. It remains solid at room temperature, and unopened ghee has a shelf life of two years. For instructions on making ghee, see page 146.

Ghee maintains youth.
Eating some ghee every day prevents aging.

—DR. T. M. GOPTE

GHEE AND CHOLESTEROL

Ghee and vegetable oils, when properly used, do not increase cholesterol. Long-term Ayurvedic research in India indicates that the regular use of ghee in the diet assumes the person lives a normally active life, and when ghee is used in combination with certain sweet or pungent spices it and other vegetable oils help maintain dietary balance and a strong agni. These researchers say that ghee heated with such spices as ground cumin, hing (asafoetida), ground coriander seeds, turmeric, and roasted, ground fenugreek enables the body to use the oils more efficiently and avoid high cholesterol levels. The spices, used singly or in combination, should be heated in the oil, then added to flavor a recipe. If you have questions about your diet and cholesterol levels, consult your doctor.

Ghee is the best food
for reducing Pitta.

—THE *CHARAKA SAMHITA*

CHOCOLATE

Although chocolate is not one of the health-promoting foods recommended wholeheartedly for everyone (eating too much chocolate is thought to create ama, which leads to other health problems), this seems to be as good a place as any to say a few words about a favorite —some would claim essential—American treat.

Chocolate is a bitter, astringent-tasting ingredient that increases Vata and, if eaten in moderation, decreases Pitta and Kapha. Sweetened chocolate increases Kapha. Even with its delectable taste chocolate should not be used as a staple in anyone's diet. Ayurveda's caution about eating chocolate primarily concerns the quantity consumed weekly and daily (hourly?) in the contemporary American diet. These concerns do not necessarily mean chocolate must be eliminated from your diet, only that anyone who cares to eat chocolate should use common sense, be aware of how you feel after eating, and enjoy it in moderation. Generally once every week or two is frequent enough, not daily.

There is concern among advocates of certain diets that the alkali used when processing chocolate into baking cocoa as well as the liqueur for candy making renders the product alkaline. Eating and drinking alkaline foods vitiates or weakens all doshas. Alkali is used in processing highly refined European cocoa (called the Dutch process), and European chocolate is considered by many gourmets to be the best-quality cocoa available. Ayurveda disagrees. The good news is that quality baking chocolate, not processed with alkali, is available at your supermarket. It's the familiar Hershey's cocoa (not their new European style).

Of course, you may avoid processing questions and purchase your own cocoa beans,* and roast and grind them yourself. You'll obtain a crumbly, slightly gritty cocoa outstanding in making hot chocolate and general baked goods.

Ayurveda does not consider carob a healthy substitute for chocolate. Certain alkaline properties in carob beans are thought to contribute to the production of ama.

HERBS AND SPICES FOR EVERYONE

Although the following spices may increase certain doshas, they are still considered good for everyone when used moderately in the regular diet. These particular ones are usually ground and combined in various proportions to make a spice blend, garam masala. It can be fried up with vegetables or added to casseroles whenever you're looking for

* Fresh Mexican cocoa beans are available by the pound with preparation instructions from J. L. Hudson, Seedsman, P.O. Box 1058, Redwood City, CA 94064.

something interesting and a little different. You can make your own dosha-balancing spice blend by using these and other spices listed in the Charts of Ingredients.

ASAFOETIDA (HING)

A powerful-smelling resinlike spice, hing is both astringent and heat-producing in the stomach after eating. It is a good intestinal antiseptic and therefore very good for Vata. The flavor and warming properties of hing are released when they are heated by frying or boiling. Lentil and bean dishes should always be made with a pinch of hing to aid digestion. When frying the other spices used in a recipe, mix a little hing with them before adding to cooked beans, lentils or mixed vegetables. Hing works best with other spices and so it should not be the only spice in a recipe. The best use of hing is in cooking dahl. Put a pinch of hing in the boiling, salted water just before adding the lentils and the spices. Then cover the pot quickly to keep its strong essence in the steam and not all over the kitchen. Using too much hing aggravates Pitta. When using Vata Churna to flavor dahl it is not necessary to add hing, as it is in the Churna.

CORIANDER

Sweet, slightly pungent, and oily, freshly ground seeds are best when fried in hot oil and added to vegetable dishes, rice, or soups. But you can also use the freshly ground seed right in soups and sauces if they are well heated to bring out the flavor of the coriander. The leaves of the coriander plant, cilantro, add pungent, astringent, and bitter tastes to salads and vegetable dishes. Cilantro is also good for anyone who likes the flavor.

CUMIN

To get the best taste from cumin seeds, dry roast them in a small pan, then grind into a powder. With sweet, bitter, pungent, and light aspects, cumin complements tomato-based dishes. It is a basic spice in both the Vata and Kapha diets, more so than for Pitta.

NUTMEG

The sweetness of nutmeg goes nicely with dairy products, cooked fruits, vegetables, and dahls. Ayurveda recommends increasing the use of nutmeg in the diet during hay fever season. When added to warm milk, nutmeg promotes sleep (as does the milk). Rice made with ghee and nutmeg has superior eating qualities. It is a nourishing spice for Vata and Pitta types.

TURMERIC

A brilliant yellow powder, turmeric is generally heated in oil before mixing with other ingredients. It plays a useful culinary role as the unifying herb among many. When cooked with other spices, turmeric tends to pull all the flavors of a dish together and turns everything a brilliant yellow. Ayurveda considers turmeric a good blood purifier and skin tonic. Slightly bitter, astringent, and pungent, hot and dry, turmeric is one of the best spices for reducing Kapha and good for Vata and Pitta in moderation.

CARDAMOM

Sweet, bitter, and astringent ground cardamom is at its best when heated with milk, included in sweet main dishes, and in baking sweet breads and cookies. Because of its sweetness, Kapha types should use less cardamom than Vata and Pitta types. It makes a good spice for a warming winter drink.

SPECIAL SPICES

The Maharishi Ayur-Ved Churnas are special blends of herbs and spices that promote health as well as add flavor to your cooking. When following Indian recipes, they can be used as garam masala, that is, 4 or 5 flavorful spices, ground and preblended for your cooking convenience. Churnas and masalas can be heated in a little oil or ghee, then added to cooked vegetables to make a curried dish. Or they can be mixed in small amounts with any of your favorite foods to taste. All three Churnas—Vata, Pitta, and Kapha—can be used by everyone to some extent. This, too, depends on taste and individual seasonal needs. We've talked about the unique way Vata Churna enhances dahls and bean dishes, but each of the Churnas provides rich and marvelous flavorings for creamy soups, gravies, marinades, dressings, and sauces. Experiments with these Churnas are sure to yield many pleasant results. They can be ordered directly from Maharishi Ayur-Ved Products International, listed on page 293.

BEST USE OF THE CHURNAS

The Maharishi Ayur-Ved Churnas come in handy when you want to be certain all six tastes—sweet, salty, sour, bitter, astringent, and pungent—are represented in a meal. When a main meal is Ayurvedically balanced, meaning that each of the six tastes can be clearly identified, then the entire meal is balanced. So the Churnas should not be sprinkled over an entire plate of food. Nor should a single Churna be used in every dish in the meal. This blurs or throws off the effect of the different tastes and the balance in the meal. Add a single Churna to only one or two dishes at a meal. Then use a different one, other herbs or spices, or simply the combined ingredients themselves to make good-tasting, well-balanced meals.

THE BEST OF THE BEST

Certain foods are so especially nutritious that Ayurveda has identified them as rasayanas, that is, foods that promote longevity. A rasayana contains all the nutrition needed for the development of every body tissue. It works on that familiar gardening principle of watering the root of a plant to develop all the parts. Rasayanas nourish the very basis of physical life.

The plump, light-colored fig known as anjier and mentioned before is a rasayana for everyone. It is sold in some supermarkets and natural food stores as the white Calmyrna fig. Other rasayanas include basmati rice, ghee, wheat, Urad gram, blanched almonds, and ground nutmeg to name a few.

Chapter 4

AYURVEDIC RECIPES

NOTE: The recipes are rated for their increasing (+), decreasing (−), or neutral (*) effects on each dosha. The effect is neutral if eaten in moderation.

Beverages

BED AND BREAKFAST DRINK

This is a nourishing and soothing milk-based drink good to have in the morning and at bedtime.

−V −P *K
Serves 1

> *1 cup milk—low-fat for Kapha*
> *½ to 2 teaspoons ghee*
> *Sugar or raw honey to taste*

Heat the milk in a small saucepan over moderate heat, stirring frequently. When just at the boiling point add the ghee and sugar. Stir and allow to come to a full boil. Cool and serve warm. For those reducing weight, eliminate the ghee and use skim milk.

CHILLED PITTA BROTH

This is a nourishing vegetable broth drink made from Pitta-reducing ingredients. Use a total of 2 cups Pitta-reducing vegetables for each quart. This recipe makes a refreshing summer beverage for Pitta when it is served chilled with a celery stick and a garnish of fresh fennel or dill.

−V −P *K
Makes 1 quart

> 1 quart water
> ¼ teaspoon salt
> ½ cup chopped broccoli
> ½ cup chopped green beans
> ¼ cup peeled and diced sweet potato
> ¼ cup chopped parsley
> ¼ teaspoon white or black pepper
> 1 tablespoon Pitta Churna
> > or
> > 1 teaspoon ground coriander
> > ¼ teaspoon crushed anise seed
> > 3 crushed green cardamom pods
> 1 small celery stick (with the leaves on)
> 1 sprig fresh fennel or dill

To a 4-quart pot of boiling salted water add the vegetables. Turn the flame to low, cover, and simmer for 15 minutes. Stir in the parsley and spices. Then turn off the heat and let the pot sit undisturbed until the broth is cool. Strain the broth through a sieve lined with cheesecloth or a damp tea towel. The cooked vegetables can be pureed and used in a creamy soup, or they can simply be eaten with a little butter.

Date Shake

If you want to gain weight, try drinking this naturally sweet milk drink every morning. It's also good to drink when you want a quick increase in energy.

−V −P + K
Serves 1

> 5 large (or 10 small) dates
> ½ cup water
> ½ cup preboiled milk cooled to room temperature

Soak the dates overnight in ½ cup of water. In the morning when the dates are softened, remove the seeds and add the dates to the milk. Blend thoroughly.

FRAGRANTLY SPICED LASSI

Lassi, a yogurt-based drink traditionally served at the end of an Indian meal, is good for everyone to drink after a main meal except late at night or in cold weather. The usual recipe for Lassi is simply yogurt thinned with water or to taste. Serve this more elaborate Fragrantly Spiced Lassi at dinner parties or on special occasions. No matter which Lassi you make, it is traditionally served at the end of the meal rather than as an accompanying beverage. If taken in large amounts, Lassi increases Pitta and Kapha. One cup or a little less per person is usually quite satisfying.

−V *P *K
Makes 1 quart

> *1 cup plain yogurt*
> *½ cup sugar or honey, or less, to taste*
> *3 cups cold water*
> *1 green cardamom pod, husked and seeded,*
>   *or ¼ teaspoon ground*
> *Pinch of saffron, crumbled*
> *⅛ teaspoon nutmeg*
> *1 teaspoon rose water*

Mix the yogurt, the sugar, and the water together in a large bowl or pitcher, beating until smooth. Add the spices. Stir well, cover, and refrigerate 2 to 4 hours. Just before serving stir in the rose water.

PINEAPPLE MINT TEA

The sweet taste of pineapple is especially useful for balancing Pitta in the summer. This fruity herbal tea is good for everyone to drink, although only those following a Pitta-reducing diet might like to drink it chilled.

*V −P *K
Makes 2 quarts

❖❖

2 cups fresh mint leaves or 4 tablespoons dried
1 quart boiling water
4 ounces frozen pineapple juice concentrate,
    defrosted, or 2 cups fresh pineapple juice
3 or 4 fresh mint sprigs for garnish

Put the mint leaves in a 4-quart pot with the boiling water. Cover right away and remove from the heat. Steep for 20 to 30 minutes. Remove the mint and strain the tea into a pitcher containing the pineapple concentrate (or pineapple juice) and 1 quart cold water. Stir well. If served as a punch, float a few sprigs of fresh mint on top.

PLAIN REFRESHING LASSI

Lassi is good for everyone, especially when served in warm weather and at the end of the meal rather than with food. Buttermilk has the same digestive usefulness. It can be diluted with water to any consistency and served in place of yogurt and water. When making Lassi for Vata types dilute one part yogurt with one part water. For Pitta use one part yogurt and two parts water. The dilution for Kapha is one part yogurt and four parts water.

−V *P *K
Makes 1 quart

1 cup plain yogurt or buttermilk
3 cups water

Shake yogurt and water in a 1-quart jar or mix well until blended. Serve immediately or very slightly chilled.

NOTE: For Vata types add to the above recipe ⅛ teaspoon ground cumin, a pinch of ginger, and salt and pepper to taste (for each 1 cup serving). Kapha appreciates even more diluted Lassi with a little pinch of ginger.

ROSE PETAL MILKSHAKE

This elegant drink soothes and cools the fires of Pitta in the summer. When served warm everyone can drink it year-round. Rose petals are said to nourish the heart. When you are finished sipping the drink, use a spoon to eat the remaining petals.

−V −P *K
Makes 2 cups

> 2 cups milk—low-fat for Kapha
> 1½ tablespoons Rose Petal Conserve
>   (a Maharishi Ayur-Ved product)
> ¼ teaspoon vanilla extract
>   (optional)

Blend or shake all the ingredients thoroughly for 1 minute. The pieces of rose petals will settle to the bottom of the container. Take care to scoop them all out when serving.

SAFFRON MILK TEA

This warm and rich drink is excellent for Vata, especially on very cold days. And, with modifications, it's good for Kapha, too. The saffron is a fine internal "heater." Although everyone can use it, it increases Pitta because of its pungent stimulating properties. In winter Pitta might enjoy a small amount of this drink.

−V +P −K
Serves 1

> 1 cup milk
> 1 teaspoon ghee
> ⅛ teaspoon crumbled saffron
> 1 teaspoon sugar

Heat the milk in a heavy saucepan just close to the boiling point. Add the remaining ingredients and simmer for about 5 minutes, or until the milk is a rich yellow color. Cool and serve.

NOTE: For Kapha types and weight watchers, use skim milk, omit the ghee, and reduce the sugar to taste.

SWEET FRUIT SMOOTHIES

This is a nourishing, cooling drink for balancing Pitta, especially in the heat of summer. It is sweet, heavy, and cold when made with very ripe, sweet fruits. Use warm milk for a Vata-balancing smoothy. Because it is heavy, sweet, and cold, this is not a drink that would benefit Kapha types.

−V −P +K
Serves 2

> *1 cup milk*
> *½ cup ice cream (optional)*
> *1 cup minced ripe fruit*
> *1 to 2 teaspoons sugar*
> *¼ teaspoon nutmeg or cinnamon (optional)*
> *½ teaspoon vanilla extract*

Whirl all the ingredients in a blender or food processor or whisk by hand until well blended. Serve in tall mugs or glasses.

NOTE: Mixed fruits such as strawberries, peaches, kiwis, cherries, and blueberries add interest and flavor. Adding some sugar helps in the digestion of the milk.

THREE-IN-ONE SUPREME

The combinations of three spices, ghee, and milk in this drink make it so nourishing that it might be considered a rasayana. It is good to drink by itself for breakfast and again before bedtime. The first version is good for Vata and Pitta. Version 2 is better for Kapha. Make up a small batch of spices ahead of time and use ½ teaspoon of the spice mixture for each cup of warm milk.

VERSION I FOR VATA AND PITTA

−V −P +K
For each serving:

> *1 cup warm milk*
> *1 teaspoon ghee*
> *1 teaspoon sugar, or to taste*
> *½ teaspoon spices in this proportion:*
> > *3 parts cardamom*
> > *1 part ground cloves*
> > *1 part cinnamon*

Heat the milk and ghee together in a small saucepan over a moderately high flame and bring just close to a boil. Quickly stir in the sugar and spices. Remove from the heat and continue stirring until it is cool enough to drink.

VERSION 2 FOR KAPHA

−V −P *K
For each serving:

> *1 cup warm milk, preferably skim or low-fat*
> *½ to 1 teaspoon raw sugar or brown sugar*
> *1 teaspoon spices in this proportion:*
> > *1 part cardamom*
> > *1 part ground ginger*
> > *1 part ground cloves*
> > *1 part cinnamon*

After heating the milk, remove it from the heat and stir in the honey and spices. Continue stirring until it is cool enough to drink.

WATERMELON-STRAWBERRY PUNCH

Watermelon is good for everyone to eat in the summer. Watermelon-Strawberry Punch is a wonderfully refreshing fruit punch for cooling off on a hot afternoon. Add small amounts of bottled juices, if you like, but there is so much fresh fruit available in the summer it is easy to make delicious fresh fruit drinks. In this recipe the hollowed-out watermelon shell is its own punch bowl, but any large bowl will do. Garnish freely with fresh herbs and flowers, but be sure to use washed flowers or leaves that you know are edible.

*V – P *K
Makes about 3 quarts

> 1 round watermelon, about 12 to 15 pounds
> 2 tablespoons sugar (optional)
> 1 pint strawberries, washed and drained
> 2 limes, thinly sliced
> Sprigs of fresh mint and lemon balm
> Blossoms from borage (blue shooting stars), nasturtiums,
>   pineapple sage, sweet violets, rose petals

To prepare the watermelon punch bowl, cut a ¼-inch slice off the bottom of the watermelon so it will stand upright. Mark the melon about one-third from the top and slice open. This small top piece can be saved for use as a cover. To save the juices, work on a cookie sheet with sides or a large shallow pan. Remove as much melon as you can in large chunks, then scrape the inside clean. Use a melon baller to make about 2 cups of balls, or cut into bite-size cubes and reserve. Be sure to remove all seeds. Juice the remaining watermelon by pounding it with a wooden spoon in a deep bowl and then straining through a sieve. You will have about 2 to 2½ quarts of melon juice.

For the punch, pour the juice into the melon shell or a serving bowl. Mix in some sugar, if needed. Juice the strawberries in a food mill or strainer and stir into the punch bowl. Add a few ice cubes or serve them in a separate bowl. Garnish with melon balls, lime slices, mint leaves, and flowers. Chill before serving.

Appetizers

CHEESE CRACKERS

These appetizers are more like soft little biscuits than crackers. Whether eaten by themselves or with soup, these little Cheese Crackers add a salty taste that is slightly pungent and sweet, which reduces Vata, is neutral for Pitta, and increases Kapha. Children seem to like them.

–V *P +K
Serves 6 generously

1 cup unbleached flour
½ teaspoon salt
½ teaspoon paprika
Coarsely ground black pepper to taste
½ cup unsalted butter
1 cup grated cheese (Parmesan, Romano,
    or cheddar in combination)
2 tablespoons heavy cream
½ tablespoon heavy cream for glaze

1. Preheat the oven to 325°F.
2. Mix the flour together with the salt, paprika, and pepper. With a pastry cutter or the steel knife of a food processor, cut in the butter and the grated cheese until mealy. Stir in the 2 tablespoons heavy cream. When you have a smooth dough, chill it for about an hour. Roll out the dough on a floured surface to a thickness of about ¼ inch. Cut into strips ½ inch by 1½ inches. Brush with the ½ tablespoon cream and arrange on ungreased baking sheets. Bake for 12 to 14 minutes until puffy and a little brown.

CURRIED HERB CHEESE DIP

Serve this sour, pungent dip with crackers, chips, or raw vegetables.

−V *P +K
Makes 1 cup

½ cup sour cream
½ cup ricotta cheese
1 tablespoon lemon juice
3 tablespoons minced fresh parsley
1 tablespoon minced fresh basil
½ teaspoon dry mustard
½ teaspoon paprika
¼ teaspoon ground white pepper
Pinch of cayenne
½ teaspoon cumin seeds

In a small bowl cream the sour cream and ricotta together thoroughly. Mix in the lemon juice, parsley, basil, mustard, paprika, and peppers. Roast the cumin seeds in a dry, hot iron pan until just turning light brown, then grind finely and add to the cheese mixture. Spoon into a serving bowl, cover, and chill in the refrigerator for 2 or 3 hours to set the flavors.

GOLDEN PANIR CUBES

Simple to make and a sweet, oily, nourishing appetizer, panir cubes prepared this way can also be tossed into stir-fried vegetables just before serving. They can be seasoned while frying with nutmeg, ground coriander, cumin, or any other ground spice of your choice.

−V *P *K
Serves 4 to 6

1 recipe Panir (pages 145–146)
½ cup ghee

Cube the panir in 1½-inch squares. Heat the ghee in a heavy 10-inch frying pan over moderately high heat. Fry the cubes, turning frequently until each side is golden brown. Skewer on toothpicks and serve hot with a dipping sauce.

GOLDEN YUMMIES

These delicious little appetizers are sweet, oily, and a little pungent. They are good for all body types when served as hot hors d'oeuvres. Allow 2 to 3 per person. The topping alone makes a delightful sweet condiment or chutney.

*V *P −K
Makes 2 cups chutney or 30 appetizers

FOR THE TOPPING

> 1½ tablespoons ghee
> ½ teaspoon cayenne
> ⅓ cup milk or cream
> 1 to 2 tablespoons sugar, or to taste
> ⅛ teaspoon allspice
> ⅛ to ¼ teaspoon crushed saffron
> ¼ cup currants or raisins
> 1 to 1½ cups coconut—finely chopped is best,
>   but flaked will do

In a small saucepan or frying pan, heat the ghee over a moderately high flame. Then add the cayenne and stir about 1 minute. Stir in the milk, the sugar, the allspice, and the crumbled saffron threads. Bring to a boil, stirring often. The milk should begin turning golden yellow. Reduce heat to simmer. Stir in the currants or raisins and 1 cup of coconut. Beat well as the mixture leaves the sides of the pan. If it is too liquid, add more coconut a tablespoon at a time until the mixture is just moist but not wet. Assemble right away or set aside until you are ready to serve.

TO ASSEMBLE

> ½ tablespoon ghee
> Unsalted wheat, mini-rice crackers,
>   or other mild-flavored crackers
> Cashew, almond, or sesame nut butter

1. Heat the ghee in a small pan over a moderate flame. Add 2 or 3 tablespoons of topping per person. Fry over high heat, stirring until heated thoroughly. Remove from the heat and spread each cracker with about ½ teaspoon nut butter, then top with 1 teaspoon hot coconut mixture. Serve warm.

2. If prepared in advance, put the yummies under a broiler for 15 to 20 seconds before serving.

NOTE: To make a Vata/Kapha Golden Yummy use a large rice cake (for Kapha) or toast instead of crackers and spread with topping.

PINEAPPLE GINGER-CREAM SPREAD

This sweet, sour, and pungent, cold and heavy sandwich or cracker spread is best for Vata, but both Pitta and Kapha can enjoy some spread on a cracker or two. It makes a fine celery stuffing.

−v *p *k
Makes 1 cup

> 8 ounces cream cheese
> 1/4 cup chopped fresh ginger
> 2 1/2 tablespoons drained crushed pineapple
> 1/2 teaspoon nutmeg
> 1/4 teaspoon ground cardamom

Mix all the ingredients together thoroughly. Cover and set aside in the refrigerator for about an hour before serving.

Salads

ASPARAGUS SALAD WITH RASPBERRY VINAIGRETTE

A colorful and unusual salad that is good for Vata, neutral for Pitta, and increases Kapha slightly. It adds sweet, a little sour, and astringent tastes to the meal.

−v *p +k
Serves 4

> 10 asparagus spears
> Lettuce leaves
> Raspberry Vinaigrette (pages 129–130)
> 1/2 teaspoon salt
> Coarsely ground pepper

Clean the asparagus, cut off the tough ends, and steam the whole stalks for 10 to 12 minutes. When the asparagus is tender yet a bright green, immediately blanch in cold water to retain the color. Refrigerate

until they are cool. When ready to serve, arrange the spears o
leaves. Pour the Raspberry Vinaigrette over the middle of th
Sprinkle with the salt and the coarsely ground pepper.

BEET AND GINGER SALAD

A colorful sweet, pungent, salty, mildly bitter and sour salad is so
good for everyone that it can be served daily as a small appetizing salad
for one or two people or as a condiment for four. For those with a
Vata imbalance or weak digestion, eat one or two mouthfuls and chew
them well.

This recipe and the Carrot Raisin Salad come from the Maharishi
Ayur-Ved Ama–Reducing Program. For information about this program and suggestions for reducing ama (toxic by-products of ineffi-
cient metabolism) and strengthening the digestive fire, contact a
physician trained in Maharishi Ayur-Ved.

−V *P −K
Serves 2

1 medium beet (or carrot),
   peeled and shredded
2 tablespoons mung bean sprouts
1 one-eighth inch piece of gingerroot,
   peeled and chopped
1 teaspoon chopped fresh basil
12 teaspoons chopped parsley
Juice of half a lemon
1/16 teaspoon salt
1 to 2 teaspoons Pitta or Kapha Churna
   or
   1/2 teaspoon turmeric
   1/2 teaspoon ground cumin
   1/4 teaspoon cinnamon
   1/8 teaspoon cardamom
   1/8 teaspoon black pepper
   1/8 teaspoon ground cloves

Toss the shredded beet, the sprouts, the ginger, and green herbs together in a small bowl. Sprinkle it with the lemon juice and the salt. Mix the spices together and lightly incorporate them into the salad. Set it aside for about 30 minutes before serving to let the flavors come together.

CARROT RAISIN SALAD

More than just a salad, Carrot Raisin Salad has a similar appetizing effect for sparking the appetite, improving digestion, and reducing ama as the Beet and Ginger Salad. It is very simple to make and is especially recommended for those with Vata or Kapha imbalances.

−V *P −K
Serves 2

> *2 medium carrots, washed and shredded*
> *¼ cup raisins*
> *1 one-eighth inch piece gingerroot, grated*
> *Juice of half a lemon*
> *¹⁄₁₆ teaspoon salt*
> *1 to 2 teaspoons Pitta Churna*
> > *or*
> > *½ teaspoon turmeric*
> > *½ teaspoon cinnamon*
> > *¼ teaspoon cardamom*
> > *⅛ teaspoon black pepper*
> > *⅛ teaspoon ground cloves*
> > *½ teaspoon raw sugar*

Toss the shredded carrots, the raisins, and the ginger with the lemon juice and the salt. Mix the spices and sugar together and lightly incorporate them into the salad. Set it aside for about 30 minutes before serving to let the flavors come together.

Coleslaw with Caraway Dressing

This salad adds the sour taste to Pitta's diet. Rather than being eaten by itself, it should be served as part of a balanced meal that includes other Pitta-reducing dishes. Although the sour tastes of caraway, sour cream, and yogurt in the dressing are good additions to Vata's diet, the cabbage makes this salad a side dish to be eaten in moderation by Vata. Kapha would infrequently eat coleslaw.

+V −P +K
Makes 4 to 6 servings

> *1 teaspoon caraway seeds*
> *1/4 cup sour cream*
> *1/8 cup plain yogurt*
> *1 teaspoon sugar*
> *1/2 teaspoon fresh lemon juice or vinegar*
> *1/2 medium head cabbage, finely shredded*

In a small heavy pan toast the caraway seeds over a low flame. Stir constantly until light brown. Remove from the heat and crush the seeds with a mortar and pestle or in a spice grinder. Whisk the sour cream, the yogurt, and the sugar together in a small bowl. Add the caraway and lemon juice or vinegar. Then toss thoroughly with the shredded cabbage. Cover and chill for at least an hour before serving.

Confetti Rice Salad

The rice in this summertime party salad is especially nourishing for Vata and Pitta. Kapha can eat some of this rice dish in moderation with a green leafy salad or separately as a light meal. This is a light, sweet, cold side dish adding some bitter, pungent, and sour tastes.

*V −P +K
Makes 4 cups

2½ cups cooked rice
½ yellow pepper, chopped
½ red pepper, chopped
1 full stalk celery with leaves, chopped
4 tablespoons chopped fresh parsley
1½ tablespoons mixed fresh finely minced herbs: basil,
  tarragon, fennel
5 tablespoons Simple Vinaigrette Dressing (page
  130)
Salt and pepper to taste
Chopped parsley and paprika (optional garnish)
12 lettuce leaves
2 medium tomatoes, cut in wedges
1 small sliced cucumber

While the rice is still warm, toss it with the chopped vegetables, the herbs, and the vinaigrette dressing. Add the salt and pepper to taste. Sprinkle on some additional chopped parsley or a little sweet paprika for color. Cover and chill for 2 to 3 hours in the summer, or set it aside for an hour, then serve while still slightly warm. Serve on a bed of lettuce with wedges of tomato and sliced cucumber.

NOTE: Sauté any leftover rice salad in a little oil with some sliced vegetables for a satisfying side dish or a light evening meal.

MACEDONIA DI FRUITA

All the fruits in this salad are good for all body types when eaten as part of a meal. But it would not be good to serve fruit salad to Kapha as the main part of a meal. Macedonia di Fruita is an excellent salad or dessert for Pitta types, especially in the middle of summer. For the culinary artist these fruits are like colors on a palette waiting to be made into something spectacular. When prepared in a grand manner it makes an impressive centerpiece for a buffet dessert or brunch.

−V −P +K

Serves 8 to 10

> *4 sweet apples*
> *3 sweet oranges*
> *1 large cantaloupe, cut into balls or cubes*
> *2 cups cubed watermelon*
> *1 medium honeydew melon, cut into balls or cubes,*
> *   or any other melon varieties in season*
> *8 to 10 small bunches red, green,*
> *   and deep purple grapes*
> *8 to 12 Calmyrna figs*
> *10 to 12 pitted dates*
> *Other seasonal fruits of choice*

Core and thickly slice the apples. Wash the oranges thoroughly and slice them with their skins on, or peel and section them. Then cube or ball the melons. Clip the washed grapes into individual bunches. Arrange the fruits on a large platter in little groups of 8 to 10 with some of every fruit in each group. Individual servings can be made ahead of time.

Spinach and Chicory Salad

The bitter, astringent, slightly pungent, light, hot, and dry properties of this salad are especially balancing for a Kapha diet. It is also a good salad to prepare when serving people with varied dietary needs. If the meal consists of several heavy or sweet dishes, then those following a Kapha diet can help themselves to a large amount of this healthy salad. Vata and Pitta types would eat smaller portions.

+V *P −K

Serves 4

¼ cup Simple Vinaigrette Dressing (page 130)
1 teaspoon dry mustard
2 teaspoons Kapha Churna
    or
    1 teaspoon coarsely ground black pepper
    ½ teaspoon ground fenugreek
    ¼ teaspoon ground cumin
    ¼ teaspoon ground coriander
2 cups spinach, washed and torn into bite-size pieces
1 small head chicory—radicchio type
½ cup thinly shredded red cabbage
3 to 4 red radishes, thinly sliced
3 tablespoons blanched, slivered almonds,
   chopped walnuts, or pine nuts

Mix the vinaigrette, the mustard, and the Kapha Churna together. If the other spice blend is used instead of the Churna, then mix the dry spices together before adding them to the vinaigrette. Place the spinach in a serving bowl and pour the vinaigrette over it. Toss well. Add the remaining vegetables. Toss again, cover, and refrigerate for at least 30 minutes. Before serving sprinkle with the slivered almonds or other nuts.

SPLENDID LAYERS SALAD

A layered, rather thick salad that is good served as a light meal in summer. The tastes are sweet, bitter, astringent, and slightly salty. It has oily, cold, and heavy qualities. This combination is good for Pitta types since the heavier vegetables provide enough substance for Pitta's healthy appetite. When eaten in small amounts, this salad is all right for Vata, but the cold and heavy qualities aggravate Kapha. When preparing, be sure to cut everything into bite-size pieces. Each vegetable can be cut in a different shape to add visual interest.

*V −P +K

Serves 6 to 8

2 *heads Bibb lettuce*

½ *head red cabbage, shredded*

6 *large artichoke hearts, steamed and quartered, or use*
    prepared artichokes: 1 14-ounce can, drained and quartered, or
    10 ounces frozen, defrosted, and quartered

1 *pound asparagus, cut in 1-inch pieces and steamed*

1 *cucumber, washed, scored with the tines of a fork, and*
    sliced very thin

1 *medium jicama or 3 sunchokes, cut in triangular shapes and sliced*

4 *tablespoons Pitta Churna Salad Dressing (page 129)*

4 *large leaves romaine lettuce, deribbed, cut in 1-inch squares*

1 *tablespoon chopped fresh mint, dill, and/or fennel*

¼ *cup small seedless grapes, currants, or raisins*

1 *cup mixed salad greens, as available, such as arugula, beet leaves,*
    hon tsai tai, chicory, and escarole, torn or chopped in small pieces

1 *red apple, cored and diced*

⅓ *cup curly parsley leaves, broken in clusters*

¼ *cup toasted croutons*

1. Line the bottom and sides of a deep, straight-sided glass bowl or other salad bowl with Bibb lettuce leaves. Sprinkle with enough red cabbage to cover the bottom. Layer with about one-third of the thick ingredients: the artichoke hearts, the asparagus, the cucumber, and the jicama. Pour 1 tablespoon Pitta Churna Salad Dressing over this layer.

2. Begin the next layer with a sprinkling of red cabbage and romaine pieces, making the layer about an inch thick. Spread on half of the chopped fresh herbs. Arrange another third of the thick ingredients and add the grapes, currants, or raisins. Then sprinkle with a little red cabbage and pour on 1 tablespoon of dressing to end this layer.

3. Cover the surface with mixed chopped greens. Sprinkle with the remaining cabbage, the herbs, the last third of the vegetables, the diced apple, and the remaining salad dressing in that order. Ring the outside with the parsley clusters and sprinkle the croutons in the center. Be sure the Bibb lettuce lines the edges of the bowl attractively. Add more leaves, if necessary, to fill in the empty spaces.

4. Cover and refrigerate for 1 or 2 hours before serving.

Tossed Green Salad

+V −P −K

An American standard, the tossed green salad is good for everyone in one or another of its many forms. In planning balanced menus a green salad becomes an essential part of the meal because it helps to contribute some of the bitter, astringent, and pungent tastes Americans sometimes have difficulty including in our main meals. An interesting tossed green salad made up of several types of lettuce and other fresh greens adds texture and color to a meal. With well-placed touches of such fresh herbs as chopped French tarragon, basil (especially cinnamon, anise, and lemon basil leaves), lemon balm, mints, chopped parsley, or cilantro, you'll enjoy many pleasant-tasting surprises as you eat.

Salad greens should be torn into bite-size pieces. You shouldn't need to chop through a tossed salad with a knife or have to try to eat large lettuce leaves whole. If the salad is to be a main part of a light meal that includes soup or bread, then allow about 1 loosely packed quart of greens for every 2 people. Use fewer greens if many dishes are to be served at the meal. It is best to dress a salad just before it is eaten or allow people to dress their own. Any greens that have been dressed with oil should not be served again as salad, although they can be stir-fried and served as an appetizer or mixed with other vegetables at the next meal.

Tossed green salads are especially good for Pitta and Kapha. Keep Kapha's salads light by using just a variety of mixed greens, herbs, and sprouts. By adding such vegetables as peeled tomatoes, avocados, and peeled cucumbers, you create a more Vata-balancing salad.

Dressings, Sauces, Dips, and Marinades

The following salad dressings are good for everyone when served on a green salad as part of a meal. Add various fruits and vegetables that are seasonally available, depending on the needs of each person. Some of the dressings also serve as excellent marinades or sauces to be poured over hot steamed vegetables.

Instead of using vinegar to dress salads Ayurveda recommends freshly squeezed lemon or lime juice, but the occasional use of vinegar is acceptable. Lemon juice stimulates agni. Because it is fresh and not fermented, it is easier to digest than vinegar. You can easily adapt any salad dressing recipe by substituting equal amounts of fresh lemon juice for the vinegar. If you are using vinegar, herbal ones add even greater interest to salad dressings.

To Make Flavored Cooking/Salad Oil

Use fresh mint, thyme, sage, tarragon, anise, marjoram, rose petals, chive blossoms, and other flavorful, edible herbs in combination or alone.

> *1 to 2 cups leaves or flower petals*
> *3 cups unflavored oil—extra*
> *light olive oil, safflower, or*
> *sunflower are most flavorless*
> *and light*

1. Wash the herbs, pat them dry, and put them in a 1-quart jar. Pour the oil nearly to the top of the jar. Cover tightly and gently turn the jar upside down 2 or 3 times.

2. The plant's oils are extracted and concentrated in the oil. Gentle heat is needed, so try just setting the bottle in the sun or on a sunny windowsill for 4 or 5 days, gently shaking each day. Strain and repeat with fresh material at least 2 or 3 times until the scent is distinctly noticeable.

3. Using good-quality, cold-pressed, light, virgin olive oil with basil, oregano, fennel, rosemary, and other pungent herbs results in a delicious oil for the Italian cuisine. You might want to add a few whole allspice or cloves.

DEANNA'S VINAIGRETTE

A delicious, very basic salad dressing to keep on hand.

Makes ⅓ cup

> *5 tablespoons olive oil or other salad oil*
> *Juice of ½ lime (about 1 tablespoon)*
> *1 teaspoon prepared mustard—stone-ground or Dijon are good*
> *1 teaspoon honey*
> *Salt and pepper to taste*

Place all the ingredients in a covered jar and shake well.

HERBED VINAIGRETTE

Use plain oil and vinegar or try different combinations of your own flavored oils and vinegars for greater variety.

*V *P *K
Makes ⅔ cup

> *2 tablespoons fresh lemon juice or vinegar*
> *½ teaspoon salt*
> *½ cup olive oil*
> *2 tablespoons warm water*
> *1 teaspoon chopped fresh herbs, such as parsley,*
> *   tarragon, thyme, or salad burnet, or*
> *   if fresh herbs are not available, use*
> *   ½ teaspoon crushed dry herbs*

Place all the ingredients in a jar, cover tightly, and shake well. Let the mixture stand for a few minutes, shake well again before serving.

PITTA CHURNA SALAD DRESSING AND MARINADE

Pitta Churna, that special blend of spices and herbs especially good for balancing Pitta dosha, does not need to be heated, as some spices do, to bring out its subtle flavors. This dressing adds a unique flavor to tossed summer salads. It is a pleasant marinade for tofu, eggplant, and other ingredients in a main dish. Both Vata and Kapha can enjoy this dressing, or substitute another Churna as you prefer.

*V − P − K
Makes ⅔ cup

> *½ cup sunflower or safflower oil*
> *2 tablespoons warm water*
> *1½ to 2 teaspoons Pitta Churna*
> *½ teaspoon salt*
> *2 tablespoons fresh lemon or lime juice*

Place all the ingredients in a jar or blender. Cover tightly and blend well. Let the mixture stand for 5 to 10 minutes and blend again. Shake well before serving.

RASPBERRY VINAIGRETTE

Raspberry dressing adds color and slightly sour and astringent tastes to green salads. It enlivens a Vata-balancing salad of steamed and cooled asparagus and peeled zucchini garnished with chopped parsley.

−V − P − K
Makes 1 cup

> *2 tablespoons fresh lemon juice or white vinegar*
> *¼ teaspoon salt*
> *½ cup safflower or sunflower oil*
> *1 cup fresh raspberries, washed, or 10 ounces*
> *frozen raspberries, defrosted*

Mix the lemon juice or vinegar, the salt, and the oil together in a jar with a tight-fitting lid. Put the raspberries in a sieve over a bowl to drain. Puree by mashing them against the sides of the sieve with a wooden spoon. Discard the seeds and pulp in the sieve and mix the raspberry puree with an equal part of the vinaigrette dressing. Shake very well before serving.

SIMPLE VINAIGRETTE DRESSING

A daily standard for all salads, Simple Vinaigrette adds astringent and oily properties to a meal.

*V − P − K
Makes ½ cup

> *¼ cup oil—preferably a good-quality olive oil*
> *1 tablespoon warm water*
> *1 tablespoon lemon juice or vinegar*
> *¼ teaspoon salt*

Place all the ingredients in a small jar, cover tightly, and shake vigorously.

NOTE: This simple vinaigrette sparks up the flavors of plain steamed vegetables and adds astringence to a meal that may be lacking it, especially if you aren't serving a tossed green salad. Just toss the cooked vegetables with 1 or 2 tablespoons of the vinaigrette before serving.

AVOCADO CHEESE SAUCE AND DIP

A warm, rich dressing for baked potatoes and other vegetables, this sauce is also good for Vata and Pitta when served warm as a vegetable crudité dip. It can be part of a light evening meal or served as a sauce to accompany a vegetable side dish. One pleasing presentation is pouring the sauce over a whole steamed head of cauliflower, centered on a large plate and ringed with a variety of tiny steamed vegetables.

Avocado Cheese Sauce is sweet, slightly sour, a little pungent, heavy, and oily. Vegetables baked slowly in the sauce are very creamy and nourishing for Vata and Pitta.

−V −P +K
Makes 2½ cups

2 medium ripe avocados
1 teaspoon fresh lemon juice
1 teaspoon sweet paprika
1 cup ricotta or soft panir cheese
2 tablespoons chopped spinach
¾ cup heavy cream
½ cup milk
1 tablespoon mixed fresh minced herbs:
    dill, chervil, cilantro, tarragon, fennel,
    parsley, marjoram, oregano, or rosemary
1 teaspoon coarsely ground white pepper
Pinch of cayenne, or more to taste

1. Peel the avocados and mash them with the lemon juice and the paprika in a bowl or food processor. Add the cheese and the spinach. Blend together until very smooth.

2. Bring the cream and milk to a boil in a 2-quart saucepan and add the herbs, pepper, and cayenne. Reduce to simmer and stir in the cheese mixture. Whisk or stir vigorously until well blended, but do not allow it to boil.

3. If the sauce seems too thick, add more cream until it pours like thick gravy. Serve warm.

NOTE: For those following a Kapha diet or watching their weight, substitute buttermilk for the cream and milk and eat moderately.

BASIC CHEESE SAUCE

An all-purpose, sweet, heavy, oily sauce that can be served on steamed vegetables and baked potatoes, this not-very-sour cheese sauce is best for Vata and Pitta. By using ricotta cheese instead of hard, very sour cheddar cheese, macaroni and cheese is more Pitta-balancing. Mixed vegetable casseroles baked with cheese sauce can be served as a side dish for everyone at a main meal. Vary the flavors by adding the spice combination or the Churna you like best.

−v *p *k
Makes 2 cups

> *2 tablespoons ghee or unsalted butter*
> *2 tablespoons unbleached white flour*
> *1 tablespoon Churna or mixed spices of your choice*
> *¾ teaspoon finely ground white pepper*
> *1 cup heavy cream or whole milk*
> *1 cup mashed ricotta cheese*
> *¾ teaspoon turmeric*

Heat the ghee in a heavy pan over low heat. Add the flour and stir to blend. Add the spices and pepper and continue stirring until well mixed and thickened. Slowly whisk in the cream or milk and stir vigorously to avoid lumps. Turn heat to moderate and add the cheese and the turmeric, cooked in the sauce, not sprinkled on after. Simmer over a low flame, uncovered, stirring frequently, until the sauce is thick and creamy. Serve warm.

NOTE: For Kapha types and those watching their weight, substitute low-fat buttermilk for the heavy cream or whole milk, and reduce the amount of butter to 1 tablespoon.

CREAM TAHINI SAUCE

This is an easy-to-make, all-purpose sauce to dress up steamed vegetables, baked potatoes, and mixed casseroles. Although it is best for Vata types, Pitta and Kapha can have moderate amounts as part of a balanced meal. This sauce adds sweet, astringent, bitter, oily, hot, and heavy aspects to a meal.

−v *p *k
Makes 1½ cups

1 cup heavy cream
½ cup (8 tablespoons) sesame tahini
  (available at Middle Eastern or natural food stores)
½ teaspoon ground ginger
  (increase to 1 teaspoon for Kapha)
¼ teaspoon ground cloves (optional)
⅛ teaspoon black pepper

Heat the cream in a small pan over moderate heat. When fully boiling turn the flame to low and stir in the tahini and spices. Continue stirring until well blended. Serve warm.

GINGER SOY GRAVY

This delicious, nourishing, nondairy gravy comes from Bruce Rash, formerly a chef at the Maharishi Ayur-Veda Health Center in Lancaster, Massachusetts. When served as part of a balanced meal, it is good for everyone. It adds salty, pungent, oily, and hot aspects to the meal. This dark, moderately thick gravy is especially good served with mashed potatoes because the ginger helps both Vata and Kapha in digesting heavy potatoes.

$-$V *P $-$K
Makes 4 cups

½ cup ghee or cooking oil
¼ cup unbleached white flour
1 tablespoon ground ginger or ¼ cup freshly grated ginger
4 cups unflavored soy milk (available at many
  supermarkets and natural food stores)
¼ cup soy sauce or tamari

1. In a 2-quart saucepan, heat the ghee over moderate heat. Add the flour and stir constantly for about 5 minutes, until blended and the flour turns light brown. Add the ginger and heat another 5 minutes, stirring frequently.

2. Meanwhile, bring the soy milk just to a boil in a separate pan. Add it slowly to the oil mixture, stirring vigorously with a whip to avoid lumps. Stir in the soy sauce. Simmer, stirring frequently, until the gravy is the consistency you like.

GOLD SAUCE

A beautiful, delicious, and easily made sauce, Gold Sauce is good for everyone, especially when it is served with appropriate dosha-balancing vegetables. Served over a bed of asparagus, this sauce is lighter and more elegant than a Hollandaise. It makes a fine dipping sauce for artichokes, and it looks beautiful when poured over a steamed head of cauliflower or baked potatoes.

−V *P *K
Makes 1 cup

> 1½ *tablespoons ghee or olive oil*
> ¾ *teaspoon ground ginger*
> ⅛ *teaspoon salt*
> *Pinch of ground white or black pepper*
> 1 *teaspoon ground coriander seeds*
> ¼ *teaspoon cinnamon*
> ½ *teaspoon licorice root powder*
> ½ *teaspoon Vata Churna*
> ½ *cup finely chopped parsley*
> 1 *cup plain yogurt*

Heat the ghee or oil in a small saucepan over moderate heat. Add the ginger, stir, then add the remaining spices and continue stirring for about 1 minute, or until they are fragrant. Stir in the parsley and allow it to sizzle for about 2 minutes. Remove the pan from the heat and vigorously stir in the yogurt. Immediately pour the sauce over steamed or baked vegetables. By not cooking the yogurt, the sauce maintains a fine creamy consistency.

RED SAUCE

A basic sour, sweet, slightly pungent, oily, and salty sauce for steamed and sautéed vegetables, Red Sauce goes particularly well with breaded eggplant, okra, zucchini, and green beans. Thick tomato-based Red Sauce is best for Vata types. By adjusting the Pitta- or Kapha-balancing spices and simmering with some appropriate Pitta or Kapha vegetables, it can be served as part of a balanced meal for anyone.

−V +P +K
Makes 2½ cups

> *1 tablespoon ground coriander seeds*
> *¼ teaspoon ground cumin seeds*
> *¼ teaspoon cinnamon*
> *⅛ teaspoon ground cloves (omit for Pitta)*
> *⅛ teaspoon cardamom (omit for Kapha)*
> *1 teaspoon black mustard seeds*
> *⅛ teaspoon salt*
> *¼ teaspoon ground black pepper*
> *¼ cup ghee or olive oil*
> *¾ cup very coarsely chopped parsley*
> *1 15-ounce can tomato sauce*
> *¼ cup dried coconut*

1. Mix all the spices together in a small dish. Heat the ghee in a small saucepan over moderate heat. Add the spices, and when the mustard seeds begin to pop, turn the flame to low and stir in the parsley. In about a minute when it looks limp and frizzy, add the tomato sauce and the coconut. Mix well. Cover and simmer over very low heat for 15 to 20 minutes. Stir the sauce occasionally.

2. Meanwhile, steam or stir-fry about 4 cups of chopped mixed vegetables. By very slowly simmering the Red Sauce for 30 to 40 minutes, the flavors become even richer. If cooking time is extended, add more water as needed to maintain a thick but pourable sauce. If this sauce is prepared early, set it aside, then reheat it just before mixing with the vegetables.

SCRUMPTIOUS SESAME-ORANGE SAUCE

This versatile recipe is great as a dip for vegetables, crackers, or for
Golden Panir Cubes (page 116). It's also a delightful condiment when
served in a small bowl to accompany an Indian dinner and, when the
recipe is doubled, as a sauce for steamed vegetables.

*v *p *K
Makes about ¼ cup

> *½ teaspoon cumin seeds*
> *5 tablespoons sesame tahini (available at Middle Eastern or
>   natural food stores)*
> *Juice of 1 medium to large orange*
> *Salt and pepper to taste*

Toast the cumin seeds in a heavy skillet over moderate heat until
just brown. Crush the seeds with a mortar and pestle or in a spice
grinder. Mix all the ingredients thoroughly. Serve warm.

Chutneys and Other Condiments

It is probably easier to eat Ayurvedically balanced meals dining on the
Indian cuisine than any other, since India is "land of the Vedas." A
feast in the Indian style includes quite an array of small dishes brimming with stewed fruits, nuts, pickles, and vegetables that offer a
splendid selection of tastes and qualities. These chutneys and other
Indian condiments, the jewels of the Indian cuisine, make any good
meal even more interesting. A chutney may contain only one taste or
all the tastes needed to balance the meal. And they can be served
effectively at nearly any meal, not just Indian ones.

When included as part of a large meal, small amounts of these
chutneys and other condiments can be eaten by anyone. Eating large
amounts of one or two chutneys would not help balance the doshas.

Varied condiments give each person a chance to select and balance
the different tastes according to his or her needs. Although there are
several recipes for chutneys and condiments in this sample menu, only
a few are actually served at each meal. For a simple dinner, one or two
chutneys are enough to enhance the meal.

APPLE-RAISIN CHUTNEY

Chutneys are good for balancing all doshas when they are served as part of a meal. This recipe is especially nourishing for Vata dosha. The addition of Kapha Churna gives it a pungent taste, making it even better for Kapha types. It is sweet, pungent, hot, and a little astringent, and it helps maintain the appetite when eaten throughout the meal.

Apple-Raisin chutney can be stored in capped, sterilized jars in the refrigerator for a month. By substituting Pitta Churna for the Kapha Churna and reducing it to 1 teaspoon, or to taste, this recipe makes a delicious turnover filling for a Vata and Pitta dessert.

−V *P +K
Makes 2½ cups

> 2 cups peeled and chopped apples
> ½ cup water
> 1 teaspoon nutmeg
> ¼ teaspoon ground cloves
> ¼ teaspoon salt
> 3 to 4 tablespoons granulated
>   sugar
> ¼ cup raw or brown sugar
> 2 tablespoons Kapha Churna
>   or
>   ½ teaspoon ground black pepper
>   1 teaspoon turmeric
>   ¼ teaspoon ground fenugreek
>   ½ teaspoon ground cumin
> 1 cup raisins

Put the apples in a 4-quart pan. Add all the other ingredients and cook over moderate heat, adding more water ¼ cup at a time to keep the chutney from drying out. Stir frequently until the apples are tender and transparent, about 30 minutes. Stir well to blend into a sauce. Cool and serve. Store in the refrigerator.

COCONUT CHUTNEY

When served as an appetizer or condiment with a meal, this rich, golden chutney adds sweet, pungent, oily, and heavy properties.

−V *P +K
Makes about 1½ cups

> 1 tablespoon ghee
> ¾ teaspoon cayenne
> ¼ cup milk or cream
> 1 to 2 tablespoons sugar, to taste
> ⅛ teaspoon allspice
> ⅛ to ¼ teaspoon crushed saffron
> ¼ cup golden raisins
> 1 cup dried coconut (finely chopped is best,
>   but flaked will do)

Heat the ghee over a medium flame in a small pan. Then add the cayenne and stir for about 1 minute. Stir in the milk, the sugar, the allspice, and the crushed saffron threads. Bring to a boil, stirring often. The milk should begin turning golden yellow. Reduce the flame to simmer. Stir in the raisins and coconut. Beat well as mixture leaves the sides of the pan. If it is too liquid, add more coconut, a tablespoon at a time, until the mixture is just moist but not wet. Serve in a small decorative bowl.

KASHMIRI MINT CHUTNEY

An authentic and most exotic way to make this fresh chutney is by collecting the wild mint that grows on the alpine hillsides of Sonmarg, "the Sun Meadow," at 10,000 feet in the Himalayas of Kashmir. But any fresh mint can be substituted until you can get the real thing. As with other chutneys, mint chutney is good for all doshas as part of a balanced meal, especially for Kapha and Pitta. The tastes in this chutney are astringent, sour, pungent, slightly sweet, and bitter. This is a chutney that keeps only for one day.

−V −P −K
Makes 1 cup

> ⅔ *cup fresh mint leaves, washed,*
>   *dried, and minced*
> ¼ *cup ground walnuts*
> *1 teaspoon plain yogurt*
> ½ *teaspoon turmeric*

Mix the minced mint leaves and walnuts together. In a small cup stir the yogurt and turmeric together, then blend with the mint-walnut mixture. Cover and allow to sit for 30 minutes before serving.

FRESH GREEN CHUTNEY

This is a fresh or "daily" chutney that should not be kept as a leftover. It is astringent, bitter, pungent, a little sweet, and salty. A little eaten with a meal is good for everyone's digestion and refreshes the palate. If you are cooking for 2 or 3 people, prepare half the recipe.

−V −P −K
Makes 1 cup

> *1 cup chopped fresh parsley, coriander leaves,*
>   *and/or spinach*
> *1 teaspoon salt*
> *Juice of 1 lemon or lime*
> *1 teaspoon cayenne or less, to taste*
> ¼ *cup water*
> ¼ *cup flaked coconut*

Put all the ingredients in a blender or food processor with a steel blade. Blend on low speed. Put in a small decorative dish and set aside for 1 to 2 hours before serving to let the flavors come together. If you're in a hurry, you can serve it right away.

GINGER LEMON CHUTNEY

A good appetizer for Vata and Kapha, this chutney is a pleasant accompaniment to many meals besides Indian ones. Ginger Lemon

Chutney is especially delicious fried with vegetables or tossed with hot rice or other cooked grains for the next meal. It keeps one day.

−V *P −K

Makes ½ cup

> *1 lemon*
> *¼ pound fresh ginger, peeled*
> *½ teaspoon salt*
> *½ teaspoon sugar (optional)*

Peel the lemon with a vegetable peeler or zester. Then mince or chop the peel very fine. Squeeze the lemon juice into a small cup. Dice the ginger or chop it into small chunks in a blender or food processor for 30 seconds. Measure ½ cup diced ginger and leave it in the blender container. Add the lemon peel, ½ teaspoon lemon juice, salt, and sugar. Blend again for 30 seconds, or until the mixture looks soft and tan. Serve in a tiny bowl or dish.

PICKLED GINGER SLICES

Chew a slice or two of this pungent fresh pickle just before eating to stimulate the appetite.

−V +P −K

> *1 3-inch piece gingerroot*
> *Juice of half a lemon*
> *¼ teaspoon salt*

Peel and cut the gingerroot into dime-size slices. Sprinkle them with the lemon juice and the salt. Tightly covered Pickled Ginger Slices can keep in the refrigerator for up to two weeks.

TOMATO CHUTNEY

Everyone can eat some of this chutney as part of a balanced meal, but it increases Pitta dosha if eaten in more than a small quantity. Tomato

Chutney has sour, pungent, astringent, sweet, salty, oily, and slightly bitter properties. It keeps well for about two weeks tightly covered in the refrigerator.

−V +P *K
Makes 2 cups

> *1 tablespoon ghee*
> *1 teaspoon brown mustard seeds*
> *1/2 teaspoon ground fenugreek*
> *1 teaspoon dry roasted and ground cumin seeds*
> *1 teaspoon ground coriander*
> *1 teaspoon freshly grated ginger or 3/4 teaspoon ground*
> *1/2 teaspoon turmeric*
> *10 medium tomatoes, peeled and mashed*
> *1 teaspoon salt*
> *1/2 teaspoon sweet paprika (optional)*
> *1 tablespoon light brown sugar, or raw sugar,*
> * or to taste*
> *1 teaspoon lemon juice*

1. Heat the ghee in a heavy pot over moderate heat. Add the mustard seeds and when they start to pop stir in the other spices. Fry for 1 minute, stirring constantly.

2. Add the tomatoes to the spices, then stir in the remaining ingredients. Simmer for 10 to 15 minutes, stirring until everything is thoroughly blended. Cover and allow to cook over low heat for another 10 minutes. Cool and serve.

QUICK CONDIMENTS

Here are a few easy condiments that add taste, texture, color, and more variety to any meal but particularly to an Indian-style dinner. Small bowls and dishes of chutneys and condiments make the meal interesting to both the eye and the palate.

LEMON AND LIME WEDGES

Wedged lemons and limes are good to serve at any main meal. They add both color and a sour taste. When eaten with the heavier parts of the dinner, they help to refresh the palate. In small quantities, lemons and limes aid digestion.

Cut a washed lemon and lime in narrow wedges and arrange in alternating colors on a small plate.

SPICED CASHEW NUTS

A few of these sweet, oily, slightly heavy nuts are good for Vata and Pitta, and increase Kapha, especially if they are eaten in excess (easy to do since they're so tasty). Spiced Cashews keep well on the kitchen shelf or in the refrigerator.

−V −P +K
Makes 1 cup

> *1½ tablespoons ghee*
> *1 cup unsalted cashew nuts, broken in pieces*
> *½ teaspoon of one of the following ground spices:*
> *cardamom, ginger, nutmeg, cinnamon, or*
> *coriander*

Heat the ghee in a small pan over moderate heat. Sprinkle in the nuts and the spice of your choice. Stir frequently until the nuts are toasty brown. Serve in a small bowl. If any are saved for another meal, reheat them briefly over a low flame just to melt the ghee.

TOASTED COCONUT CONDIMENT

Serve a small dish of coconut plain or toasted so it can be sprinkled over some favorite curry on the dinner plate. If Toasted Coconut is served as a condiment, do not serve Coconut Chutney as well. A little of the sweet, heavy, and oily properties of coconut go a long way. They are good for Vata and Pitta and increase Kapha.

−V −P +K
Makes about ½ cup

> *1 tablespoon ghee*
> *½ to ⅔ cup flaked coconut*
> *¼ teaspoon crumbled saffron (optional)*

Heat the ghee in a small pan over low heat. Toss in the coconut and the saffron. Stir frequently until the coconut is just brown on the tips. Put in a serving dish immediately.

SIMPLE RAITA

Raita (RAI-tah) is a yogurt-based side dish that serves as a sour, cold, refreshing foil to a spicy meal. As part of a whole meal and when eaten in small amounts, it is good for everyone to eat. In large quantities it increases Pitta and Kapha. Finely shredded carrots or radishes make a colorful raita, but almost any minced or shredded raw vegetable mixed with yogurt qualifies as raita.

Cool and refreshing to the palate, yogurt-based raita can be blended with various shredded raw vegetables and ground spices and it will never appear the same at any meal. But this is just about the simplest way to make it.

−V *P *K
Makes 1 cup

> *1 cup plain yogurt*
> *¼ teaspoon freshly roasted and ground cumin*

Stir the yogurt into a serving bowl. Sprinkle most of the cumin on top and stir it in. Sprinkle the rest of the cumin on top. Cover and refrigerate 30 minutes before serving.

TOMATO AND CUCUMBER RAITA

This is a refreshing raita that adds sour and slightly salty tastes to the meal and cold, heavy qualities.

−V *P *K
Makes 2 cups

> 1 small cucumber, peeled, seeded, and
>   chopped
> ¼ teaspoon salt
> 2 cups plain yogurt
> 1 medium tomato, skinned and chopped
> ½ teaspoon roasted and ground cumin seeds

Mix the cucumber and the salt together in a small glass or stainless steel bowl. Set it aside for about 15 minutes to extract the liquid out of the cucumber. Mix the yogurt and tomato together in a serving bowl. Drain and squeeze the juice from the cucumber until it feels dry and add the dry cucumber to the yogurt. Discard the juice. Stir in ¼ teaspoon cumin. Sprinkle the rest on top. Cover tightly and refrigerate 30 minutes to an hour before serving.

WILTED GINGER LETTUCE

You can quickly make this hot condiment to help balance a meal that may be lacking in pungent, bitter, and astringent tastes. In small amounts it is good for everyone's digestion. Adjust the amount of fresh ginger you use according to how pungent-tasting you want this condiment to be. If serving a mixed group, use 2 tablespoons. If cooking for Pitta or in the heat of summer, 1 tablespoon of ginger should be enough.

*V *P −K
Makes 1 cup

> 2 tablespoons sunflower, safflower, or other light oil
> 1 to 2 tablespoons freshly grated ginger
> 2 cups chopped and loosely packed Romaine,
>   other lettuce, or bitter greens
> ¼ teaspoon salt
> Pinch of black pepper
> ½ teaspoon lemon or lime juice

Heat the oil in a small, heavy frying pan over moderate heat. Add the ginger and stir for 1 minute. Then stir in the lettuce, tossing it well with the ginger. Sprinkle with the salt and the pepper and immediately turn the heat off and cover tightly for 1 or 2 minutes. As you put the Wilted Ginger Lettuce in a small decorative serving bowl, sprinkle it with the lemon or the lime juice.

Other Basics

PANIR AND RICOTTA SOFT CHEESE

This is a delicate, easily digestible cheese for Vata types to eat regularly. Its slightly sour, oily, and cold aspects make it the only cheese Pitta and Kapha should use because it is not as sour and indigestible as hard cheeses. Panir and Ricotta are made in almost the same way, except Ricotta usually contains more liquid and is drained for less time than Panir. Ricotta does not have to be kneaded and refrigerated, but can be used right away. Ricotta, a soft "stuffing" cheese, is used in fillings for manicotti and pasta shells. The firmer Panir is generally fried in ghee until crisp, then tossed with spiced vegetables or in sauces.

−V *P *K
Makes 1½ cups

> 2 quarts milk
> 2 tablespoons lemon juice or white vinegar
> ½ cup plain yogurt (optional)

1. In a heavy pot bring the milk to a boil over moderately high heat. Watch it carefully so it doesn't boil over. As foam begins rising, remove the pot from the heat and stir in the lemon juice or vinegar and the yogurt. Continue stirring gently as the curds separate from the whey. Set the pot aside for 5 minutes and line a large sieve or colander with enough muslin cheesecloth or a clean, loosely woven towel to tie into a bag.

2. Pour the cheese into the lined sieve, reserving the whey separately in lidded jars. Drain until cool. Then wrap the cloth tightly around the curds and squeeze out excess liquid. Hang the bag over a bowl or above the sink for an hour until most of the liquid is gone. If you are making Ricotta, put the cheese in a bowl, cover tightly, and refrigerate or use right away. For Panir, press the remaining liquid out of the cheese. Remove it from the bag and slightly knead it. Press it flat into a shallow pan or sealable container. Cover and refrigerate for 5 or 6 hours or overnight.

NOTE: Use the protein-rich, easily digested whey for the liquid in soups, rice, vegetable casseroles, and when baking bread. Don't throw it away—it's valuable. (Tightly covered, whey will keep in the refrigerator for 2 or 3 days.)

To Make Ghee
Makes about 2 cups

1. Melt a pound or more of unsalted butter over moderate heat in a heavy, uncovered saucepan. When the butter becomes liquid and foamy, turn the heat to low. Simmer slowly for about an hour, skimming the froth off every once in a while. Take great care not to burn the ghee when the boiling becomes less vigorous. Also, if ghee is left unattended it may be flammable. Unless the ghee is made from freshly churned, unsalted butter (not the commercial variety), discard the skimmings. Otherwise these are a nutritious addition to rice, bread, or dahl.

2. When the ghee turns a golden yellow and little brown bits of milk solids lie at the bottom of the pan, it is ready to be filtered into a clean jar. Pour the hot oil through a fine sieve lined with a coffee filter. Lacking a paper filter, the fine sieve will do. A double sieve is even better. If the oil does not flow through the filter easily, it is too cold and should be briefly rewarmed. It is not necessary to refrigerate ghee when all the milk solids have been removed, but keep it tightly covered after using.*

* Ghee can be ordered from Maharishi Ayur-Ved Products International, Inc. See Appendix 5, page 293.

To Sprout Whole Beans and Seeds
Makes 1 cup sprouts

Use whole lentil beans or seeds when sprouting. Wash ½ cup of lentils that have been sorted for small stones. Place them in a covered bowl or jar, set in a warm place, and rinse in tepid water 3 or 4 times a day. They are ready to use when just slightly sprouted, about 24 hours. For cooking purposes use just-sprouted beans, except in the Chinese cuisine.

Some whole legumes and seeds that are good for sprouting are mung beans, black gram (Urad), brown lentils, chick-peas, sunflower seeds, radish seeds, and pumpkin seeds. Seeds should be purchased only at food stores. Do not use seeds prepared for gardening, as they are sometimes treated with fungicides and are inedible.

To Prepare Rice
Serves 4

Boil 2 cups water for each cup of washed brown or basmati rice. Do not wash enriched rices since the enrichment is on the surface of the grains. When the water comes to a boil, add 1 teaspoon salt and the rice (and a tablespoon of ghee for Vata and Pitta cooking). Cover and simmer for 20 minutes. Fluff with a fork before serving.

AN EASY BAKING METHOD: Use the same proportion of ingredients but place in a covered baking dish and bake for 20 to 30 minutes at 350°F. Fluff immediately and then cover until ready to serve. If you are baking a vegetable casserole or Perfect Lentil Soup, it's easy to prepare the accompanying rice in the same oven. When you're making rice for more than 4 people and you want it to come out light and fluffy, baking it in a shallow casserole is the most reliable way. Baked rice never comes out sticky.

Vata Broth

This basic broth is useful as a soup stock or an all-purpose gravy and sauce base. When mixed with ¼ teaspoon tamari or soy sauce per cup, it makes a warming bouillon drink. As with the other dosha-specific broths, the flavors will change depending on which Vata-reducing combination of vegetables and spices you use. Consult the Charts of Ingredients (pages 283–290) for more choices.

−V *P +K

Makes 2½ quarts

> *2 quarts boiling water*
> *1 teaspoon salt*
> *½ teaspoon pepper*
> *1 cup sliced carrots*
> *½ cup chopped tomatoes*
> *½ cup chopped parsley*
> *½ cup diced celery*
> *1 cup green beans, cut in 1-inch pieces*
> *1 bay leaf*
> *½ teaspoon ground fenugreek*
> *¼ teaspoon crumbled saffron*
> *½ teaspoon ground cumin*
> *2 tablespoons Vata Churna (optional) or to taste*
> *1 tablespoon ghee*

Bring the water to a boil in a heavy pan. Add the salt, pepper, and the vegetables. Simmer, covered, for 15 minutes. Then add the remaining ingredients. Stir, cover, and simmer for another 5 minutes. Cover and turn off the heat. Allow to sit undisturbed for half an hour. Strain the carrots, celery, and green beans and use the broth. The vegetables can be eaten separately with a little salt, pepper, and butter.

PITTA BROTH

Pitta Broth, a combination of Pitta-reducing vegetables, herbs, and spices, is a basic soup stock. The flavor of the broth will vary depending on the combination of ingredients you use. When making this broth, choose at least three different Pitta-reducing vegetables, herbs, and spices. Use 3 or 4 cups of mixed vegetables—bitter- and astringent-tasting ones are best. Pitta Broth is useful as a gravy base, for the beginning of a vegetable cream sauce, in other soups, or as a refreshing summer beverage.

+V −P *K
Makes 2 quarts

> *2 quarts water*
> *1 teaspoon salt*
> *1 cup chopped broccoli*
> *1 cup chopped green beans*
> *1 cup peeled and diced potatoes*
> *1 cup chopped celery or lovage leaves*
> *½ teaspoon white or black pepper*
> *2 tablespoons Pitta Churna*
> > *or*
> > *2 teaspoons ground coriander*
> > *½ teaspoon crushed anise seed*
> > *3 or 4 crushed green cardamom pods*
> > *or other Pitta-reducing spices, to taste*
> *1 tablespoon ghee (optional)*

In a large pot of boiling salted water put the vegetables and spices. Turn the heat to low, cover, and simmer for 15 minutes. Stir in the ghee if you are making an oily broth. Then turn off the heat and let the pot sit undisturbed for 30 minutes. Use a colander to strain out the vegetables and use the broth. The vegetables can be pureed and used in a creamy soup (such as Creamy Summer Garden Soup, page 156), or they can be eaten with a little butter.

NOTE: Pitta Broth makes a refreshing drink and summer appetizer when served chilled with a celery stick and a garnish of fresh fennel or dill. Strain the warm broth through a coffee filter for extra clarity before chilling.

KAPHA BROTH

A light, pungent appetizer as well as the basis for other soups and light Kapha-reducing sauces, Kapha Broth is easy to make.

+V +P −K
Makes 2 quarts

2 quarts water
1 teaspoon salt
½ teaspoon ground black pepper
¼ cup chopped parsley or celery leaves
2 teaspoons Kapha Churna, or to taste
3 cups Kapha-reducing vegetables—select at least
   3 different kinds from this list:
   broccoli
   beet greens
   Brussels sprouts
   cabbage
   green beans
   lettuce
   parsnips
   peas
   spinach
   squash
   Swiss chard
2 tablespoons mixed fresh chopped herbs: thyme, basil,
   oregano, marjoram

Bring the water to a boil in a large pot. Add the salt and pepper, the parsley, the Kapha Churna, and the vegetables. Chopping or shredding them first makes for faster cooking. Cover and bring to a boil. Lower to simmer and sprinkle chopped herbs on top. Stir once gently. Cover tightly, turn off the heat, and do not lift the lid for 20 to 30 minutes.

TO MAKE YOGURT

There's no commercial substitute for your own freshly made yogurt. This is a simple way to prepare homemade yogurt. There are also electric yogurt makers available that work quite well. Or gently pour the warm yogurt mixture into a one-quart thermos and leave it overnight. Then in the morning uncap it for a few minutes, reseal, and refrigerate. This makes an exceptionally smooth, rich-tasting yogurt.

−v *p *k
Makes 1 quart

> *1 quart whole milk*
> *2 tablespoons plain yogurt*

Heat the milk just to the boiling point in a 2-quart saucepan. Cool to 105°F. to 110°F. Use a candy thermometer to test the temperature. Pour into a deep bowl or a 1-quart jar, then very gently stir in the yogurt. Cover, and without shaking too much, place in a warm spot for 4 or 5 hours. An oven with a pilot light works well, or the top of the refrigerator near the back. The amount of setting time will determine the taste. The longer it sets, the more sour yogurt becomes. Refrigerate to set it more firmly. Reserve 2 tablespoons of yogurt to begin the next batch.

EVERYDAY GRANOLA

Both as a snack and a breakfast food this sweet, heavy, dry cereal is good for all doshas. Eating a one-cup serving adds extra fiber to the diet and helps regulate digestion. If you would like more bulk in your diet, add extra oat or wheat bran. Wheat bran makes granola (and other baked goods) a little more moist, and oat bran makes it smoother with more body. For a crumbly mixture make it with less syrup. This granola is recommended as a breakfast food for those following a Vata-reducing diet. Simply soak the cereal in heated cream or whole milk until it is soft. This makes it easier for Vata's digestion. Those reducing Kapha and weight would use skim or low-fat milk and they do not need to let it get soggy before eating it. Dry granola makes a good snack for Kapha types. They can eat it dry right out of the jar. Pitta can enjoy granola either way, as a snack or a cereal with milk.

VERSION 1 FOR VATA AND PITTA

−v −p *k
Makes 2½ quarts

4 cups quick oats
½ cup sunflower seeds
½ cup pumpkin seeds
½ cup sesame seeds (less for Pitta)
¾ cup flaked coconut
½ cup bran, oat, or wheat
½ cup wheat germ
½ cup slivered almonds
1 tablespoon poppy seeds (optional)
½ cup melted ghee or unsalted butter
½ to ¾ cup brown rice syrup or corn syrup
2 teaspoons vanilla extract
1½ cups raisins or currants
½ cup pine nuts (optional)

Preheat oven to 300°F. In a large bowl mix all the ingredients except the raisins and pine nuts. If you use less syrup the granola will be more crumbly. Spread the granola on two large cookie sheets with sides. Bake for about 30 to 35 minutes, turning the granola with a long-handled spatula every five minutes until it is uniformly brown. Granola bakes faster around the edges of the pan, so be sure to move it from the sides to the center and spread it evenly on the pan at every turning. As soon as it is done turn into a large mixing bowl and toss with the raisins and pine nuts, if you are using them.

While the granola is still warm, store it in quart jars or plastic containers. You can also freeze it in Ziploc bags or sealed containers for up to a month.

KAPHA-PITTA VERSION: This recipe for granola is less sweet than the first one. The use of barley flakes and barley malt syrup makes for a more bitter and astringent-tasting cereal good for both Kapha and Pitta. The small amount of rye flakes gives it a slightly sour taste.

*V − P − K
Makes 2 quarts

> 2 cups quick oats
> ½ cup rye flakes
> 1½ cups barley flakes
> ½ cup sesame seeds (or less for Pitta)
> ¼ cup flaked coconut
> ½ cup sunflower or pumpkin seeds
> ½ cup oat bran
> ½ cup wheat germ
> ½ cup slivered almonds
> ½ cup melted ghee or unsalted butter
> ½ cup barley malt syrup
> 2 teaspoons vanilla extract
> 1 cup raisins, currants, or dried sour cherries

Follow the directions as given in the Vata-Pitta version.

Breads

LIGHT CORN BREAD

Corn bread is a sweet, salty, hot, light bread that is good for both Kapha and those wanting to reduce weight. The light quality increases Vata a little. Because of its "heating" quality, this is not the best bread choice for Pitta. As with many Kapha-reducing foods, corn bread is good to eat during a light fast or as part of a light evening meal. Vata should eat this corn bread spread with ghee or butter to help in digestion. For Kapha, spreading with a little honey will aid digestion.

*V +P − K
Serves 6 to 8

1¼ cups unbleached white flour
¾ cup cornmeal
1½ tablespoons baking powder
¾ teaspoon salt
1½ cup buttermilk
2 tablespoons unsalted butter or ghee
1 tablespoon sugar, or to taste

1. Preheat the oven to 375°F.

2. Sift all the dry ingredients together except the sugar. Heat the milk, ghee or butter, and the sugar in a saucepan and stir until the sugar is dissolved. Then stir into the mixed dry ingredients until *just* moistened. The batter will look thick and a little lumpy.

3. Spread the batter in an oiled 9-inch pan and bake for 30 to 35 minutes, until it's a light brown color and pulls away from the sides of the pan.

NOTE: When cooking for Pitta, reduce the cornmeal to ½ cup, increase the white flour accordingly, and add ½ teaspoon licorice root powder.

FRENCH BREAD

The taste and crunchy texture is authentically French. This bread, like most breads made from wheat flour, is sweet-tasting and good for general nutrition. Eaten in moderation, it reduces Vata and Pitta and is neutral for Kapha. Because it is both sweet and heavy, too much bread will increase Kapha. It's best to eat bread spread with butter for ease of digestion. Vegetables and bread complement each other. That means they are most efficiently digested when eaten during the same course of the meal.

−V −P *K
Makes 2 to 3 loaves

2 packages yeast
3 cups tepid water
7½ cups unbleached bread flour
4 teaspoons salt

1. In a small bowl dissolve the yeast in the tepid water. In a large bowl mix the flour and the salt together. Form a well and with a wooden spoon incorporate the yeast and water into the flour. Work the flour into a ball by hand, and then transfer to a floured work surface. The dough will feel tacky. Knead dough for about 10 minutes, adding small amounts of flour as necessary. Occasionally throw the dough on the work surface. After 10 minutes it will become elastic but remain a bit sticky. Grease a large bowl and place the dough in it. Cover tightly with plastic wrap and set it in a warm place; allow to double in volume. This will take about 1½ to 2 hours. When it has risen, punch it down, cover, and let it rise again.

2. Turn out on a floured surface and knead briefly. Divide the dough into as many loaves as desired. If you are using a French baguette pan, divide the dough into thirds, and make 2 baguettes and 1 oval loaf. Otherwise, 2 nicely rounded loaves can be made.

3. Place the loaves, covered lightly with a towel, in a warm place and let rise to double volume.

4. Preheat the oven to 425°F.

5. Place a shallow pan of water on the lowest oven shelf. Before putting the loaves in the oven, slash the tops diagonally with a razor blade or a very sharp knife point. Then spray the loaves lightly with water before placing in the oven. Bake on a preheated baking tile or on baking sheets sprinkled with a little cornmeal. During the first 18 minutes of baking, open the oven door and spray the loaves again with a light covering of water several times. This will make them very crispy. Then remove the pan of water and finish baking until the loaves are golden brown. Total baking time is 25 to 30 minutes. Remove the loaves and cool on a wire rack.

LITTLE FLAT BREADS

These chewy disks are useful as food pushers to accompany Moroccan Delight (pages 175–176) and other vegetable dishes. They also make an unusual breakfast bread. Their sweet and slightly bitter tastes decrease Pitta and increase Kapha a little.

−V −P +K
Makes 8 small disks

1 package dry yeast
1½ cups warm water
2 tablespoons oil or ghee
1 teaspoon salt
1 cup whole wheat flour
3 to 4 cups white flour
4 tablespoons poppy seeds or sesame seeds

1. In a large bowl dissolve the yeast in the warm water. When it is frothy stir in the oil, the salt, and the whole wheat flour. Begin adding the white flour, a cup at a time, until a stiff dough is formed. Turn out on a floured surface and wash the bowl.

2. Oil your hands a little and knead the dough for about 10 minutes, adding small amounts of flour as necessary to make it smooth and elastic. Return the kneaded dough to the bowl. Cover with plastic wrap or a damp towel and place it in a warm place to rise. In about 1 to 1½ hours it will be doubled in bulk.

3. Oil 2 baking sheets.

4. Preheat the oven to 450°F.

5. If using sesame seeds, roast them in a heavy skillet over low heat until they are just light brown and starting to pop. Set aside. Do not brown the poppy seeds. Turn the dough out on a clean work surface. Oil your hands. Punch it down and divide it into 8 equal parts. Press each part into a circle with a thin middle and higher outer lip. They will look like little piecrusts. Mark the centers a few times with the tines of a fork. Brush with water and sprinkle some seeds on each disk, pressing the seeds lightly into the dough.

6. Place them, sides not touching, on baking sheets. Bake 10 minutes, or until just brown. They are best when eaten warm.

PURIS AND CHAPATIS

These are fried unleavened breads used in the Indian cuisine for pushing the food and sopping up the delectable juices. They are good for everyone, although the sweet and heavy qualities can increase Kapha if too many are eaten. While the ingredients are identical, chapatis (chah-PAH-tees) are fried on a hot griddle and puris (POO-res), puffy breads, are deep-fried in oil.

−V −P +K
Makes 15 to 20 puris or 10 large chapatis

> 1½ cups whole wheat flour
> ½ cup white flour
> ½ teaspoon salt
> 1 tablespoon ghee
> ¾ cup hot water
> 3 to 4 cups oil for frying puris

1. In a large bowl stir the flours and salt together. Rub in the ghee with your fingertips until it is evenly combined with the flour mixture. Add the water and stir into a dough. Add a little more water by teaspoons, if needed, to completely blend all the flour smoothly. Knead for 4 or 5 minutes in the bowl. Cover with plastic wrap and allow to rest 1 or 2 hours. The consistency of workable dough should be pliable and firm but not sticky.

2. To make puris, pinch off 1-inch balls of dough, roll in a little flour, then gently roll out on a wooden surface with a rolling pin. Roll in one direction only. Turn the dough over and roll in the opposite direction until it is 4 to 5 inches across and about as thin as a penny, not thinner.

3. Heat the oil in a deep, heavy pan or wok over moderately high heat. When it is hot gently ease a puri in so it goes under the surface to the bottom of the pan. When it rises to the top use a pair of tongs and gently push it back under the oil. It should blow up like a balloon. Turn it over and cook 30 seconds more. Remove and drain on paper towels. Cook each puri separately and drain.

4. To make chapatis, pinch off 2-inch pieces of dough. Roll out evenly and fry on a hot greased griddle or a heavy skillet for about 30 seconds on each side. Then hold each chapati with tongs over a moderate gas flame for 30 seconds on each side. Serve immediately.

SQUASH ROLLS

These tender rolls decrease Vata and Pitta and increase Kapha. If you have some Ginger Carrot Soup, Curried Squash, or other thick soup left from lunch, substitute it for the cooked squash and serve the rolls at supper. These rolls are sweet, oily, a little heavy, and very moist.

−V −P +K
Makes 1½ dozen

> ⅓ cup ghee or unsalted butter
> 1 cup milk
> ½ teaspoon crushed saffron
> ¼ teaspoon nutmeg
> ¼ teaspoon ground cardamom
> ⅓ cup brown or raw sugar
> 1 cup cooked and pureed yellow squash
> 1 package dry yeast
> ¼ cup warm water
> 6 to 7 cups unbleached flour

1. Preheat the oven to 375°F.

2. In a saucepan heat the ghee, the milk, the saffron, the spices, and the sugar. Bring to the boiling point. Remove from the heat and stir in the squash puree. Set aside to cool.

3. In a large bowl dissolve the yeast in very warm water (100°F.) and wait 2 to 3 minutes for it to foam. Pour in the warm (not hot) squash mixture. Stir the flour into the squash mixture, a cup at a time, until the dough starts to come away from the sides of the bowl. It will be very soft and tender to the touch.

4. Turn the dough out on a floured board, rub your hands with ghee or oil, and knead about 5 minutes until the dough is smooth and not too sticky to handle. Add flour as needed. Let it rest while you wash and oil the bowl. Put the dough in the bowl and turn it to coat with the oil.

5. Cover with plastic wrap or a damp towel and let rise in a warm place for 45 minutes to an hour, or until doubled. Push the dough down gently and turn out on a floured board. Shape golf ball–size pieces into rolls. To avoid tearing, do not stretch them too much. Place on a greased baking sheet. If the sides are touching, softer rolls result. Placing the rolls 1 inch apart on the sheet makes them crispier. Cover the rolls with a damp towel and let rise until doubled (about 40 minutes) or until they are the size you want. Bake 15 to 20 minutes, until just golden brown on top. Remove and brush with a little ghee. Serve warm.

Soups

CREAMY SUMMER GARDEN SOUP

Jade-green in color and delicate in flavor, this sweet, slightly bitter, astringent, and oily soup is both refreshing in summer or winter and good for reducing Pitta. Because it is cold and heavy this soup increases Vata and Kapha. The vegetables can vary with the seasons.

+V −P +K
Serves 6 to 8

> *4 cups chopped Swiss chard, loosely packed*
> *2 small zucchini, thinly sliced*
> *1 cup chopped bok choy or Napa cabbage leaves*
> *1 cup chopped beet greens*
> *1 small parsnip, peeled and sliced*
> *5 cups unsalted Pitta Broth (pages 148–149)*
> *1 very ripe avocado, mashed*
> *1 cup heavy cream (½ pint)*
> *1 teaspoon minced fresh French tarragon or ½ teaspoon dried*
> *½ teaspoon ground white pepper*
> *6 or 7 mint leaves, chopped*
> *½ cup shredded raw beets or thinly sliced red radish*
> *8 to 10 sprigs fresh fennel, dill, or small mint leaves*

1. Steam the vegetables for 12 minutes, or until the zucchini is very soft. Or cook the vegetables in a pressure cooker for 4 minutes. Cool slightly and puree in a food processor or blender until creamy.

2. Heat 5 cups of Pitta Broth in a large heavy pot and add the vegetable puree. Simmer and stir until well blended. Use a hand mixer in a small bowl or a food processor with a steel blade to blend the mashed avocado with half of the cream. Slowly blend in until smooth and creamy. Add the tarragon, the pepper, and the mint. Stir vigorously into the vegetable soup. Serve it warm or cover it, cool for an hour, then chill for at least 3 hours before serving.

3. Serve in a large decorative glass bowl with a shredded beet, radish, and fresh herb garnish. Or garnish each bowl individually as you serve it.

NOTE: This recipe can be cut in half if you are cooking for less than 6 persons with Pitta dosha. Kapha types can substitute buttermilk for the heavy cream and add extra ground pepper or picante sauce to taste. Vata types would always eat this soup warm and substitute spinach, with its hot quality, for bok choy or Napa cabbage leaves.

CURRIED SQUASH SOUP

When served as part of a balanced meal, this sweet, salty, slightly pungent soup is good for everyone. Curried Squash Soup is on the menu for New Mothers and Their Babies (see page 274); new fathers say this is one of their favorites, too.

−V *P −K
Serves 4 to 6

>2 acorn or 1 large butternut squash
>2¼ cups water or Vata Broth (or broth of your choice)
>½ teaspoon salt
>2 tablespoons ghee
>½ teaspoon ground cumin
>½ teaspoon cinnamon
>¼ teaspoon ground cardamom
>¾ teaspoon ground ginger
>1 cup orange juice (use apple juice when cooking for Pitta)

1. Preheat the oven to 400°F.
2. Split the squash lengthwise and bake it facedown on an oiled tray for 30 or 40 minutes, or until it is soft. Cool and scoop out the insides. This makes about 3 cups.
3. Puree the cooked squash in a food processor or blender with the water or broth and the salt. Then pour the mixture into a 4-quart pan and heat it over a low flame. In a small pan heat the ghee and sauté the spices for about 1 minute. Add them to the soup as it is heating. Stir in the orange juice and simmer gently, stirring frequently. Serve when it is steaming hot.

Ginger Carrot Soup

This is a pungent, sweet, oily, and salty soup that is a good appetizer for Vata and can be eaten in moderation by Kapha, but it increases Pitta. A great soup to serve as part of a light meal on a "winter-almost-spring" day, it begins with a Vata broth that serves as a basis for many other Vata-balancing main dish recipes, gravies, and sauces.

−V +P *K
Serves 6 to 8

> 2 cups Vata or Kapha Broth made without salt
>   (pages 147–148, 149–150)
> 2 cups milk
> 2 tablespoons ghee
> 2 teaspoons sugar (optional)
> 3/4 teaspoon pepper
> 1/2 teaspoon cardamom
> 1/4 cup chopped fresh ginger
> 2 cups shredded carrots
> Juice of 1/2 orange
> 1/2 to 3/4 cup heavy cream
> Butter for Vata servings

1. Bring the broth and the milk to a boil in a heavy 4-quart pan. Add the ghee, the sugar, the pepper, and the cardamom. Stir well for a minute over moderately high heat. Add the ginger and cook for an additional 2 or 3 minutes, until you can smell the ginger clearly. Stir in the carrots and the orange juice. Simmer over low heat, stirring frequently, for about an hour, or until the carrots are pulpy. Turn off the heat. Cover, set aside, and let cool.

2. When ready to serve, puree the mixture in a food mill or food processor until creamy. Then return it to the pot. Reheat just to the boiling point and turn down to simmer. Add the cream. If it seems too thick, add a little water until it seems to be a moderately thin consistency. To further enrich the soup for Vata, a pat of butter or dollop of whipped cream can be floated on top of each bowl.

NOTE: When cooking for Kapha, omit the sugar and use low-fat milk, not heavy cream.

KHICHARI

Khichari (KITCH-er-ee), a nutritious and traditional Indian food for soothing diets, is simply rice and lentils cooked so thoroughly together that they make a creamy stew. This recipe makes a satisfying soup for an evening supper or a light meal, as well as a nourishing food to serve to new mothers and convalescents. If doubling the recipe, do not increase the salt, ghee, or spices. If you are using spice combinations other than the Vata Churna, it is important to include a pinch of hing (asafoetida) with the spices to aid in the digestion of the lentils. The total cooking time is about 1½ hours.

−V −P +K
Serves 2 to 3

> 2¾ *cups water*
> ¼ *cup mung lentils, cleaned and washed*
> *1 teaspoon salt*
> *1 teaspoon Vata Churna or a blend of other spices*
>   *(such as ground coriander, licorice root powder, and ground*
>   *fennel seeds), and a pinch of hing*
> ¼ *cup rice*
> *3 tablespoons ghee*
> ¼ *to* ½ *teaspoon crushed saffron threads (optional,*
>   *but omit for Pitta)*
> *1 teaspoon ground cumin*
> *1 teaspoon mustard seeds*

1. Bring 1½ cups water to a boil in a 4-quart pan. Add the lentils, the salt, and the Vata Churna or other spices. Cover and bring back to a boil, then reduce the flame to very low and simmer for about an hour.

2. Add the rice, 2 tablespoons ghee, the remaining water, and the saffron. Increase the heat to high and bring to a boil again. Then reduce the heat to low and simmer for half an hour. Stir frequently to avoid sticking and add more water if it becomes too thick. Khichari should have the consistency of thick gravy. When ready to serve, heat the remaining ghee in a small pan with the cumin and mustard seeds. When the mustard seeds pop, stir the spices into Khichari and serve.

MASOOR DAHL

Dahl (sounds like "doll") is good for people of all body types. It is a traditional Indian lentil soup. For more information about other lentils used in making dahl, see Chapter 3, Something for Everyone. Masoor Dahl is made from thin, coral-colored lentils that cook faster than any others. Other lentil soups are prepared in this way; they simply take longer to cook. Although dahl can be flavored with various spice combinations, an easy and most delicious way is by using Maharishi Ayur-Ved Vata Churna. It never fails to produce a rich and authentically Indian dahl.

−V −P *K
Serves 4 to 6

> *5 cups water*
> *1 cup red lentils*
> *1 teaspoon salt, or to taste*
> *1 tablespoon ghee*
> *1 tablespoon Vata Churna or a choice of ground*
> *   spices and a pinch of hing (asafoetida)*
> *2 teaspoons brown mustard seeds*
> *1 teaspoon ghee or oil*

1. Bring the water to a boil in a 4-quart pot. Put the lentils in a shallow dish and pick through them to remove any tiny stones that might be hiding there. Wash the lentils in several changes of cool water until the water runs clear. Pour them into the boiling water. Bring back to a boil, lower the heat to simmer, and add the salt, the ghee, and the Vata Churna. Or if you are using other spices, put the pinch of hing in the boiling water and heat the ground spices in the ghee and add to the cooking lentils.

2. Cover and simmer gently for 20 to 30 minutes, stirring occasionally.

3. When the lentils are tender and the dahl is a thick soup, fry the mustard seeds in ghee or oil until they just start to pop. They will make a swooshing sound as you add them to the dahl. Serve with a bowl of rice.

PERFECT LENTIL SOUP

This extraordinarily neat and easy method of making a delicious, creamy dahl is good for everyone. Make it with plenty of water for an extremely soupy dahl that is best for Vata and Kapha to digest. Those following a Pitta-balancing diet might want to double the amount of lentils. Although you bake it at least 2 hours, it's very creamy and splendid after slowly baking for 5 or 6 hours. This is a basic dish you can put in the oven after breakfast and serve at lunch.

Vata Churna is an important ingredient that adds to the balance and flavor of this recipe. You can substitute other spices, but be sure and put a pinch of hing in with them to aid in the digestion of the lentils. If you do bake it for 5 to 6 hours and it's too thick, just add some boiling water before serving.

To save time, bake some rice in a separate covered casserole, either at the beginning or end of the Perfect Lentil Soup's cooking time.

−V −P *K

Serves 3 to 4

> ½ to ¾ cup mung lentils, washed and cleaned
> 4 cups boiling water
> ½ teaspoon salt
> 1 teaspoon ghee
> 1 teaspoon Vata Churna, or more to taste
>   or
>   ½ teaspoon turmeric
>   ½ teaspoon ground cumin
>   ½ teaspoon ground coriander
>   Pinch of hing (asafoetida)
> 1 teaspoon mustard seeds (optional)
> 1 teaspoon ghee (optional)

1. Preheat oven to 325°F.
2. Place all the ingredients in a 2-quart casserole, cover tightly, and bake for 2 to 5 hours. It will make a very thin, easily digested lentil dahl. If you would like, just before serving, fry a teaspoon of brown mustard seeds in a teaspoon of ghee in a small pan, and when the seeds start to pop stir them into the soup. Serve with rice.

POTAGE PRINTANIER/FRENCH POTATO SOUP

This is a light, flavorful potato soup in the French style. It takes less than an hour to make and your guests will think it took much longer. Within the context of the whole menu this soup is nourishing for everyone. A steaming bowl of Potage Printanier, a tossed green salad, and a slice of lightly buttered bread makes a good light supper for Kapha types. Tastes in this recipe are sweet, salty, and a little astringent.

−V −P *K
Serves 8

> *2 tablespoons unsalted butter or ghee*
> *1 green pepper, chopped*
> *1½ quarts hot water*
> *2 potatoes, pared, quartered, and sliced thin*
> *2 carrots, sliced*
> *¼ cup white rice*
> *6 stalks asparagus, cut in ½-inch pieces*
> *½ pound spinach, washed and chopped*
> *1 cup light cream*
> *Ground pepper to taste*

Melt the butter or ghee in a large pot over moderate heat. Add the green pepper and sauté until it is soft. Add the water, the potatoes, and the sliced carrots. Bring to a boil, then reduce the heat and simmer for 15 minutes, stirring occasionally. Add the rice and the asparagus. Cover and simmer over very low heat for 25 minutes. Then stir in the spinach. Simmer for another 10 minutes. Finally, just before serving, add the light cream and just heat through, but do not boil. Sprinkle with ground pepper and serve immediately.

FOR WEIGHT WATCHERS AND KAPHA: Decrease the recipe to 1 potato, ½ cup cream mixed with ½ cup water or 1 cup skim milk, and 1 tablespoon butter or ghee.

SWEET POTATO SOUP

This soup is a soothing dish to serve as a light meal for those with Vata and Pitta constitutions, new mothers, and convalescents. It is sweet, heavy, and oily. As with all milk- or cream-based soups, if you make this soup with cream instead of broth omit the salt.

−V −P +K
Serves 4 to 6

6 to 7 cups water
4 medium sweet potatoes
2 carrots (use 1 for Pitta)
1 bay leaf
½ to 1 cup heavy cream or
  1 cup Vata or Pitta Broth and ½ teaspoon salt
2 tablespoons ghee
White pepper, to taste
Cardamom, to taste

1. Bring the water to boil in a large pot. Meanwhile, peel and chop the potatoes and the carrots. When the water is boiling, add a bay leaf and the vegetables. Reduce heat to medium, cover, and cook until the vegetables are very soft, about 40 minutes.
2. Cool for about 15 minutes, or until comfortable enough to puree until smooth in a food processor or blender. Return to the pot. Add enough cream to make a thin soup, then add the ghee and seasonings to taste. Heat thoroughly and serve.

NOTE: By substituting the broth for the cream and reducing the ghee to 1 teaspoon, this soup becomes useful for Kapha types and those watching their weight.

VEGETABLE SOUP WITH FRESH HERBS

This light and pungent soup is excellent for Kapha. It is a highly nutritious and tasty soup that can be enjoyed as an appetizer before a main meal for all body types, although when served by itself it increases Pitta and Vata slightly.

+V +P −K
Serves 6 to 8

> *2 quarts water*
> *2 teaspoons salt*
> *1 teaspoon coarsely ground black pepper*
> *4 cups cauliflower, cut in bite-size pieces*
> *1 large carrot, sliced*
> *1 cup green beans, cut in 1-inch pieces*
> *¼ cup chopped parsley*
> *1 teaspoon minced French tarragon or ½ teaspoon dried*
> *1 to 2 teaspoons minced lemon basil or lemon thyme, or 1 teaspoon*
> * dried thyme leaves*
> *¾ cup tiny semolina pasta or cooked barley*

1. Bring the water to a boil in a large pot. Add the salt, the pepper, and the vegetables. Cover and bring just close to a boil. Lower to a simmer and sprinkle the chopped herbs on top. Stir once gently. Cover and turn off the heat. Do not lift the lid for 20 to 30 minutes.

2. When ready to serve, bring the soup to a boil and add the tiny pasta or cooked barley. Simmer for 8 to 10 minutes and serve.

Main Dishes

ARTICHOKES STUFFED WITH HERBED CHEESE

Available from late winter to early summer, artichokes are at their best and most affordable when most of the popular spring herbs are growing. Fresh herbs impart a superior flavor to this Vata- and Pitta-decreasing filling. If the artichokes were stuffed with Roasted and Spiced Barley (pages 182–183), then Kapha dieters could enjoy them as well. This dish adds sweet, sour, slightly pungent, cold, heavy, and oily properties to a meal. A pungent appetizer, such as a bowl of hot soup, should precede the meal. And the more varied the bed of herbs and greens used in the salad garnish, the better this dish is for Pitta and Kapha.

Whether served as part of a main meal in springtime or alone as a light meal, complemented by various condiments, stuffed artichokes are impressive to behold. When individually presented, centered on a large plate, surrounded by torn lettuce, feathery dill and fennel, young purple basil leaves, and some colorful nasturtium and blue borage flowers, these beautiful artichokes can establish a fine cook's reputation forever.

−V −P +K
Serves 4

> *4 large artichokes*
> *Juice of 1/2 lemon*
> *2 bay leaves*
> *3 to 4 whole allspice*
> *1 1/2 tablespoons ghee*
> *1/2 cup chopped sunflower or pumpkin seeds*
> *3 cups soft bread crumbs*
> *1 cup chopped parsley*
> *1/2 teaspoon salt*
> *1 1/2 cups ricotta cheese or soft panir*
> *1 tablespoon grated Parmesan cheese*
> *1/2 cup tofu*
> *1 tablespoon minced fresh French tarragon*
> *1 tablespoon minced mixed fresh herbs: thyme, savory,*
>   *sorrel, mint, or basil*
> *1 teaspoon black pepper*
> *1/2 teaspoon crushed anise seeds*
> *1/2 teaspoon ground cardamom*
> *2 teaspoons sweet paprika*
> *2 teaspoons olive oil*
> *Lettuce varieties, fennel, dill, tarragon, basil, orange,*
>   *pineapple, or lemon mint, chive blossoms, edible*
>   *flowers (as a garnish)*

1. To prepare the artichokes, bring 2 to 3 quarts of water to a boil in a large pot. Rinse the artichokes and trim the bottom stems even

with the bottom leaves. Working from the bottom up, use s⟨
clip the sharp pointed leaf tips. Fit the artichokes into the po⟨
boiling water, add the lemon juice, the bay leaves, and the allspice.

2. Cover and simmer over moderate heat for 40 minutes. Remove the artichokes and drain them upside down on a rack. Reserve 2 cups of the cooking liquid.

3. To make the filling, heat the ghee in a large pot over moderate heat. Stir in the seeds and fry until they are light brown, about 2 minutes. Add the bread crumbs, the parsley, and the salt. Toss well until mixed. Cover and set aside while preparing the cheese mixture.

4. In a large bowl mash the cheeses and tofu together. Using a mortar and pestle, crush the spices and herbs together in the olive oil. Form a thick paste (pesto). Mix the cheese and the pesto thoroughly together in a large bowl, and then combine with the bread crumbs.

5. To stuff the artichokes, set the cooked artichokes upright and carefully open each one until the center choke is exposed. Pull this out with your fingers or use the tip of a sharp knife to get started.

6. Place a large spoonful of filling in the center. Then slip some between all the leaves except the most outward ones. Divide the filling equally among the artichokes. When thoroughly stuffed, tie a cotton string around each one to hold the stuffing and leaves together. Pour 1 cup of the reserved liquid into a large pot. Lay a metal or bamboo steamer in the pot. Gently set the artichokes in the steamer so the sides touch. Cover and simmer over low heat for 20 minutes. If the liquid evaporates before the time is up, add more. Remove the artichokes from the pot and set aside for 15 minutes before handling. Cut and remove the strings. Set each artichoke on a bed of lettuce and decorate with herbs and flowers. Serve warm.

SAVORY WILD RICE CASSEROLE

Although wild rice, seed of a native north American aquatic grass, is not truly a rice, it has similar properties. Because it is a thicker and rougher grain it takes longer to cook than rice. It can be eaten in greater quantities by those following Pitta and Kapha diets.

+V −P −K

Serves 4 to 6

❖❖❖

1 tablespoon ghee or butter
1/4 cup thinly sliced celery
1 cup wild rice, washed
2 cups vegetable broth (Vata, Pitta, or Kapha) or
  2 cups water and 2 teaspoons Kapha Churna
1/2 teaspoon salt
1 teaspoon ghee or butter
1 tablespoon sliced almonds
1 tablespoon ghee or olive oil
1/2 cup coarsely chopped sweet red pepper
1/2 teaspoon salt
1/2 cup shredded carrots

1. Preheat the oven to 350°F.

2. Melt 1 tablespoon ghee or butter in a heavy casserole over moderate heat. Add the celery and wild rice, frying until they are well coated. Pour the broth over the rice and sprinkle on the salt. Bring just close to a boil, then cover tightly and bake in the middle of the oven for 1 hour. Remove from the oven and allow to rest, covered, for 15 minutes. Meanwhile, in a small heavy pan, melt 1 teaspoon ghee or butter and brown the almonds. Set aside. Then heat the remaining tablespoon ghee or olive oil in a skillet, add the red peppers and salt, tossing well, until the peppers are limp. Stir in the carrots and fry for 2 minutes. To serve, toss the peppers and the carrots with the rice. Sprinkle the almonds on top.

NOTE: For those reducing weight, omit the almonds and reduce the ghee and oil by one-half.

CURRIED VEGETABLES AND PANIR

A mixture of spiced vegetables and crisply fried panir served on a bed of basmati or other long-grain white rice, this dish is a basic standby that can be made for any constitution by using an appropriate blend of vegetables and spices. When serving a group with varied dietary needs, use many different vegetables so everyone has several to choose. This recipe is just an example of proportions and cooking methods you can use.

−V −P −K

Serves 4 to 6

> 1½ *tablespoons ghee*
> 1½ *cups 1-inch Golden Panir Cubes (page 116)*
> 2 *tablespoons sunflower or safflower oil*
> 1 *cup diced sweet potato*
> 2 *stalks celery, sliced*
> 1 *carrot, thinly sliced*
> 2 *stems broccoli, chopped*
> 1 *medium turnip, diced*
> 1 *medium parsnip, peeled and diced*
> 1 *cup green beans, cut in 1-inch pieces*
> 1 *medium tomato, peeled and cut in wedges*
> ¼ *cup raisins*
> ½ *teaspoon salt*
> 2 *teaspoons ghee or oil*
> 1 *teaspoon ground coriander*
> ½ *teaspoon ground cumin*
> ½ *teaspoon ground fenugreek*
> ½ *teaspoon ground cardamom*
> 1½ *cups water or whey (left from making the panir)*

1. Heat the ghee in a large, heavy skillet over moderately high heat. Add the panir cubes and allow to fry without turning for 3 or 4 minutes. When slightly crispy, use a metal spatula to turn. Continue frying until all sides are richly browned. Remove from the pan and set aside on a plate lined with paper towels. In the same skillet heat the 2 tablespoons of oil. Add the vegetables, one kind at a time. Fry each for 1 minute, stirring well, before adding the next one. Add the raisins and the salt.

2. Push everything to the sides of the pan to make a small well in the center. Pour in 2 teaspoons ghee or oil and sprinkle in the mixed ground spices. Stir until heated, then blend with all the vegetables. Gently add the panir and pour the water or whey over everything, cover tightly, and turn the flame to low. Allow to slowly simmer, covered, for 15 minutes. Serve on a bed of hot rice.

NOTE: If you prefer the panir cubes with a crispy covering, don't steam them with the vegetables but serve them separately or lay them over the top of the vegetables just before serving.

GREEN AND GOLD BAKED SQUASH

With predominantly astringent, bitter, slightly sour, and slightly pungent tastes and hot, light, and slightly oily qualities, this colorful main dish is a good choice for reducing Kapha. Vata or Pitta may have a moderate amount as part of a balanced meal or as a side dish. Allow ½ squash per serving. You can either stuff each half separately, or peel the squash, cut it into 2-inch cubes, and mix it together in an oiled baking pan with the stuffing.

*V *P — K

Serves 4

> *2 teaspoons ghee*
> *½ teaspoon turmeric*
> *½ teaspoon ground thyme*
> *1 teaspoon licorice root powder*
> *1 teaspoon shredded fresh ginger (reduce for Pitta), or*
>   *¼ teaspoon ground*
> *½ cup skim milk ricotta cheese*
> *1 cup cooked millet (use cooked rice for Vata)*
> *1 cup fresh spinach, washed and chopped fine*
> *1 medium Granny Smith, Greening, or other tart apple, diced*
> *1 teaspoon nutmeg*
> *2 acorn or trimmed butternut squash, halved and seeded*
> *1 cup hot water*

1. Preheat the oven to 375°F.
2. Heat the ghee in a small heavy pan over moderately high heat. Add the turmeric, thyme, licorice root, and the ginger. Stir in the ricotta with a sharp chopping motion and just blend together. Toss with the millet, the spinach, the diced apple, and the nutmeg. Pile the stuffing into the squash halves and set in a 7 × 11-inch oiled pan or other baking casserole. Pour the water around the squash. Cover the pan tightly and bake for 45 minutes, or until the squash is tender when pierced with a fork.

GREEN BEANS IN TOMATO SAUCE
(FAGIOLONI IN UMIDO VOLPONI)

A delicious and colorful northern Italian dish, this has properly balanced tastes and qualities that reduce all doshas. It is pleasantly sweet and salty. The green beans must be very well cooked for Vata to be able to eat.

−V −P −K
Serves 4

> *1 pound fresh green beans*
> *1 pound ripe tomatoes or 1 14-ounce can of tomatoes, chopped*
> *2 tablespoons olive oil or vegetable oil*
> *½ teaspoon each crushed oregano, thyme, and basil*
> *Salt and pepper to taste*
> *½ cup water, as needed*

Wash, destring, and cut the beans into 1-inch pieces. Blanch and peel the fresh tomatoes, then chop them into chunks, keeping as much of the juice as possible. Heat the oil in a 2-quart saucepan. Add the beans, the tomatoes, and the crushed herbs. Stir a few times, then add the salt and pepper to taste. Cover and simmer over low heat for about 45 minutes, until the beans are quite tender and the tomatoes saucy. If the sauce starts to stick, add a little water during cooking. Serve hot with pasta or rice.

NOTE: Heavy Kapha types and those reducing weight would eat this as a simple side dish without pasta or perhaps with a little rice.

LAYERED VEGETABLE LOAF

Lightly breaded eggplant slices layered with a variety of Kapha-decreasing vegetables in a loaf pan makes this entrée light in quality with the astringent, bitter, pungent, and slightly sour tastes good for Kapha diets. It can be eaten as it is by Vata and Pitta types as a side dish. Otherwise use the sliced eggplant layered with Vata- or Pitta-decreasing vegetables and herbs.

Serve plain. Those following Vata and Pitta diets might enjoy it with Avocado Cheese Sauce (pages 130–131).

*v *p — k
Makes 1 loaf

> 1 medium eggplant
> 3 tablespoons buttermilk
> 1½ cups fine bread crumbs
> 1 tablespoon olive oil
> 1 teaspoon minced fresh basil or ½ teaspoon dried
> 1 teaspoon minced fresh oregano or ½ teaspoon dried
> ½ teaspoon black pepper
> ½ teaspoon salt
> 1 cup shredded carrots
> 1 cup peas, steamed
> 1 cup chopped spinach or chard
> 2 tablespoons diced sweet red pepper
> ¼ cup chopped celery leaves
> 1 medium tomato, peeled, seeded, and thinly sliced
> ¼ cup chopped roasted sunflower seeds
> ½ cup water

1. Preheat the oven to 350°F.
2. Peel the eggplant and cut 10 to 12 slices about ½ inch thick. Pour the buttermilk in a shallow bowl and dip each slice first in the buttermilk and then in the bread crumbs. Tightly fit a layer of breaded eggplant on the bottom of the pan. Mix the remaining ingredients together in a mixing bowl, except the tomato, the sunflower seeds, and the water, and pat a third of the mixture on the eggplant. Lay a couple of tomato slices on top. Make 3 such layers, ending with eggplant. Sprinkle the chopped seeds on top. Pour the water around the sides. Cover tightly and bake 45 minutes. Let the loaf rest 10 minutes before slicing it.

LIGHTLY SEASONED VEGETABLES

Vegetables prepared this way make a good side dish or a light evening meal for anyone following a Vata-reducing diet, new mothers, or any children who like mixed vegetables.

−v *p *k
Serves 4

> 1 cup diced potatoes
> ½ cup thinly sliced carrots
> ½ cup thinly sliced beets
> 1 cup thinly sliced yellow squash
> ½ cup chopped Swiss chard leaves or spinach, or more to taste
> 2 tablespoons ghee
> ½ teaspoon brown mustard seeds
> ½ teaspoon ground cardamom
> 8 fenugreek seeds, lightly roasted and ground
> 1 teaspoon Vata Churna
>> or
>> ¼ teaspoon ground cumin
>> ½ teaspoon turmeric
>> ¼ teaspoon ground ginger
> ⅛ teaspoon salt

Steam the vegetables in a pressure cooker (2 to 3 minutes) or steamer (5 to 10 minutes) until they are tender. In a large skillet heat the ghee and the mustard seeds. When the seeds start to pop, add the remaining spices and the salt. Stir for 30 seconds and then add the vegetables. Sauté for about 2 minutes, or until they are well coated with the spices.

MOROCCAN DELIGHT

An elaborate and beautiful dish to serve at a party, this recipe reduces Pitta and Vata and increases Kapha (although it is nourishing for Kapha). The "delight" is in savoring a variety of stimulating flavors and exotic color combinations. By preparing groups of ingredients separately, the tastes remain distinct from one another even after they are finally combined just before serving. A little of every taste is represented, but it is mostly sweet in taste and heavy and oily in quality.

−v −p +k
Serves 4 to 6 generously

❖❖❖

2 cups Marinated Tofu (recipe follows)
2 cups broccoli florets
2 cups cauliflorets
4 tablespoons ghee
2 tablespoons sesame seeds
1 large sweet pimiento pepper, cut in bite-size pieces
1 8-ounce can artichoke hearts, not marinated,
  quartered
2 tablespoons olive oil or other cooking oil
1 tablespoon turmeric
½ teaspoon ground coriander
1 teaspoon ground cardamom
½ teaspoon to 1 teaspoon salt, to taste
½ cup warm water
½ cup sliced bright orange dried apricots
¼ cup chopped pitted dates
6 cups cooked couscous or rice
¼ cup sliced blanched almonds

1. Drain the tofu. Steam the broccoli and cauliflower for 10 minutes. Set aside.

2. Heat 3 tablespoons ghee in a wok or a heavy frying pan over moderately high heat and sauté the tofu cubes until they are lightly browned, about 10 minutes. Set the browned tofu aside in a large bowl. In the same pan heat the remaining 1 tablespoon ghee over medium heat. Add the sesame seeds and stir until they begin to turn brown and start popping.

3. Immediately add the pepper pieces and the artichoke hearts. Sauté for 2 minutes, tossing to cover the vegetables with the sesame seeds. Then gently mix the peppers and artichoke hearts in with the tofu. Set aside and cover.

4. Again in the same pan heat 2 tablespoons oil over medium heat. Then add the turmeric, the coriander, the cardamom, and the salt. Stir until any turmeric lumps disappear. Then slowly stir in ½ cup warm water. This makes a bright gold sauce.

5. Add the steamed broccoli and cauliflower to the sauce. Stir until the cauliflower is uniformly golden, then add the apricots and the dates. Add more water as needed to keep the sauce from drying out. Simmer over low heat for another minute, stirring frequently. Then

gently fold in the tofu cubes and stir-fry another minute or 2 until they are dark brown. Arrange on a bed of steaming couscous or rice and sprinkle with sliced almonds.

6. If you are not serving it immediately, cover the platter tightly and keep it warm in a 175°F. oven.

7. To prepare this dish for a celebration or a large party, allow ½ cup tofu and ½ cup vegetables per person. For an authentic ethnic touch, serve with Little Flat Breads or pita bread.

MARINATED TOFU

1 quart sweet red fruit juice, such as raspberry, pomegranate, plum, strawberry, or a blend of these
¼ teaspoon each nutmeg, ground coriander, and cinnamon
1 tablespoon tamari or soy sauce
1 pound firm tofu, water pressed out and cubed

In a 2-quart saucepan, heat the juice, the spices, and the tamari. Remove from the heat and mix in the tofu cubes. Cover and marinate for 2 or 3 hours at room temperature, or overnight in the refrigerator. For a quick marinade, omit the spices and simply pour the juice and the tamari mixture over the tofu. Cover and set aside for at least 2 hours before you are ready to use it.

COUSCOUS

Couscous can be served with any vegetable dish or as a rice substitute. Made from semolina flour, it is a sweet-tasting addition to any meal and is good for decreasing Vata and Pitta and increasing Kapha a little. Whole wheat couscous, available at natural food stores, is more nourishing than the creamy yellow variety, but it does not come out as light and fluffy.

−V −P +K
Serves 6 to 8

2½ cups couscous (about 1 pound)
3½ cups water
1 teaspoon salt
1 tablespoon oil or ghee (optional)

Add the couscous to boiling salted water and stir vigorously with a fork for about a minute. Cover the pan tightly and let it stand for 10 to 15 minutes. Before serving, fluff with a fork and stir in oil or ghee. While the couscous is resting, sauté some vegetables to serve with it.

EASY COUSCOUS—THE OVEN METHOD
Serves 4 to 6

2 cups couscous
1 tablespoon ghee or light oil
1 teaspoon salt
3 cups water

1. Preheat the oven to 400°F.
2. Spread the couscous in a 2-quart glass or ovenproof casserole. Add the ghee or oil and sprinkle with the salt. Pour the water over the couscous. Seal tightly with foil and a lid. Bake for 15 to 20 minutes. Uncover and fluff with a fork while it is steamy.

NOTE: Make a salad of leftover couscous tossed with chopped celery, herbs, spices, and lemon juice on a bed of lettuce.

OVEN-BAKED FRENCH FRIES

Baking French fries makes them less oily than those cooked using the deep-frying method, but even these French fries are heavy, oily, and fat-increasing, so Kapha should eat less of them.

−V −P +K

1 potato per person
½ tablespoon butter per person
Salt and pepper to taste

1. Preheat the oven to 350°F.

2. Slice the potatoes in long, thin, "frenched" shapes. Melt the butter and coat the potatoes. Arrange them on baking sheets 1 or 2 layers thick. Bake for at least 1 hour, turning the potatoes after about 30 minutes. They are done when they turn golden brown. For large amounts (more than 5 potatoes) baking may take longer.

PASTA AND GREEN SAUCE

The green herbs make this sauce a flavorful accompaniment to spaghetti or linguini. When served with pasta, this dish decreases Vata, is neutral for Pitta, and increases Kapha. Kapha can eat more of this as a main dish if cooked barley is substituted for the pasta. Parmesan cheese can be used in moderation by both Vata and Kapha. The combined qualities of this recipe are sweet, salty, oily, and heavy.

−V *P +K

Serves 3 to 4

> *1 cup minced parsley*
> *3/4 cup minced fresh basil or 1/2 cup dried crushed*
> *1 teaspoon salt*
> *1/2 cup chopped nuts (pine nuts are best)*
> *1/2 cup olive oil*
> *1 pound vermicelli or other pasta*
> *Grated Parmesan cheese (optional)*

1. Grind the herbs, the salt, and the nuts with a mortar and pestle, or chop in a food processor with a steel blade. Add the oil and combine until smooth. This makes about 1½ cups of simple pesto.

2. Cook the vermicelli or other pasta according to package directions. Drain and toss with the green sauce and sprinkle with the cheese.

0

PETIT POIS BRAISÉ LAITUE
(PEAS BRAISED WITH LETTUCE)

This recipe from the French cuisine is a delightful blend of sweet and sour tastes. It combines a delicate consistency with the refreshing lightness of spring vegetables and makes a satisfying entrée when served with Simple Rice Pilaf (page 184), pasta, or plain rice. The recipe has a neutral effect on Vata and Pitta and increases Kapha slightly.

*V *P +K
Serves 4 to 6

> *1 firm head Boston lettuce*
> *3 sprigs each:*
>   *parsley*
>   *thyme*
>   *marjoram*
> *1 red bell pepper or pimiento, diced or chopped*
> *2 cups fresh peas*
> *1 cup chopped spinach*
> *1/2 cup water*
> *1/2 teaspoon salt*
> *1/2 teaspoon sugar*
> *2 tablespoons butter*

Wash the lettuce and cut it into 4 to 6 wedges. Tie each wedge together with cotton string to keep its shape. Tie the herb sprigs together. In a heavy 3-quart saucepan, put all the ingredients except 2 tablespoons butter. Bring to a boil over moderate heat, tossing lightly. Cover the pan and simmer over very low heat for 30 minutes, stirring frequently, until the vegetables are tender and the liquid is just cooked away. Remove the herbs and the strings from the lettuce wedges. Add 2 tablespoons butter, toss, and serve on a bed of rice or pasta.

NOTE: The sugar and butter can be reduced by half for Kapha and others watching their weight.

RICH STUFFED PEPPERS

A delicious main dish that is nourishing for Vata with its sweet, salty, bitter, and slightly astringent tastes. The warm, rich, heavy stuffing can be baked separately in a buttered casserole and served as a side dish for Pitta and Vata.

−V −P +K
Serves 6

> *3 large green peppers, halved and*
> *   blanched*
> *½ cup ghee or unsalted butter*
> *¾ cup chopped celery stalks and leaves*
> *2 small zucchini, cubed*
> *¼ cup chopped parsley*
> *½ cup chopped sweet red pepper*
> *¼ cup coarsely chopped pecans or cashews*
> *4 cups soft bread cubes*
> *½ teaspoon salt*
> *1 teaspoon crushed sage*
> *½ teaspoon thyme*
> *¼ to ½ teaspoon coarsely ground pepper*
> *1 large tomato, peeled and cut in 6 wedges*

1. To blanch the peppers, bring 2 quarts of water to a boil. Meanwhile, halve the peppers and remove the seeds and membrane. Drop them into boiling water and allow to boil for 3 minutes. Remove the soft peppers from the pot, place them in a colander, and immediately run them under cold water. Drain them, hollow sides down, on a towel until you are ready to stuff them.

2. Preheat the oven to 350°F.

3. For the stuffing, heat the ghee in a large frying pan or deep pot. Add the vegetables and sauté, stirring frequently, for about 20 minutes, or until they are soft. Add the chopped nuts, then the bread cubes and seasonings. Toss well and heat through. Mound the stuffing into the pepper halves and place them in a lightly oiled 7 × 11-inch baking pan or other deep casserole. Bake, uncovered, for 10 minutes.

NOTE: Stuff green peppers with plain or Roasted and Spiced Barley (recipe below; omit vegetables) for Kapha and those watching their weight. Instead of tomato wedges, a simple tomato sauce can be served along with the peppers for Vata.

QUICK VEGETABLE MEDLEY

A colorful sweet, oily, slightly pungent vata-decreasing dish that is very easy to make, it can be served with rice or couscous. New mothers find this vegetable combination colorful and delicious.

−V +P *K
Serves 4

> *2 tablespoons ghee*
> *½ teaspoon ground cumin*
> *1 teaspoon Vata Churna*
> *½ teaspoon salt*
> *1 medium cucumber, peeled, seeded, and diced*
> *1 cup shredded beets*
> *1 cup shredded carrots*

Heat the ghee in a skillet over a moderate flame. Stir in the spices and salt and fry for 1 minute. Then add the vegetables. Cover and reduce the heat to low. Simmer, stirring frequently, until the vegetables are well cooked and soft.

ROASTED AND SPICED BARLEY WITH VEGETABLES

Everyone can eat this dish as part of a balanced meal, but it is a first choice for Kapha and good to eat on days when you are eating a lighter diet. The outstanding tastes of this recipe are pungent, sweet, and salty. It should be served as a side dish rather than the main course for Vata and Pitta. If you substitute cooked brown rice or kasha for the barley, it would make a more substantial main dish for thin people and Vata.

*V +P −K
Serves 6 to 8

3 tablespoons ghee
½ teaspoon cayenne
1 cup barley, rinsed and drained
1½ teaspoons salt
3½ cups hot water
1 cup bite-size broccoli florets
2 tablespoons olive oil
1 teaspoon minced fresh ginger or ½ teaspoon ground
¼ cup sesame seeds
¼ cup roasted pumpkin seeds
1 sweet red pepper, cut in 1-inch squares
1 cup washed and chopped Swiss chard
   (mixed ruby and white look best)
½ cup washed and chopped beet greens
2 teaspoons salt
½ teaspoon coarsely ground black pepper

1. To prepare the barley, heat the ghee in a heavy iron skillet or a 2-quart pot over moderate heat. Stir in the cayenne. Lower the flame to simmer and after the cayenne is heated, about 1 minute, stir in the barley. Roast the barley by continuously stirring it until the grains are medium brown. Watch carefully not to burn it. Then sprinkle on the salt, add the hot water, and stir once or twice. Cover tightly and simmer over very low heat for about 1 hour. It's all right if some liquid remains. Fluff up the barley with a fork, cover, and set it aside while you prepare the vegetables. Or make the barley ahead of time and prepare the vegetables just before serving.

2. To prepare the vegetables, steam the broccoli for 3 to 4 minutes and set it aside.

3. Heat the oil in a wok or a large heavy frying pan. Add the ginger and the sesame seeds. Fry over moderate heat until the seeds just start to pop. Add half the pumpkin seeds, stir, add the red peppers, and stir well. Stir in the chard and the beet greens. Add the steamed broccoli, the salt, and the pepper. Toss well and cover tightly. Turn off the heat and let the vegetables steam while you reheat the barley over medium heat, stirring until any remaining liquid is gone.

4. Fold in the remaining pumpkin seeds and spread the barley on a serving platter. Arrange the vegetables on the bed of barley and serve.

SIMPLE RICE PILAF

This easy-to-make dish adds sweet and salty tastes to the meal. It is best served with steamed or sautéed vegetables. As part of a balanced meal, this pilaf is good for everyone.

−V −P *K
Makes abut 2 cups

> 3 tablespoons ghee or unsalted butter
> 1 stalk celery, chopped
> 1 cup white rice or brown as a substitute
> ½ teaspoon crushed dried basil or 1 teaspoon chopped fresh
> 1 tablespoon chopped parsley
> ½ teaspoon salt
> ½ teaspoon pepper, or to taste
> 2 cups water or Vata or Pitta Broth

Melt the ghee in a 2-quart saucepan and sauté the celery. Add the rice and stir about 1 minute, or until the rice is transparent. The ghee should just cover the rice. Add the basil, the parsley, the salt, and the pepper. Then stir in the water or broth. Bring to a boil, reduce the heat to low, and simmer, covered tightly, for about 20 minutes, or until all the water is absorbed. Fluff with a fork and serve.

NOTE: For Pitta, omit the basil and increase the parsley to taste.

SIMPLY BAKED CARROTS

This simply made side dish is nourishing for a Vata, new mothers, and convalescents. Children who like carrots really like them this way. Reducing the ghee to 1 tablespoon makes it a good side dish for Kapha.

−V +P *K
Serves 2 to 3

❖❖❖

½ pound carrots
¼ cup water
¼ teaspoon salt
¼ cup sesame seeds or ground blanched almonds
4 tablespoons ghee

1. Preheat the oven to 350°F.
2. Julienne the carrots or cut into narrow finger-length pieces. Place them in a saucepan with the water and the salt. Boil over a moderately high flame just until they are tender (test with a fork). Arrange the carrots in a small deep baking pan and pour in any remaining cooking liquid along with them. Sprinkle with the sesame seeds and the ghee. Bake, uncovered, for 30 minutes, or until they are golden brown, basting several times with the juices.

SPICY VEGETABLE CURRY

Great to serve in springtime, Kapha's season, Spicy Vegetable Curry decreases Kapha and Vata and increases Pitta somewhat. It makes a good side dish for Pitta when served as part of a meal with other Pitta-reducing selections. The predominant tastes are pungent, sour, sweet, slightly bitter, and astringent with hot and oily qualities. This combination makes it a good main dish anytime for those following a Kapha-reducing diet.

Wash, peel, chop, and grind all the ingredients before beginning to cook. Select fresh, seasonally available vegetables. If you omit those vegetables not available listed in this recipe, be sure to substitute others in the correct quantity to make up the total amount. Although fresh vegetables are always the best choice, buying good-quality fresh tomatoes, peas, and other summer favorites might not be practical in winter. The occasional use—once every week or two—of canned or frozen ingredients is all right as long as they make up a small part of the recipe.

−V +P −K
Serves 6 to 8

❖✦❖

3 tablespoons ghee
1 tablespoon Kapha Churna or prepared curry powder
   or
    ½ teaspoon ground ginger
    ¼ teaspoon licorice root powder
    ¼ teaspoon ground cloves
    ½ teaspoon ground coriander
4 medium carrots, sliced
4 small zucchini, sliced thin
1½ cups green beans, cut in ½-inch pieces
½ cup fresh or frozen peas
1 teaspoon salt
½ cup water, or more as needed
3 tablespoons olive oil or other cooking oil
1 teaspoon turmeric
¾ teaspoon ground cumin
1 small cauliflower, broken into florets
1 small eggplant, peeled and diced
3 to 4 medium tomatoes, skinned and diced,
   or 1 18-ounce can peeled tomatoes, chopped

1. In a large pot, heat 3 tablespoons ghee over moderate heat. Add the Kapha Churna, stir briefly, then add the carrots and the zucchini slices. Turn the heat to low and stir until well coated with ghee. Cover and allow the vegetables to simmer for 3 minutes. Add the green beans, peas, salt, and ½ cup water. Cover and continue simmering on low while preparing the other ingredients. If the water evaporates, add more.

2. In a frying pan or large wok, heat 2 tablespoons oil over moderately high heat. Add the turmeric and the ground cumin. Mix well together for about 30 seconds, then stir in the cauliflower. Stir-fry about 2 minutes, or until the cauliflower is evenly coated and bright gold. Push the cauliflower to the sides of the pan and add the remaining tablespoon of oil to the center. When it is hot, stir in the eggplant. Cook 1 minute. Then mix the tomatoes in with the eggplant and the cauliflower. Stir until everything is well blended. It should become very liquid, like a tomato sauce. If not, add water gradually. Cover and turn the heat to low and simmer 3 to 4 minutes.

3. About 10 minutes before serving, stir the tomato mixture into the large pot. Mix gently and simmer on low. Serve with rice.

NOTE: If any curry is left after the meal, save it until evening and heat it by frying in hot oil. Then stuff it in folded chapatis, tortillas, or pita bread. Serve these with a tossed salad for a light meal.

STUFFED SHELLS WITH ARTICHOKE CREAM SAUCE

Easily made, this elegant entrée is best for Vata and Pitta. Because it is so rich Kapha should eat a small portion of this sweet, oily, heavy, slightly sour, slightly pungent dish.

−V −P +K
Serves 4 (3 shells per serving)

> 12 large pasta shells
> 1 tablespoon olive oil or ghee
> 1 tablespoon basil pesto (see Green Sauce, page 179)
> 1 medium sweet red pepper, cut in 1-inch pieces
> 2 cups heavy cream
> 1/4 cup grated Parmesan cheese
> 1 cup soft tofu
> 1 cup ricotta cheese
> 1 cup chopped parsley
> 1/2 cup chopped spinach
> 1 teaspoon black or white pepper
> 1/2 teaspoon nutmeg
> 1 can artichoke hearts, drained and quartered
> 1/2 teaspoon paprika
> 1 tablespoon grated Parmesan cheese (optional)

1. Boil the pasta shells in a large pot of rapidly boiling salted water for 10 minutes. Drain and run under cold water to cool. Prepare the sauce while the shells cook. Heat the oil in a heavy 2-quart saucepan. Add the pesto and the peppers. Fry until the peppers are soft. Add the cream and stir in the cheese. Simmer until the sauce bubbles and is slightly thickened. Cover and set aside while you stuff the shells.

2. Preheat the oven to 400°F.

3. Mix the tofu, ricotta, parsley, spinach, pepper, and nutmeg together and stuff each cooled shell. Pour a cup of the sauce in the bottom of an 8-inch square baking pan. Arrange the stuffed shells closely together and fill in the spaces with the quartered artichoke hearts. Sprinkle with the paprika and the grated Parmesan, if you like. Cover and bake for 30 minutes.

SWEET SUMMER CURRY

This sweet, unctuous, astringent, warm, heavy, and a little salty curry makes a good main dish for Pitta and Vata. Kapha can eat very moderately of this curry. The more pungent ones suit Kapha better. If you increase the spinach and decrease the raisins, grapes, and potatoes, this sweet curry would make a better side dish for Kapha types. The Fried Spiced Potatoes is a Kapha side dish also.

When preparing sprouted lentils for frying, soak them in warm water, cover, and allow them to sit in a warm place overnight or just long enough for the sprouts to begin coming out. Wash them well in cool water before using.

−v −p +k

Serves 4 to 6 generously

> 6 tablespoons ghee
> 3/4 cup toasted dried coconut
> 1/2 teaspoon brown mustard seeds (or poppy seeds for Pitta, if desired)
> 2 tablespoons Pitta Churna, or a mixture of ground licorice root, cardamom, fennel, and coriander seeds
> 1 cup sprouted whole Urad gram
> 2 apples, peeled and diced
> 2 medium yellow summer squash, diced
> 3/4 teaspoon salt
> 1/2 cup raisins
> 1/2 cup seedless green or red unsprayed grapes
> 1 cup sweet fruit juice: pineapple-coconut, mango, or white grape
> 1 recipe Fried Spiced Potatoes (recipe follows)
> 3/4 cup washed and chopped spinach

1. To toast coconut, heat 2 tablespoons of ghee in a small pan over moderate heat. Add the coconut and toss it well to coat. Heat it slowly, stirring constantly, until it is light brown. Remove from the heat and set aside.

2. In a large frying pan or wok heat 2 tablespoons ghee over medium-high heat. Add the mustard seeds (or poppy seeds). When the seeds begin to pop, add the Pitta Churna. Stir 1 minute. Add the sprouts. Cook 2 to 3 minutes, stirring frequently. Push the sprouts to the sides of the pan and add 2 more tablespoons ghee in the center. When the ghee is hot, add the chopped apples and the squash. Stir in the salt. Gently sauté the apples and the squash for 3 to 4 minutes, then mix together with the sprouts. Add the raisins, the grapes, and the fruit juice. Cover and simmer on low heat for 10 minutes. Gently toss in the Fried Spiced Potatoes, mixing well. Stir in ½ cup toasted coconut, reserve ¼ cup for garnish. Spread the spinach evenly on top and sprinkle with the remaining coconut. Cover. Turn off the heat and let the spinach steam for 10 minutes.

3. Serve on a platter of Saffron Rice (recipe follows below) or plain rice for Pitta in hot weather.

Fried Spiced Potatoes

¼ cup safflower or sunflower oil
½ teaspoon nutmeg
½ teaspoon ground cardamom
½ teaspoon ground coriander
4 medium red-skinned potatoes, scrubbed and diced
½ teaspoon salt
½ cup warm water

1. Prepare Fried Spiced Potatoes and allow them to steam while you cook the fruits and vegetables.

2. In a heavy frying pan heat the oil over medium-high heat. Add the nutmeg, the cardamom, and the coriander. Stir in the potatoes. When they are coated with the oil and the spices, sprinkle them with the salt. Fry over moderate heat, stirring frequently, for 10 minutes. Pour in the water, cover, and simmer on low heat for 5 minutes. Turn off the heat and leave the potatoes covered until you are ready to combine them with the remaining ingredients.

Saffron Rice

Rice is cold, sweet, and heavy. It reduces Vata and Pitta and increases Kapha. But this is a good way to prepare rice for Kapha types because the saffron is a heating herb, and by frying the rice in a little oil before boiling, it becomes less heavy. Vata types can use the heat of saffron, but the rice does not need to be fried first. Those with Pitta constitutions do not need to lighten the rice by frying either. Saffron can be eaten in moderation by Pitta in cold months. Baking rice in a casserole is easy and makes dependably fluffy rice.

−V *P +K
Makes 2 cups

> 2 tablespoons ghee
> 1 cup washed basmati rice or other long-grain white rice
> 2 cups boiling water
> ½ teaspoon salt
> ¼ teaspoon crumbled saffron, or to taste

1. Preheat the oven to 350°F.
2. Heat 1 tablespoon ghee in a frying pan over moderate heat. Add the washed rice and stir to coat each grain. Fry for 3 to 4 minutes. Pour the water, the salt, and the saffron into a 2-quart casserole. Stir in the remaining ghee. Spread the rice evenly on the bottom. Cover tightly with foil and bake for 30 minutes. Fluff the rice with a fork when it is done and again before serving.

TOFU NUT BURGERS

A good main dish that is both sweet and nourishing, Tofu Nut Burgers have a tonic (healthfully nourishing) effect. They are a body-building food that decreases Vata, is neutral for Pitta, and increases Kapha. When eaten with the usual selection of condiments—pickles, olives, mustard, catsup, and so forth—they are more easily digested. Choose from condiments according to your taste.

−V *P +K
Makes 8 burgers

1 pound firm tofu
2 cups cooked brown rice
1 cup ground nuts (medium
   grind)
3 tablespoons tamari, or to taste
1 stalk celery, chopped and sautéed

1. Preheat the oven to 350°F.

2. Combine the tofu with 1½ cups cooked rice in a food processor, blending thoroughly. Add the remaining ingredients, mix, and form into patties. Bake the burgers on a greased baking sheet for 25 to 35 minutes. A nice brown crust will form on the outside, but they will stay moist on the inside.

3. Serve hot or save them and reheat by putting in a 350°F. oven for 5 minutes.

NOTE: Tofu burgers can be baked at the same time as Oven-Baked French Fries (pages 178–179).

VEGETABLE WHOLE GRAIN SAUTÉ

Anyone can enjoy this recipe as part of a balanced meal. It's a light, easily digested main dish that is just right for Kapha when barley is used. Bulgur, cracked wheat, or brown rice are better whole grains for those following Pitta and Vata diets. This recipe adds sweet, astringent tastes and light and oily qualities to the complete menu. Even when prepared with cooked barley it can be served to anyone as the main part of a light meal. The use of sprouted Urad beans (whole black gram) adds a sweet, nutty flavor. These sprouts are very nourishing and somewhat weight-producing. They are especially useful for Vata and Pitta diets. For those who are reducing weight, mung bean or brown lentil sprouts can be used instead of the more fattening Urad.

−V −P −K
Serves 4

FOR THE VEGETABLES

> *2 teaspoons sesame oil*
> *2 tablespoons sunflower seeds*
> *½ teaspoon salt*
> *½ teaspoon coarsely ground black pepper*
> *½ cup shredded zucchini*
> *¾ cup shredded carrots*
> *½ cup minced celery*
> *1 cup sprouted Urad beans (page 147)*

Heat the sesame oil in a large wok or a large heavy frying pan over a moderately high flame. Stir in the sunflower seeds, the salt, and the pepper and sauté about 1 minute, or until the seeds are just browning. Add the zucchini and carrots and toss with the seeds, frying for about a minute. Then add the minced celery and the sprouts, and cook another minute. Turn off the heat, cover, and prepare the barley or bulgur for serving.

FOR KAPHA

> *2 cups water*
> *½ teaspoon salt*
> *¾ cup pearled or hulled barley*
> *2 teaspoons olive oil*

In a heavy 1-quart pan bring the water to a boil. Add the salt and the rinsed barley. Cover and simmer gently for 40 minutes, or until the barley is soft but still holds its shape. When it is done, toss it with the olive oil, cover, and set aside until ready to serve.

FOR VATA AND PITTA

> *2 cups water*
> *1 cup bulgur or cracked wheat*
> *2 teaspoons olive oil*

Bring the water to a boil. Place the bulgur in a 1-quart bowl. Pour the water over. Cover and set aside for about 15 or 20 minutes until the bulgur is tender. Drain off any excess water. Pour on olive oil and toss with a fork. Cover until ready to serve.

JUST BEFORE SERVING

> *½ teaspoon olive oil*
> *1 teaspoon crushed sage*
> *2 teaspoons minced fresh thyme or*
> *½ teaspoon crushed dried*
> *Lemon wedges*

In a heavy frying pan heat ½ teaspoon olive oil. Add the cooked barley, the sage, and the thyme; mix well and heat thoroughly. Mound on a serving plate with an indentation in the center. Pile the sautéed vegetables on top. Decorate with lemon wedges.

ZUCCHINI AND TOMATO FRY

A satisfying and colorful main dish with sweet, sour, bitter, salty, and slightly pungent tastes, this dish can be enjoyed by Vata and in moderation by Kapha when served with couscous, pasta, or rice. It increases Pitta.

−V +P *K
Serves 4

> *2 tablespoons ghee*
> *1 teaspoon black mustard seeds*
> *1 teaspoon cumin seeds, roasted and crushed*
> *1 teaspoon ground coriander*
> *¼ teaspoon lightly roasted and ground fenugreek*
> *1 teaspoon turmeric*
> *½ teaspoon ground ginger*
> *4 medium zucchini, peeled, quartered, and sliced*
> * thin*
> *2 to 3 tomatoes, peeled, seeded, and sliced*
> *½ teaspoon salt, or to taste*

Heat the ghee in a large frying pan or wok over moderate heat. Add the mustard seeds. When they begin to pop, add the remaining spices. Stir-fry over low heat for 1 minute. Then add the zucchini and increase the heat to moderately high. Fry, uncovered, until just tender. Stir frequently. Add the tomatoes and the salt. Stir and cook for 3 or 4 minutes more. Serve with rice or pasta.

Pies and Pastries

ALMOND CUSTARD FRESH FRUIT PIE

A sweet, easily digested pie that is good for building muscles, bones, brain, and body tissues as well as fat, this dessert reduces Vata and Pitta rather than Kapha. When served warm, the filling alone makes a delicious custard that is also a nourishing dessert, especially for children and convalescents.

−V −P +K
Makes one 10-inch deep-dish pie or tart

FOR THE BUTTER CRUST

> *1¾ cups unbleached flour*
> *¼ teaspoon salt*
> *½ cup (1 stick) unsalted butter*
> *2 to 3 tablespoons cold water*

1. Preheat the oven to 425°F.
2. Mix the dry ingredients together in a 1-quart bowl. Cut in the butter until it is just mealy looking. Sprinkle 2 tablespoons water over the mixture and blend lightly with a fork. Add the remaining water as needed to make the dough form a ball. Roll it gently between wax paper or on a lightly floured surface. Place the dough in a pie pan or a tart shell, flute the edges, prick it a few times on the bottom and sides with a fork, and bake for 12 to 15 minutes. Cool the crust before filling.

FOR THE FILLING

> *¼ cup cornstarch*
> *½ cup sugar*
> *2 cups half-and-half*
> *2 cups whipping cream*
> *1½ cups very finely ground blanched almonds*
> *2 teaspoons almond extract*
> *1½ cups fresh fruit, such as whole or sliced*
>   *strawberries, raspberries, or sliced*
>   *kiwifruit and apricots*

Mix the cornstarch and the sugar in a heavy 2-quart pan. Cook over moderate heat, slowly stirring in the half-and-half and cream. Stir constantly and when just beginning to thicken, add the ground almonds. Lower the heat and simmer, stirring until the mixture is thick and just at the boiling point. Do not allow it to boil. Remove from the heat and stir in the almond extract. Pour into the baked pie shell. Refrigerate at least 4 hours before serving. Decorate with fruit just before serving.

AMERICAN APPLE PIE

This pleasantly spicy pie is sweet, heavy, and very easy to make. If you reduce the sugar and the cardamom, Kapha can eat some of this pie. Or use the Apple Pie Filling Without Sugar recipe (page 198).

−V −P +K
Makes one 10-inch pie

> *Piecrust dough for top and bottom of a 10-inch pie (page 202)*
> *3 to 4 cups apples (about 6 to 8 large), peeled, cored, and chopped*
> *½ cup granulated sugar*
> *4 tablespoons light brown sugar, packed*
> *1½ teaspoons cinnamon*
> *¾ teaspoon cardamom*
> *¼ teaspoon nutmeg*
> *Juice of 1 lemon*

1. Preheat the oven to 375°F.
2. Mix all the ingredients together in a large bowl.
3. Roll out half the piecrust dough on a floured surface. Carefully place it in a pan without tearing it. Heap the apple mixture toward the center of the pan. Roll out the rest of the dough and lay it on the apples. Seal the edges well and slit vents in the top to allow steam to escape. Bake on a cookie sheet for about 1 hour, or until the crust is nicely browned.

APPLE DUMPLINGS WITH VANILLA SAUCE

Everyone loves apple dumplings. They are sweet and heavy, good for Vata and Pitta and increasing for Kapha. (Kapha can have a small dumpling without the sauce.) This recipe's been tried and tested by many generations of the Weller family of Ohio. Try whole ripe peaches that are peeled and pitted for unforgettable dumplings, too. The Rich Dumpling Crust makes an excellent pastry for all cream and fruit pies because it doesn't get soggy.

−V −P +K
Serves 4 to 5

FOR THE RICH DUMPLING CRUST

> *¾ cup (1½ sticks) cold unsalted butter or shortening*
> *1½ cups unbleached flour*
> *½ teaspoon salt*
> *1 teaspoon plain yogurt*
> *1½ teaspoons white vinegar*
> *2½ tablespoons cold water*

Cut the butter into the flour and the salt. Mix the yogurt, the vinegar, and the water together, then stir the liquids into the dough. Form into a ball, cover, and chill while preparing the apples.

FOR THE FILLING

> *½ cup light brown sugar, packed*
> *1 teaspoon cinnamon*
> *4 to 5 baking apples, peeled and cored*
> *4 to 5 tablespoons unsalted butter*
> *Vanilla Sauce (recipe follows)*

1. Preheat the oven to 425°F.
2. In a small bowl mix the brown sugar and the cinnamon together.
3. Roll out the dough on a floured surface to about ⅛ inch thick. Cut it into 4 or 5 equal squares, about 4 inches by 4 inches. Place an apple in the center of each square, fill each cored apple with a tablespoon of the brown sugar mixture, and top it with a tablespoon of butter. Wrap the pastry over the apple, sealing it well. Use a little milk or water to seal the edges closed.
4. Place dumplings on a baking sheet with sides and bake for 10 minutes. Reduce the heat to 350°F. for 30 more minutes, or until nicely brown. Serve warm with plenty of Vanilla Sauce.

Vanilla Sauce

When served warm in a pitcher or a small gravy boat, Vanilla Sauce makes something special of fruit dumplings, unfrosted cakes, waffles, pancakes, and apple pie. The sweet taste decreases Vata and Pitta and increases Kapha.

−V −P +K
Makes 2½ cups

> *¾ cup sugar*
> *2 tablespoons cornstarch*
> *¼ teaspoon salt*
> *2 cups boiling water*
> *¼ cup raisins or currants (optional)*
> *1 tablespoon vanilla*
> *4 tablespoons unsalted butter*
> *Dash of nutmeg*

Mix the dry ingredients in a heavy saucepan. Add the boiling water and the raisins. Stir constantly over moderate heat until the sauce shimmers and looks clear and thickened, about 5 to 10 minutes. Remove from the heat and stir in the vanilla, the butter, and the nutmeg. Continue stirring until the butter is melted. Serve warm. Refrigerate and reheat as needed. This sauces keeps for 2 or 3 days, covered, in the refrigerator.

APPLE PIE FILLING WITHOUT SUGAR

For those watching their weight but still wishing to eat a delicious slice of apple pie or a turnover, this is the filling to choose. The wheat flour crust will add to its Kapha-increasing properties, but not very much. It reduces Vata and Pitta.

−V −P +K
One 9- or 10-inch pie

> *Piecrust dough for top and bottom of 9- or 10-inch pie*
>   *(pages 202–203)*
> *10 medium baking apples (8 to 9 large),*
>   *Granny Smith, Jonathan, Winesap, or Rome*
> *Juice of 1 large lemon, or 1 orange, or 2 limes*
> *¾ cup raisins*
> *3 tablespoons cornstarch*
> *2 tablespoons cinnamon*
> *¾ teaspoon nutmeg*
> *¼ teaspoon freshly ground cardamom*

1. Preheat the oven to 425°F.
2. Peel and slice the apples very thinly. Add the remaining ingredients and mix thoroughly.
3. Roll out half the piecrust dough on a floured surface. Carefully place it in a pan without tearing. Heap the apples toward the center of the pan. Roll out the rest of the dough and lay it on the apples. Seal the edges well and cut slits in the top. Bake on a cookie sheet for 15 minutes at 425°F., then reduce the heat to 350°F. and bake 45 minutes longer.

CHOCOLATE CUSTARD PIE

This delicious, sweet, unctuous (oily), astringent, bitter pie filling decreases Vata and Pitta and increases Kapha. It is useful for increasing weight. For a simple dessert that serves 6 to 8 people, prepare the chocolate custard as a pudding and top with a dusting of confectioners' sugar, whipped cream, or fresh fruit.

−V −P +K
One 9-inch pie

> *Dough for 9-inch pie (pages 202–203),*
>   *halve recipe for single crust*
> *¼ cup semisweet chocolate chips*
> *¼ cup cornstarch*
> *½ cup sugar*
> *1 pint half-and-half*
> *1 pint whipping cream*
> *½ teaspoon vanilla extract*
> *6 ounces semisweet chocolate chips*
> *1 cup sweetened whipped cream*
> *Shaved bitter chocolate (optional)*

1. Prepare one-half recipe of piecrust dough.

2. In a small bowl mix the cornstarch and the sugar together and set aside. Heat the half-and-half and cream over low heat or in the top of a double boiler. Add a small amount, about a tablespoon, of steaming cream to the dry ingredients and whisk to blend. When smooth, pour the mixture slowly into the rest of the warm cream, whisking all the time. Stir constantly until thickened. Remove from the heat and add the vanilla and the 6 ounces semisweet chocolate chips. Stir until blended. Cover with plastic wrap placed directly on the filling and refrigerate until cold, about 4 hours.

3. Meanwhile, bake the piecrust. When it comes out of the oven, spread the ¼ cup chocolate chips evenly on the bottom and let cool. If the chips do not melt entirely, slip the pan back in the turned-off oven for a minute or two. Then spread them evenly across the crust.

4. When ready to serve, fill the cooled shell with the custard and top with the sweetened whipped cream and the chocolate shavings.

SWEDISH CHOCOLATE CREAM PIE

A luscious, richly creamy, slightly sour pie made sweet and very unctuous with white chocolate. This is a real winner for Vata and Pitta. It
is a quick, no-bake pie that uses any sweet, seasonally available fruits
to advantage.

−v *p +k
Makes one 10-inch pie

> *1 prebaked 10-inch piecrust*
> *2½ tablespoons cornstarch or arrowroot*
> *2 cups milk*
> *3 tablespoons sugar*
> *4 ounces white chocolate, broken in pieces*
> *1 teaspoon vanilla extract*
> *8 ounces sour cream*
> *2 cups berries, sliced peaches, or other sweet fruit*
> *1 cup stiffly whipped cream*

Mix the cornstarch and ⅓ cup milk in a heavy saucepan. Add the
remaining milk and sugar, then stir over moderately low flame until at
the boiling point. Stir vigorously for 5 minutes to cook the cornstarch.
Add the white chocolate and continue stirring for 5 more minutes.
Remove from the heat and beat in the vanilla and the sour cream.
Turn into the piecrust and freeze for 30 minutes if you are in a hurry,
or chill the pie in the refrigerator for at least 2 hours. Then decorate it
with whole or sliced fruit, pipe on whipped cream, and refrigerate
until ready to serve.

STRAWBERRY YOGURT PIE

This makes a pretty pie that is not too filling to eat after a big meal. Its
sour, sweet, cold, oily, and heavy properties decrease Vata, are neutral
for Pitta, and increase Kapha. It is a good pie to serve as a luncheon
dessert or in the afternoon with tea. Because of the sour yogurt, it
should not be eaten too late at night.

−v *p +k
One 9-inch pie

1 prebaked 9-inch pie shell, cooled
1 4-ounce package cream cheese
8 ounces kefir cheese or ricotta cheese
1 8-ounce container strawberry yogurt
4 tablespoons sugar
1 cup sliced strawberries
10 to 12 whole strawberries, or more to taste,
   washed and stemmed

Blend the cheeses together. Add the yogurt and the sugar. Blend well. Refrigerate until just firm (about 30 minutes). Spread the sliced fruit on the bottom of the baked piecrust and cover it with the yogurt mixture. Refrigerate until ready to serve (about 3 to 4 hours) and decorate with the whole strawberries before serving.

SWEET POTATO–APPLE PIE

This is a sweet, heavy dessert for Vata and Pitta diets. When made without the sugar and the piecrust, it's a tasty side dish to a main meal.

−V −P +K
Makes one 8-inch pie

1 unbaked 8-inch single piecrust
1 large sweet potato, baked
1 large sweet apple, peeled and shredded
⅛ cup sweet orange, pineapple, or apple juice
¼ cup light brown sugar, packed
¼ cup finely ground blanched almonds or
   ¼ cup dried coconut
¼ teaspoon cinnamon
⅛ teaspoon ginger and nutmeg, combined

1. Preheat the oven to 350°F.
2. Peel the potato and mash it with the other ingredients. Spread on the piecrust. Bake for 30 to 40 minutes, or until the crust is nicely browned and the tines of a fork poked in the center come out clean. Cool at least 10 minutes before cutting.

SOME FAVORITE PIECRUSTS

All these piecrusts are made from wheat flour. They all decrease Vata and Pitta and increase Kapha.

BUTTER PIECRUST

Use all white flour or, for a nicely browned, nutritious crust, two-thirds white flour and one-third whole wheat flour.

−V −P +K
Makes two 10-inch crusts

> *3 cups unbleached flour*
> *¼ teaspoon salt*
> *1 cup (2 sticks) cold unsalted butter*
> *3 to 4 tablespoons ice water*

Mix the flour and the salt together, then cut in the butter with a pastry cutter, a steel blade in a food processor, or chop with a knife until the pieces are the size of currants or small peas. Add the ice water a tablespoon at a time, and stir lightly just until the dough will hold together to form a ball. Roll out on a floured surface to about ⅛ inch thick. Try not to stretch or handle the dough more than necessary or it will become tough. Lay it gently in the pie pan, fill, then lay the other crust on top. Seal the edges by pinching them together, slit a steam hole in the top, and bake.

OIL PASTRY

This is a flaky crust that can be made quickly in a food processor using the steel blade; it can also be made by stirring with a fork. Use a very mild-flavored oil for dessert pies.

−V −P +K
Makes two 9-inch crusts

> *2 cups unbleached flour*
> *1 teaspoon salt*
> *½ cup oil*
> *4 to 5 tablespoons cold water*

1. Preheat the oven to 425°F.

2. In a food processor bowl, mix the flour and the salt. In a separate cup, first pour the oil, then 4 tablespoons water, but do not mix. Pour them slowly into the processor while it is running. It should make a soft dough. Add a little more water, if necessary. Roll out on a floured surface, or press right into the bottom of the pie pan with your fingers.

3. Halve the recipe for a single filled pie. Prick with a fork and bake for 12 minutes. Cool before filling.

SIMPLE COOKIE CRUST

This basic, sweet crust can be used for all cream pies. Sweet and oily, it increases Kapha but is good for Pitta and Vata. You can make this piecrust ahead of time and freeze it for an instant crust when you're unexpectedly entertaining or in a hurry.

−V −P +K
Makes two 8-inch crusts or one 10-inch crust

> 2 cups graham cracker or other cookie crumbs
> ½ cup ghee or unsalted butter
> 4 tablespoons granulated or raw sugar

1. Preheat the oven to 400°F.

2. Mix all the ingredients in a food processor with a steel blade or in a large bowl. Press the mixture into a pie pan and bake for 5 to 8 minutes, until just tan-colored. Cool and fill.

Cookies

CASHEW NUT BALLS OR SQUARES

Cashew Nut Balls, in the Indian cuisine known as laddus (LAH-dooz), are melt-in-the-mouth, unbaked sweets like a cookie and candy combined. The dough of these stovetop cookies, if not made in balls, can be pressed into a 9-inch square pan, dusted with confectioners' sugar, and cut into 1-inch squares when hardened. This nutritious, sweet, astringent, unctuous, and slightly heavy dessert is nourishing for Vata and Pitta, and one or two are good for Kapha, too.

−V −P +K

Makes 1½ to 2 dozen

> *1 teaspoon ghee*
> *¼ cup broken unsalted cashews*
> *¼ cup ghee*
> *1 cup besan (garbanzo or chick-pea) flour, from Asian*
>   *or natural food store, and ½ cup whole wheat flour*
>   *or 1½ cups whole wheat flour*
> *½ teaspoon cardamom (6 green cardamom pods),*
>   *seeded and ground*
> *¼ teaspoon licorice root powder (optional)*
> *¾ cup raw sugar or packed light brown sugar*
> *2 tablespoons ghee*

1. Melt 1 teaspoon ghee in a small pan over low heat. Sprinkle the nuts evenly over the bottom of the pan and stir-fry until lightly toasted. Remove from the heat and finely chop them with the ghee in a nut grinder. Set aside.

2. In a large skillet or heavy pan, heat ¼ cup ghee over moderate heat. Add the besan and cook over low heat, stirring constantly, until the mixture is a golden tan color, about 5 minutes. Watch carefully not to allow the flour to get too dark. It can easily burn once it turns brown. Roasting the flour makes it more digestible. Remove the pan from the heat and add the other ingredients, stirring well. The dough will leave the sides of the pan and be thick when well mixed. Spread the dough evenly over the bottom of the pan and allow it to cool until it can be handled, about 10 minutes. It will look somewhat crumbly. Using your fingertips, press and roll each cookie into a small ball, smaller than a golf ball. Rub your hands with a little ghee if the dough sticks too much.

3. Arrange cookies on a large plate as they are rolled. Set the cookies aside for at least an hour, or until they are hard, before serving.

4. Store in a tightly sealed container.

FRESH GINGER COOKIES

Here is a cookie that is easy to make and good for all doshas. It's one of those rare desserts that Kapha can eat in more than small amounts. These cookies reduce Kapha and Vata and have a neutral effect on Pitta when eaten in moderation, but the decidedly pungent taste may not appeal to the Pitta palate. They are sweet, pungent, salty, and astringent. Made entirely of barley flour, one of Kapha's best grains, and a generous amount of ginger, eating them actually benefits weight watchers. Both Vata and Pitta may prefer substituting some whole wheat flour for the barley. Fresh ginger makes these cookies sparkle!

These cookies travel well for sending as gifts.

−V *P −K
Makes about 2 dozen

> 4 cups barley flour or 3 cups barley flour
>   and 1 cup white or whole wheat flour
> ½ cup unbleached flour
> 2 teaspoons baking soda
> ¼ teaspoon salt
> 1 teaspoon cinnamon
> ¼ teaspoon cloves (omit for Pitta)
> ½ cup oil or ghee
> 1⅓ cups light molasses or corn syrup
> 2 tablespoons finely grated fresh ginger
>   or 1 tablespoon ground

1. Preheat the oven to 325°F.
2. Mix all the ingredients together in the given order and let the batter rest for 5 or 10 minutes until it can be rolled into 1-inch balls. Or drop the batter in heaping teaspoonfuls on a greased baking sheet. Bake the cookies for 12 to 15 minutes, or until they are lightly browned. The centers will be soft. Cool on a rack and store securely when they are completely cool.

NOTE: To make these more enjoyable for Pitta types, reduce the amount of ginger by half. Even then, Pitta should eat only 1 or 2 of these pungent cookies. There are many other cookies better for Pitta to eat than these.

❖❖

ITALIAN HAZELNUT COOKIES

These delicate cookies are sweet, bitter, astringent, dry, and good for all doshas. When they are made with a blend of wheat and barley flours, they are better for Kapha to eat. If you don't have barley flour, use all white flour. The anise flavor develops best when the cookies are stored in a sealed container for a day or two before eating.

−V −P *K
Makes 2½ dozen

> *1 cup (2 sticks) butter, softened at room temperature*
> *¼ cup granulated sugar*
> *2 teaspoons anise extract*
> * or 3 teaspoons finely ground fresh anise seeds*
> *½ cup barley flour and 1½ cups unbleached white flour*
> * or 2 cups unbleached white flour*
> *¼ teaspoon salt*
> *¾ cup finely ground hazelnuts or pecans*
> *¾ cup confectioners' sugar*

1. Preheat the oven to 300°F.
2. Cream the butter and the sugar together. Mix in the anise extract or the freshly ground seeds. Measure the flour and salt in a separate bowl and mix together thoroughly. Stir in the nuts, then add the dry ingredients to the butter mixture. Shape into balls or 2 × 2½-inch crescents. Spread the confectioners' sugar on a large plate and roll each cookie in it. Bake on ungreased cookie sheets in the center of the oven until they are faintly brown, about 10 to 12 minutes. (Gently turn one cookie over to test for color.) When they are cool, roll each one again in confectioners' sugar.

JAM DIAGONALS

A fancy and easily made bar cookie that is a fine treat for Vata and Pitta, it adds sweet and heavy aspects to a meal. These cookies are quickly made using a food processor with a steel blade.

−V −P +K
Makes about 2 dozen cookies

¼ cup sugar
½ cup (1 stick) unsalted butter, softened
1 teaspoon vanilla extract
⅛ teaspoon salt
1¼ cups flour
½ cup strawberry or raspberry jam
⅔ cup confectioners' sugar
1 tablespoon lemon or orange juice

1. Preheat the oven to 350°F.

2. For the dough, beat the sugar, the butter, the vanilla, and the salt together in a mixing bowl until fluffy. Stir in the flour and blend well. Divide the dough into thirds. Using your hands, roll each third into a 9-inch rope. Place each rope 3 inches apart on an ungreased cookie sheet. Using your fingertips, make a ½-inch depression down the center of each rope. The ropes will flatten to 1-inch-wide strips. Fill the depressions with the jam. Bake for 12 to 15 minutes, or until they are golden. Cool on the sheet.

3. For the icing, blend the confectioners' sugar and the lemon juice in a small bowl until smooth, then drizzle over the thoroughly cooled jam. When the icing is set, cut diagonally in 1-inch bars.

NOTE: If you are in a hurry, there is an alternate way of making these. Simply spread the dough in a pie pan or 8-inch square pan, then fill with jam, bake, and frost as directed. Cut into squares before removing from the pan.

LEMONY DATE BARS

These sprightly-tasting bar cookies are not only sweet and delicious, but they are good for you, too. The fruit and grain combinations are especially nourishing for Vata and Pitta, but they also increase Kapha by building muscles and tissues. Because they are so nutritious everyone can eat them in moderation. When they are cut in 3- or 4-inch squares and served in small bowls with heavy cream poured over the top, they make a fine dessert for Vata and Pitta.

−V −P +K
Makes 1½ dozen

> 2 cups (20 ounces) chopped pitted dates
> ⅔ cup granulated or raw sugar
> 1 cup water
> Peel of a large lemon to yield ¼ cup, coarsely chopped
> Juice of ½ lemon
> 1 cup unbleached flour
> 1 cup whole wheat flour
> 2 cups packed light brown sugar
> 1 teaspoon salt
> 1 cup (2 sticks) unsalted butter
> 3 cups quick-cooking oats
> ⅓ cup buttermilk or ½ cup yogurt
> 2 teaspoons vanilla extract

1. Preheat the oven to 350°F.
2. In a heavy saucepan, cook the dates, the granulated sugar, and the water until thick and well blended. Add the lemon peel and juice to the date mixture. Stir well and cool. Mix the flours, the brown sugar, and the salt together in a large bowl. Cut in the butter until well blended. Add the oats and mix well. Stir the milk and the vanilla together, then blend into dough. Pack a thin layer of dough on the bottom of a greased 13 × 9-inch pan or two 8 × 8-inch pans. Spread the fruit on top and pat the remaining dough over the fruit. The dough does not have to cover the fruit completely; it will spread during baking. Bake 30 to 40 minutes, until top is brown. Cool, cut into bite-size bars.

MOTHER'S LADDU

These sweet, unctuous (oily) cookies are both nourishing and satisfying. They are recommended for a new mother's diet, but anyone can eat them, especially those following a regular Vata- or Pitta-reducing diet. Kapha could have one or two. If there is not enough time to roll them into balls, just pat the dough into an 8-inch square pan and allow it to set until firm, then cut into 1-inch squares. The Cashew Nut Balls (pages 203–204) recipe is a variation on this one.

−V −P +K
Makes about 1½ dozen

> ¼ cup ghee
> 3 tablespoons finely ground blanched almonds
> ¾ cup unbleached white flour
> ½ cup besan (garbanzo or chick-pea flour)
> ½ cup whole wheat flour, or if besan is
> unavailable, 1 cup whole wheat flour
> ½ teaspoon cardamom (6 green cardamom
> pods), seeded and ground
> ¼ teaspoon ground ginger
> ¾ cup packed light brown sugar, or raw sugar
> 2 tablespoons ghee

1. In a large skillet or heavy pan heat ¼ cup ghee over moderate heat. When just steamy, add the almonds and flour(s) and cook over low heat, stirring frequently, until golden. Watch carefully not to allow the flour to get too dark; it can easily burn once it gets brown. Remove from the heat and add the other ingredients, stirring well. The dough will leave the sides of the pan and be thick when it is well mixed. Spread the dough evenly over the bottom of the pan and allow it to cool until it can be handled, about 10 minutes. Roll each laddu into a bite-size ball smaller than a golf ball. Rub your hands with some ghee if the dough sticks too much.

2. Arrange the laddus on a plate as they are rolled. Before serving, set them aside for at least an hour, or until they are hard.

3. Store in a tightly sealed container.

OATMEAL RAISIN COOKIES

Highly nutritious and tasty, these cookies ship well and are very good for dunking. Both Vata and Pitta can eat these sweet, heavy, slightly salty cookies. They increase Kapha but are so nutritious that Kapha can occasionally have a couple.

−V −P *K
Makes 4 to 5 dozen

½ cup (1 stick) butter or vegetable shortening
⅓ cup oil
1 cup granulated sugar
1 cup packed light brown sugar
⅓ cup yogurt
2 tablespoons water
2 teaspoons vanilla extract
1½ cups unbleached white flour
1 cup whole wheat flour
1 teaspoon baking soda
1 teaspoon baking powder
1 teaspoon salt
3 cups quick-cooking oats
1 cup raisins
½ cup broken walnuts

1. Preheat the oven to 350°F.
2. Cream the butter and the oil. Then add the sugars and cream together well. Add the yogurt, water, and vanilla. In a separate bowl mix together the flours, the baking soda, the baking powder, and the salt. Stir these dry ingredients into the sugar mixture. Add the oats, the raisins, and the nuts. Mix with your fingers if it is too thick to stir. Shape the dough into balls and flatten slightly. Place them close together, but not touching, on greased baking sheets. Bake 15 minutes, or until they are just turning brown underneath.

SIMPLE SHORTBREAD

A rich unleavened dessert for everyone, although in moderation for Kapha shortbread can be served most festively with jam spread on top and then dusted with powdered sugar.

−V −P *K
Makes 1 dozen

½ pound (2 sticks) unsalted, slightly softened butter
½ cup raw or granulated sugar, or more to taste
2 cups unbleached flour
¼ teaspoon salt

1. Preheat the oven to 350°F.
2. Cream the butter thoroughly with the sugar. A food processor with a steel blade does this job well. Mix the flour and the salt together, then add them to the butter mixture. Roll or pat out the dough to a ¼-inch thickness, cut into 1 × 2-inch rectangles, and prick several times with a fork. Place on an ungreased baking sheet with the sides not touching. Bake 20 to 25 minutes, or until they are light brown on the edges.
3. Or pat the dough into a 9-inch pie pan, prick all over the top with the tines of a fork, and bake 25 to 30 minutes. Cut when warm.

NOTE: For Kapha and Vata, fold in ½ cup coarsely chopped crystallized ginger. For a Kapha-reducing diet, omit jam and sugar.

SUPER CHOCOLATE BROWNIES

For some people brownies are a popular picnic dessert. The particular combination of bitter, astringent, and sweet tastes, and the slightly dry quality of this rich cookie recipe is a good one for anyone who loves to eat chocolate. Kapha types should still eat moderately of them. The only thing wrong with these delicious brownies is that they are so moist when they first come out of the oven that you have to wait until they are completely cool to cut them. They are best made by hand and not in a food processor or with an electric beater.

*V *P *K
Makes 1 dozen

> 2 squares (2 ounces) unsweetened chocolate
> ½ cup (1 stick) unsalted butter or ghee
> ⅓ cup unbleached flour
> 1¼ cups cool water
> ½ teaspoon salt
> 2 teaspoons vanilla extract
> ½ cup cocoa (best quality available)
> 2 cups unbleached flour
> 2 teaspoons baking powder
> 2 cups sugar
> 1 cup coarsely chopped pecans or blanched almonds

1. Grease a 7 × 11-inch pan. Preheat the oven to 350°F.

2. Melt and stir the chocolate and the butter together in a small heavy pan over low heat. Set aside when it is well blended. In a small saucepan, mix ⅓ cup flour with a little water to make a paste, then add the remaining water and cook over moderate heat, whisking constantly, until thickened, about 5 minutes. A few lumps are okay. Remove from the heat and stir in the salt, the vanilla, and the chocolate mixture.

3. Measure the cocoa, unbleached flour, and baking powder into a large bowl. Stir well or sift together. Mix in the sugar, the liquid mixture, and the nuts. Stir until just blended, about 1 minute. The mixture will look very thick. Spread it into the pan and bake for 30 to 40 minutes on the center oven rack. The brownies are done when they just start to leave the edges of the pan. For moist brownies, a knife inserted in the middle will not come out completely clean. Remove from the oven and cool completely before cutting.

TOASTY CINNAMON BAR COOKIES

Good for Vata and Pitta and increasing Kapha, these cookies are delicious but simple treats to make. They just seem to disappear as soon as they are cut into bars.

−V −P +K
Makes 1½ dozen

FOR THE BATTER

>*2 cups unbleached flour*
>*1 cup sugar*
>*2 teaspoons baking powder*
>*1 cup milk*
>*1 tablespoon ghee or unsalted butter, melted*
>*1 teaspoon vanilla extract*
>*½ cup raisins*
>*½ cup chopped pecans*

Preheat oven to 350°F. Combine all the ingredients. Spread in a 15 × 10-inch sheet pan. Bake 20 minutes. While the bars bake, mix the topping.

FOR THE TOPPING

> ½ cup ghee or melted butter
> ½ cup sugar
> 1½ teaspoons cinnamon

Mix together and drizzle over the baked cookie dough, spreading evenly. Bake 10 more minutes. Cool and cut into bars.

FRUIT SHORTCAKE

A favorite American dessert, shortcake is quick to make and good for Vata and Pitta. With sweet, astringent, slightly salty tastes, and heavy and dry qualities, the cake alone is good for all doshas. But the addition of whipped cream and sweet fruit increases the sweet, cold, and heavy qualities. Since these increase Kapha, eating this dessert in moderation is necessary. This is not a dessert for weight watchers.

Sweet fruits like berries, sweet cherries, and ripe peaches are the best choices to serve with whipped cream. For strawberry shortcake select only the sweetest variety and lightly sprinkle them with sugar before using.

−V −P +K
Serves 6

FOR THE CAKE

> 2½ cups unbleached white flour or substitute
> ½ cup besan (garbanzo or chick-pea),
> whole wheat, or barley flour for ½ cup
> white flour
> 2 teaspoons baking powder
> ¼ cup sugar
> 4 tablespoons unsalted butter or ghee
> ½ cup milk

1. Grease an 8-inch square or round pan. Preheat the oven to 450°F.

2. In a large bowl sift or stir the dry ingredients together. Rub the butter in with your fingers. Add enough milk to make a soft dough. Pat the dough into a baking pan and bake for 15 to 20 minutes, or until the cake is slightly brown on top.

3. Cool and remove the cake from the pan.

BEFORE SERVING

> *4 cups fresh fruit, peeled and cut in bite-size pieces*
> *½ cup confectioners' sugar*
> *1 cup whipping cream*
> *1 teaspoon vanilla extract*

Sprinkle the fruit with the sugar (less than 1 tablespoon) and set it aside for at least 20 minutes. Whip the cream, adding the reserved sugar and the vanilla. Using a serrated knife, split the shortcake in half, then fill it with most of the fruit. Serve with whipped cream on top and the remaining fruit.

MARBLE CRUMB CAKE WITH VANILLA SAUCE AND ENGLISH CREAM

This heavenly cake, simply made by layering a crumb cake mixture with sweet syrup and then tracing swirls in the batter with a knife to marble, is served with a pitcher of warm Vanilla Sauce and English Cream, unsweetened heavy cream whipped with cream cheese. Its tastes, sweet, oily, slightly sour, are all good for Vata, with neutral effects for Pitta. Kapha would eat just a small slice of this cake without the sauce and whipped cream.

−V *P +K

Serves 4 to 6

2½ cups unbleached flour
1 teaspoon baking powder
Dash of salt
¼ cup granulated sugar
¾ cup firmly packed dark brown sugar
¾ cup (1½ sticks) unsalted butter
½ cup corn syrup
½ cup light molasses
1 teaspoon baking soda
1 cup boiling water
Vanilla Sauce (pages 197–198)
English Cream (recipe follows)

1. Grease an 8 × 8 × 2-inch baking pan. Preheat the oven to 375°F.

2. Measure the flour into a mixing bowl or a food processor with a steel blade. Add the baking powder, the salt, and the sugars. Blend well. Cut in the butter until it resembles coarse crumbs. In a small bowl combine the corn syrup, the molasses, the baking soda, and the boiling water.

3. Press 1 cup of the crumb mixture firmly into the bottom of the baking pan. Pour in ⅔ cup of the syrup mixture. Spread another crumb layer on top, followed by syrup. Make 3 layers in all. Sprinkle the remaining crumb mixture on top. Using a knife or spatula, gently cut through the batter in swirling motions to marble. Avoid cutting through to the bottom pressed crumb layer. Bake in the center of the oven for about 45 minutes, until it looks firm and brown and a cake tester comes out clean. Cool on a rack.

4. When ready to serve, cut into 3- or 4-inch squares, pour on generous amounts of Vanilla Sauce, and top each serving with a dollop of English Cream.

English Cream

As an unsweetened garnish for cakes and for spreading on scones, this sour, cold, heavy cream is better for Vata than for Pitta or Kapha.

−V *P +K

Makes 1 cup

3 tablespoons cream cheese
½ pint heavy cream
¼ teaspoon vanilla extract

Whip ingredients together until soft and fluffy.

GINGER SPICE CAKE WITH LEMON SAUCE

This is a simple cake to make for Vata and Kapha. Pitta would eat less of this pungent and sweet unfrosted cake. It's one of those cozy, old-fashioned cakes especially nice to serve on a cold winter afternoon.

−V +P −K
Makes an 8-inch square cake

1½ cups unbleached flour
½ cup sugar
¾ teaspoon baking powder
¾ teaspoon baking soda
½ teaspoon salt
1 teaspoon cinnamon
¼ teaspoon allspice
¼ teaspoon nutmeg
¼ cup warm ghee or unsalted butter, melted
¼ cup light corn syrup
½ cup buttermilk
2 teaspoons grated fresh ginger or 1 teaspoon ground
3 tablespoons plain yogurt
Lemon Sauce (recipe follows)

1. Grease and flour an 8-inch square pan. Preheat the oven to 350°F.
2. Mix the dry ingredients and the spices together. In a small pan, thoroughly heat the ghee and blend the corn syrup, the buttermilk, and the grated ginger. Add the yogurt to the dry ingredients and beat for 2 minutes until smooth. Add a little water if the batter is too thick to pour. Pour into the pan and bake 30 minutes, or just until it leaves

the sides of the pan and the center comes out clean when tested with a toothpick. Allow the cake to cool before cutting. Serve with a small pitcher of Lemon Sauce.

Lemon Sauce

This is a refreshing topping for plain and spicy cakes that is good for Vata. The sour taste of this sauce increases Pitta and Kapha somewhat.

−V +P +K
Makes about 1 cup

> ¾ *cup sugar*
> *1 tablespoon plus 2 teaspoons cornstarch*
> *Pinch of salt*
> ½ *cup boiling water*
> *1 teaspoon grated lemon peel*
> *3 tablespoons lemon juice (juice of ½ large lemon)*
> *3 tablespoons unsalted butter*

Mix the sugar, the cornstarch, and the salt in a small saucepan. Whisk in the boiling water and simmer for 10 minutes over moderate heat. Add the remaining ingredients and stir over low heat until the butter melts. Serve warm.

OLD-FASHIONED ORANGE TEA CAKE

A wonderfully rich, orange-flavored, moist old-fashioned cake, its sweet, nourishing, heavy, and oily properties are best for Vata and Pitta. Dates add to the elegant heaviness of this cake, but currants or raisins give it a little more delicacy. Be sure to use just the zest, the orange-colored part of the peel.

−V *P +K
Makes one 9-inch tube cake or 2 loaves

Zest of 3 oranges
1 cup chopped dates, raisins, or currants
1 cup sugar
½ cup unsalted butter
6 tablespoons plain yogurt
¾ cup buttermilk
1 teaspoon vanilla extract
2 cups unbleached flour
2 teaspoons baking soda
2 teaspoons baking powder
½ teaspoon salt
½ cup walnuts
2 tablespoons water

FOR THE ORANGE MARINADE

1 cup fresh orange juice
½ cup sugar
2 teaspoons vanilla extract

1. Grease a 9-inch tube pan or 2 loaf pans. Preheat oven to 325°F.

2. In a food processor or blender grind the orange peel and the dates together until they are chopped fine. Cream the sugar and the butter together. Add the yogurt, the buttermilk, and the vanilla and mix thoroughly. Fold in the fruit. Mix the dry ingredients separately and stir into the butter mixture. Finely grind the nuts and the water together and fold into the batter. Pour into pan(s). Bake for about 50 minutes, or until the cake tests done inserting a toothpick or a wooden skewer into the center. Do not open the oven before 40 minutes are up to check. This is one of those cakes that collapses if bothered too early. Let the cake stand for 15 minutes before removing it.

3. While the cake is baking mix the orange marinade. In a small pan heat and stir the marinade ingredients over a moderate flame until the sugar is dissolved. Then slowly pour the marinade over the cake a tablespoon at a time. Prick the cake all over with a long, thin skewer to let the marinade penetrate the cake. Cover the cake and set it aside until it is completely cool. Serve with softly whipped cream.

SWEET CHOCOLATE CAKE WITH CHERRY SAUCE

Like an elegant Black Forest cake but easier to make, this dessert is sweet, slightly bitter, oily, and heavy. It reduces Vata and Pitta and increases Kapha. The tofu and banana make it especially nourishing for body tissues. It can be made as an elaborate layer cake with a Rich Quick Chocolate Mousse filling, or simply in one layer topped with warm dark cherry sauce.

−V −P +K
Makes one 8-inch layer cake or a single sheet cake

FOR THE CAKE

> *½ cup (1 stick) unsalted butter*
> *3 ounces sweet baking chocolate*
> *2 cups unbleached flour, sifted*
> *1 cup sugar*
> *⅓ cup cocoa (the best quality)*
> *1 teaspoon baking powder*
> *1 teaspoon baking soda*
> *½ pound tofu*
> *½ cup milk*
> *1 small ripe banana*
> *1 teaspoon vanilla extract*
> *½ cup chopped pecans (optional)*

FOR THE CHERRY SAUCE

Makes 2 cups

> *1 package (16 ounces) frozen dark,*
>   *sweet cherries, defrosted*
> *2 tablespoons sugar*
> *1 tablespoon cornstarch*
> *1 tablespoon cool water*
> *½ teaspoon almond extract*
> *Rich Quick Chocolate Mousse (page*
>   *229)*

1. Preheat the oven to 350°F. Grease and dust with flour two 8-inch pans or a 7 × 11-inch sheet pan.

2. Melt the butter and the chocolate in a small pan over low heat. Stir until blended, then set it aside while preparing the other ingredients.

3. In a large bowl mix the dry ingredients together. Blend the tofu, the milk, and the banana in a food processor or with an electric mixer until it is thick and creamy.

4. Combine all the ingredients, including the vanilla and nuts, and pour the batter into the pans. Bake for 30 minutes, or until a knife inserted in the middle comes out clean. Allow the pans to rest for 5 to 10 minutes before removing the cakes. Cool before filling.

5. Meanwhile, make the Cherry Sauce. Heat the cherries in a saucepan over moderate heat. Add the sugar and stir until dissolved. Turn the heat to low and mix the cornstarch with the water in a cup, then stir into the cherries. Return to moderate heat and continue stirring for about 1 minute, until thickened. Remove from the heat and add the almond extract. Cool for 10 minutes before using.

6. The single-layer sheet cake can be cut in squares and served with warm Cherry Sauce and whipped cream. Or prepare the more elaborate layer cake.

7. To assemble the layer cake, spread 1½ cups Rich Quick Chocolate Mousse out to half an inch from the edge of the bottom layer. Gently place the second layer on top (this cake is very tender to handle), then spread the warm Cherry Sauce on top, allowing it to drizzle over the sides. Pipe the remaining mousse or plain, slightly sweetened whipped cream and shaved bitter chocolate over the top.

SWEET FRUIT AND SPICE TEA BREAD

The particular combination of fruits and spices in this sweet bread gives it all the qualities of food that is fundamentally nourishing for everyone as the basis of digestion. The preparation time is longer than for many other desserts, but this one is worth it. It is a sweet, astringent, slightly bitter dessert/breakfast bread good for nourishing all doshas. Although the ghee and the butter increase weight a bit, this delicious bread is very good for Vata and Pitta and nourishing for Kapha when eaten moderately.

−V −P *K
Makes 1 large loaf

FOR THE FILLING

½ cup dried apricots
½ cup dried peaches
½ cup pitted prunes
1 cup boiling water
1½ cups chopped blanched almonds
¾ cup poppy seeds
½ cup unsalted butter
½ cup packed dark brown sugar
2 teaspoons cinnamon

FOR THE DOUGH

2 tablespoons dry yeast (rapid rise–type works best)
¼ cup granulated or raw sugar
1½ cups heated apple juice
½ cup warm water
¼ cup ghee or unsalted butter, melted
1 teaspoon lemon peel
½ teaspoon cinnamon
½ teaspoon allspice
½ teaspoon nutmeg
¼ teaspoon cloves
1 teaspoon salt
2 cups whole wheat flour
3 to 4 cups unbleached white flour

FOR THE ICING

1 tablespoon orange juice
3 tablespoons confectioners' sugar

1. To make the filling, chop the dried fruit and place it in a 1-quart bowl. Pour enough boiling water over the fruit to cover. Cover and let stand for 4 or 5 hours or overnight. Soak the fruit until very soft.

When you are ready to mix the bread, measure 2 cups of the softened, drained fruit into a large mixing bowl with the remaining ingredients. Stir everything well. Set it aside while making the sweet dough.

2. Preheat the oven to 350°F.

3. To make the dough, blend the yeast, the sugar, the warm juice, and the water in a large bowl. Let sit for 5 to 10 minutes, until frothy. Add the ghee, the lemon peel, the spices, the salt, and the whole wheat flour. Blend everything together and then stir vigorously for 2 or 3 minutes. Stir in the white flour a cup at a time until a stiff dough is formed.

4. Turn it out on a floured board and knead until it is smooth and not sticky, about 10 minutes. Wash the bowl and rub it with a little ghee. Put the dough in the bowl, spread a little ghee on top to keep it moist, and cover it with plastic wrap or a clean towel. Let it rise in a warm place until double in bulk, about 1 hour. Punch it down, cover, and let it rise again until double in bulk, another hour. Or let it make the second rising in the refrigerator overnight if you are baking it as breakfast bread for the next morning.

5. Punch the dough down and turn it out on a lightly floured board. Roll into a long rectangle with a rolling pin. The size will be about 16 × 10 inches. Stir the filling again and spread evenly over the dough. Roll tightly, beginning at the long end. Pinch the ends together to close. Place on a greased baking sheet, cover, and let it rise about an hour, or until it is evenly puffy.

6. Bake the bread for 25 to 35 minutes, or until it is golden brown on top and sounds a little hollow when tapped on the bottom. Cool on a rack.

7. To make the icing, mix the orange juice and the confectioners' sugar together. Drizzle the icing over the top of the finished bread.

CREAMY RICE PUDDING

This rich, nourishing dessert is sweet, heavy, and slightly pungent. Rice pudding and other milk-based puddings are best for the digestion when served warm. Long, slow cooking over low heat allows the rice grains to blend so well with the other ingredients that it becomes a creamy, easily digested treat. This pudding is especially recommended for convalescents, new mothers, and young children.

−V −P +K
Serves 4 to 6

> *3 cups water*
> *2 cinnamon sticks*
> *1 cup long-grain rice*
> *3 cups boiled milk*
> *1 cup sugar*
> *½ cup raisins*
> *¼ teaspoon crumbled saffron threads*
> *½ cup very finely ground blanched almonds*

1. Bring the water and the cinnamon sticks to a boil in a large pot. Add the rice and simmer on low, covered, for about 15 to 20 minutes, or until the water evaporates and the rice is soft. Meanwhile, mix the hot milk, the sugar, the raisins, the saffron, and the ground almonds in a bowl and set aside.

2. When the rice is soft, add the milk mixture to the pot and cook over moderately high heat until just boiling. Reduce the heat to low and allow the pudding to simmer, uncovered, for 20 to 30 minutes. Stir frequently. The pudding is done when everything is well blended and the rice grains can barely be seen. Pour into dishes and serve warm.

KAFFA'S DREAM

An exceptionally rich dessert that is sweet, heavy, oily, bitter, and slightly sour, this is the kind of chocolate pudding, cream-filled with crunchy crust confection, that you would serve at the conclusion of a very special dinner or as a party treat. Children love it. Eating some of Kaffa's Dream reduces Vata and has a neutral effect on Pitta. Eating any more than a bite or two should remain a "dream" for Kapha.

−V *P +K
Makes 16 ramekins or one 7 × 11-inch pan

FOR THE CRUST

2¼ cups graham cracker crumbs
½ cup (1 stick) unsalted butter, melted
½ cup granulated sugar
½ to ¾ cup flaked coconut
¼ cup finely chopped pecans
1 15-ounce can sweetened condensed milk
8 ounces semisweet chocolate chips

1. Combine all the ingredients except the milk and the semisweet chocolate chips. Press two-thirds of the mixture into the pan or divide it evenly among the 16 ramekins or custard cups. Reserve one-third of the mixture.

2. Preheat the oven to 375°F.

3. Heat the milk in a saucepan over moderate heat. Blend in the chocolate chips and stir until the mixture thickens and the chocolate is well blended. Pour it over the crust, dividing it equally among the cups. Sprinkle with the remaining crumb mixture and press down lightly. Bake for 12 minutes. Set aside to cool while preparing the next 2 fillings.

FOR THE FILLINGS

8 ounces cream cheese,
*   softened*
1 cup confectioners' sugar
½ pint heavy cream, whipped
1 teaspoon vanilla extract
½ cup coarsely chopped
*   pecans*

Beat the cream cheese and the sugar together in a small bowl. Fold in the whipped cream and the vanilla. Spread it on top of the cooled chocolate crumb crust. Sprinkle this layer with nuts. Refrigerate while making the pudding.

FOR THE PUDDING

> *1 7-ounce package dark chocolate pudding, or make*
> *Chocolate Custard Pie filling (page 199), if*
> *you have time*
> *2¾ cups milk*
> *½ cup semisweet chocolate chips*

Mix the pudding with the milk following the package directions. Mix in the chocolate chips while the pudding simmers. Let it cool and then pour over the chilled cream mixture. Chill for 2 or 3 hours.

OPTIONAL FINISH: In case this is not *yet* rich enough, top with great dollops of sweetened whipped cream and garnish with some shaved bitter chocolate and a few fresh whole strawberries, raspberries, or other favorite fruit.

PINEAPPLE ICE

This is a perfect dessert for Pitta, especially on a hot day. It is easy to make and so like authentic Italian ices that for Pitta a dish of Pineapple Ice is a fine way to end an Italian meal. Because it is so cold and sweet, both Vata and Kapha should have much less of this dessert.

+V −P +K
Makes 1½ quarts

> *2 cups water*
> *¼ to ½ cup sugar, to taste*
> *2 cups cored and chopped fresh pineapple or 1 14-ounce can*
> *crushed pineapple*
> *¼ cup lemon juice*

Boil the water and the sugar together in a heavy saucepan for 4 to 5 minutes, stirring until the sugar is completely dissolved. Remove from the heat; stir in the pineapple and the lemon juice. When it is cool enough to touch pour the mixture into a shallow bowl. Put it in the freezer part of the refrigerator. After half an hour remove and stir vigorously. After about 30 minutes or when it is about half-frozen, whip with an electric mixer on medium for 1 minute. Freeze until firm, about 2 hours.

LEMON SCONES

Scones, a pleasant breakfast or teatime treat, are made like shortcake. Slivers of lemon peel, or orange peel if you prefer, add a delightful surprise. These scones are sweet, astringent, slightly salty, heavy, and dry. The astringent and dry aspects are good for Kapha. When eaten in moderation, scones are good for all doshas.

−v *p −k
Makes 1 dozen

> *2 cups unbleached flour and ½ cup besan (chick-pea)*
> *   or barley flour, or 2½ cups unbleached flour*
> *2 teaspoons baking powder*
> *¼ cup sugar*
> *4 tablespoons unsalted butter*
> *1 to 2 teaspoons coarsely chopped lemon peel*
> *   or any of the following:*
> *¼ cup raisins or currants*
> *2 large dates or prunes, chopped*
> *2 teaspoons chopped fresh or crystallized ginger*
> *¼ cup slivered dried apricots*
> *2 teaspoons chopped orange peel*
> *¼ cup toasted coconut*
> *2 tablespoons fennel seeds*
> *½ cup milk or buttermilk*

1. Grease a large baking sheet and preheat the oven to 475°F.
2. In a large bowl sift or stir the dry ingredients together. Cut the butter in with a pastry cutter or rub it with your fingers until the flour is mealy feeling. Add the lemon peel and enough milk to make a soft dough.
3. Roll or pat the dough out on a floured board to at least ½ inch thick. With a serrated or very sharp knife, cut it into triangles. Bake 10 to 12 minutes, until lightly brown. Serve warm.

PÊCHE CARDINAL

A recipe from the French dinner menu, this dessert is a combination of sweet tastes and heavy qualities that is good for both Vata and Pitta. Kapha types should eliminate the Chantilly Cream and eat lightly of this dish.

−V −P +K
Serves 6

> *4 cups water*
> *1½ cups sugar*
> *6 large peaches, peeled, halved, and pitted*
> *2 tablespoons vanilla extract*

In a heavy saucepan bring the water and the sugar to a boil over high heat, stirring constantly until the sugar dissolves. Boil for 3 minutes, then reduce the heat to simmer. Add the peaches and the vanilla. Simmer for 15 minutes, or until the peaches are barely tender when tested with a fork. Cover and refrigerate while preparing other ingredients.

FOR THE CARDINAL SAUCE

> *2 10-ounce packages frozen raspberries or 2 cups fresh raspberries, washed*
> *2 tablespoons fine granulated or confectioners' sugar*

Drain the raspberries in a sieve and puree with a wooden spoon. Discard the seeds and the pulp. Stir the sugar into the raspberry juice and refrigerate in a tightly covered container.

FOR THE CHANTILLY CREAM

> *½ cup heavy cream, chilled*
> *1½ tablespoons sugar, fine granulated or confectioners'*
> *2 teaspoons vanilla extract*

Whip the cream until it is thick. Sprinkle in the sugar and the vanilla. Continue beating until it is firm enough to hold soft peaks.

To serve, arrange the peach halves in individual dishes or on a platter. Spoon the Cardinal Sauce over each peach. Top with Chantilly Cream. Use the remaining peach cooking syrup for poaching other fruit or reduce it to a thick syrup and serve over pancakes or waffles.

R&S COUSCOUS

R & S (Rich and Satisfying) Couscous is a special Vata- and Pitta-reducing cereal to serve for breakfast or as a rather homey dessert.

For those who want a warm, filling start to the day, a quick, light evening meal, or something soothing on a day of light eating, prepare oatmeal, farina, rolled rye, or other cooked breakfast cereal with 1 or 2 teaspoons of ghee in the boiling water. Serve with warm milk or cream and sugar. It is a recommended recipe for convalescents.

−V −P +K
Makes 2½ cups

> 2 cups milk, or light cream for those who need to gain weight
> 1 cup couscous
> 1 tablespoon ghee
> ¼ to ½ cup raisins, currants, or chopped dates
> Warm light cream or milk
> Sugar to taste

Heat the milk over moderate heat until it is just ready to boil. Add the couscous and the ghee. Stir it vigorously with a wooden spoon until the liquid is almost absorbed. Stir in the fruit. When the cereal is steamy and begins to sizzle, remove from the heat. Cover and let sit for 5 to 10 minutes. Serve with warm cream or milk, and sugar.

RICH QUICK CHOCOLATE MOUSSE

This light chocolate mousse is useful either as a cake and pie filling or served by itself at the end of an elegant dinner. With its sweet, bitter, oily, and heavy properties, it is better for Pitta and Vata than Kapha. Kapha would only have a very small portion, if any at all.

*V − P + K
Makes 2 cups

> *2 cups heavy cream*
> *4 ounces (1 bar) sweet baking chocolate*
> *1 teaspoon vanilla extract*

Heat the cream in a heavy saucepan over low heat. When it is just simmering, add the chocolate in broken pieces. Stir until the chocolate is melted and well blended. Cover and refrigerate 3 to 4 hours or overnight. When ready to serve, add the vanilla and whip until stiff. Whipping this mixture will take less time than plain whipped cream does, about 2 minutes.

FOR MOCHA MOUSSE: Add 2 tablespoons strong, cold coffee or Raja's Cup (a MAPI product and coffee substitute*), with the vanilla extract.

WHITE FIGS À LA KAPHA

Although other figs like black or Mission figs are nourishing, none is held in such esteem by Ayurveda as Calmyrnas—known in Sanskrit as anjier. These white, dried figs are sold at most supermarkets and natural food stores.

− V − P *K

Plump some white Calmyrna figs in a vegetable steamer for 5 minutes. Serve warm. One or two figs and a few fresh ginger cookies make a good dessert for Kapha.

---

* Raja's Cup can be ordered from Maharishi Ayur-Ved Products International, Inc. See Appendix 5, page 293.

❖❖❖

White Figs in Apricot Cream Sauce

Plain steamed figs are good for everyone who likes figs. This recipe makes a beautiful, more elaborate dessert that's best for Vata and Pitta and that can also be served at a breakfast, brunch, or teatime party.

−V −P +K

Serves 5 to 6

> *10 to 12 Calmyrna figs*
> *1½ cups heavy cream*
> *¼ teaspoon nutmeg*
> *½ teaspoon cinnamon*
> *1 tablespoon apricot preserves*
> *Fresh mint, lemon balm leaves, or small violets or*
>   *other edible flowers, if available*

1. Steam the figs for 5 minutes and set aside. When they are cool enough to handle slice each in half lengthwise with a sharp knife. Then prepare the sauce.

2. In a heavy 2-quart saucepan heat the cream over a moderately high flame. Stir in the spices and the apricot preserves, whisking thoroughly. When the cream just comes to a boil, gently stir in the figs, coating them completely. Simmer over a very low flame for 2 or 3 minutes. Serve immediately, garnished with mint, lemon balm leaves, or little flowers.

Chapter 5

PLANNING GOOD MEALS, PARTIES AND CELEBRATIONS, AND DINING WELL

Planning Good Meals

MENU PLANNING

Now it is time to put everything together to make a memorable meal. Since successful Ayurvedic cooking is a matter of knowing how food influences each of the different body types and planning well-balanced meals accordingly, it is important to undertake Ayurvedic menu planning with variety in mind. Even those menus in this book specifically designed for Vata, Pitta, or Kapha contain a wide enough range of tastes and qualities so anyone can choose from them and feel satisfied. Now we'll look at some basic ideas for menu planning, different seasonal considerations, and we'll examine a few festive menus with a variety of tastes and qualities for all constitutions.

THE VARIED MENU

When planning and preparing a full dinner menu, especially for family members or friends with all types of dietary needs, the universal principle of "the whole is more than the sum of the parts" should be your guide. All the various herbs and spices, vegetables, fruits, grains, and cooking techniques combine to make a finished recipe with an overall effect that is greater than that of any single ingredient or preparation method. And four or five dishes served in combination at a meal interact to produce an effect that is greater than that of any single dish. Usually the ingredient used in the greatest amount has a dominant influence in a recipe.

❖❖❖

**POINTS TO REMEMBER
WHEN PLANNING A MEAL**

- Meals Look:
  Colorful
  Smell Delicious
  Taste Wonderful
- Choose Ingredients:
  Appropriate to the
  Season
  As Fresh as Possible

- Include:
  Six Tastes
  Six Qualities
  Three Categories
- Always Follow:
  Seasonal
  Considerations
  Dictates of the
  Body's Needs
  Common Sense

Different cooking processes—frying or roasting compared with boiling or steaming—may change the predicted quality of an individual ingredient or the whole recipe. Boiling or steaming a potato makes it moist and somewhat lighter in quality, deep-frying produces a heavier, oily potato, and dry roasting makes the potato light and dry. But the effect of the taste in the menu does not change with the cooking technique—pungent remains pungent and sweet stays sweet, no matter how the ingredient is prepared.

Whenever possible use more than one method of heating/cooking in each main meal. An all-boiled meal seems rather bland or uninteresting, and a meal where everything is stir-fried and deep-fried is heavy to digest. Varied menus are interesting, balanced, and satisfying for everyone and a goal of Ayurvedic cooking.

THREE CATEGORIES OF DIET

Ayurveda organizes the various elements of the menu or diet into three broad categories called *gunas* in Sanskrit. These *gunas* interact to influence the mind and body, but they especially affect one's feelings and behavior. Their action is one of the main reasons you feel happy after a meal, or irritable, or dull and sleepy.

The chart on page 233 describes these categories or *gunas* in dietary terms. *Sattva* (SUT-wuh) contains all the best elements of a menu that are good for everyone no matter the body type. Foods in the category,

Sattva	Rajas	Tamas
Diet which develops mental and physical strength, and longevity, health, creates happiness and love. Filled with rejuvenating value for mind, body, and nature. Characteristics: sweet, light, oily, contains all 6 tastes, balanced protein, vitamins, and nutrients.	Stimulates activity in the mind and body. If eaten in excess creates burning feeling, unhappiness, anger, discomfort, or disease. Characteristics: dry, hot, sour, salty.	More than a small amount in diet will create dull, listless mind and behavior, and serious illness. Characteristics: *extremely* cold, hot, heavy, dry, or sour. Spoiled, stale, leftover, burned food.
FAVOR	**REDUCE**	**AVOID**
Cow's milk, buttermilk, ghee, sweet fruits and juices, butter, cream. Mung beans and lentils, wheat, rice. Fresh whole food.	Very pungent, sour, salty, or dry vegetables and spices. Too much hing, black pepper, vinegar, tofu, peanuts, chicken, meat, fish, cheese. Canned, frozen, or bottled foods.	Extremely hot, sour, pungent tastes. Cooked food sitting out many hours. Cold and dry, tasteless, burned, spoiled, dirty food. Food already tasted by others. Onions, mushrooms, garlic, alcohol. *Large amounts* of meat, fish, chicken, cayenne peppers, other chilies.

Every meal contains something from each category. Most of the diet is from the Sattvic category, a small part is Rajasic. Tamas should be avoided.

rajas (RUH-jus) stimulate activity in the mind and body. When rajasic foods are eaten excessively the resulting high level of stimulation shows up as irritability and discomfort. *Tamas* (TUM-us) creates inertia making one feel dull and listless, or lethargic.

As we saw in Chapter 1 no matter who you are cooking for always be sure each menu for a main meal has some sweet, salty, sour, bitter, pungent, and astringent tastes. Include some of each of the six qualities hot, cold, dry, oily, heavy, and light as well. In addition to that consider the *gunas* when planning your meals. A large proportion of any menu comes from the sattvic category, much less from rajas and only a tiny bit might appear from the tamasic group. A sattvic diet minimizes the amount of impurities taken into the body. But just as exclusively eating only one or two food tastes, or limiting the diet to only a few favorite foods like apple juice or pizza creates an imbalance in the body, so too, in the Ayurvedic view only eating sattvic food (as salutary as it is) would not represent all the balance found in nature. The human body is seen by Ayurveda as a small, complete version of the universe in which every element in creation can be found. The interaction of the three *gunas* play an important role in creation. Since rajasic foods aren't as healthful when eaten in any other than moderate amounts so they would make up a small part of the balanced diet. Maharishi Ayur-Ved does not recommend eating tamasic food.

MENU PLANNING: FIRST CONSIDER THE WEATHER

When following an Ayurvedic diet, we don't eat the same thing day in and day out all year long. It makes good sense since the environment and our bodies change with the weather and the seasons. Whether the weather is hot and muggy, or icy cold with dry winds chapping your face and hands, raining and foggy, or just plain blazing hot, the changing seasons and different kinds of weather have predictable influences on your appetite, your body's energy level, and the kinds of foods you'll want to eat. Consider the weather when planning your menus and you will stay healthy.

Seasonal cooking follows the principle of Similarities and Differences that we discussed in Chapter 1. That means during the season or

SEASONS AND WEATHER AFFECT THE DOSHAS

SEASON	DOSHA	WEATHER
Late Autumn/Winter	Vata	Increases in cold, dry, windy weather
Spring	Kapha	Increases in humid, heavy, wet, cold weather
Summer/Early Autumn	Pitta	Increases in sunny, dry, hot weather

❖-❖

weather most like your dominant dosha, eating too much of those foods that have qualities similar to the weather aggravates that dosha and sends the system out of balance. It can take a month or two, or sometimes until the next season, before the accumulated imbalance shows up as illness. By eating meals with a high proportion of ingredients that are opposite to your doshas, you can stay healthy year round. One of the best things anyone can do to prevent illness is to plan meals that tend to maintain doshic balance during the seasonal changes while at the same time nourishing the body at its most fundamental level.

MENU PLANNING BY CONSTITUTION AND SEASON

In Chapter 2 we described the influences of the seasons and seasonal cooking for each of the three body types. Menu planning for someone who is purely Vata, Pitta, or Kapha is not very complicated. When the weather changes, the diet gets a few alterations. Many people, however, are a combination of doshas, usually two.

In reading the following chart to help you plan your meal according to your constitution and the changing seasons, please note that during the weather and season most like your nature it's best to eat meals that balance your dominant dosha(s). Very thin people with Vata-Kapha constitutions should follow a Vata-decreasing diet year round rather than lose weight on a Kapha-reducing diet. But a Kapha-Vata—that means more Kapha than Vata imbalance—or an equally balanced Vata-Kapha should eat Vata-reducing foods in spring and summer and Kapha-reducing foods in winter. Kapha-Vatas who gain weight easily, most noticeably on the hips, abdomen, and thighs, should favor a diet that reduces Kapha in the summer as well.

Those Kapha-Pitta or Pitta-Kapha types who gain weight easily or need to lose weight maintain a "very tender balance" by continuing to follow a Kapha-decreasing diet even in summer, but they should add cooling fruits and other foods to their menus. And most important, they should avoid such Pitta-aggravating ingredients as tomatoes, peppers, chilies, vinegar, cheeses, and so forth.

This chart is a general menu-planning guide. You are the one who knows your physiology best, and with experience and increasing attention you'll know how you feel when you eat certain kinds of foods,

GUIDE FOR MENU PLANNING BY CONSTITUTION AND SEASON

CONSTITUTION	WINTER	SUMMER/FALL	SPRING
Vata	V	V	V
Pitta	P	P	P
Kapha	K	K	K
Vata-Pitta/Pitta-Vata	V	P	V
Kapha-Vata	K	V	V (if thin)
Vata-Kapha	V	K	V (if thin)
Pitta-Kapha/Kapha-Pitta	K	P	P/K K (if heavy)
Vata-Pitta-and Kapha	V	P	K

V = Vata-balancing diet, P = Pitta-balancing diet, K = Kapha-balancing diet.

especially those that balance your doshas. And you'll become more sensitive to the things you want to change in your diet as the seasons change.

SERVING LARGE GROUPS

Serving a great variety of foods, with many condiments in small decorative bowls, buffet style, is an easy solution to large group needs for variety and balance. Each person can select greater amounts of the foods most nourishing for him or her and less of those that he or she simply needs to nibble on for overall balance. Preparing simple entrées or side dishes accompanied by a variety of toppings or sauces is not only easy on the cook, but abundant choices give a feeling of opulence, making even simple meals festive for everyone. You might serve a large group of people one large mixed vegetable and pasta casserole, baked potatoes and halves of baked squash or yams with ghee or butter, accompanied by a selection of sauces: a broccoli cream sauce, sour cream mixed with Mexican picante sauce, pureed curried vegetables, spicy dahl, and, to aid digestion, other pungent-tasting toppings for the potatoes, a tossed green salad and a fruit salad, breads, and two or more desserts—one very light one for Kapha. Such a menu gives everyone plenty to choose from.

SPARKING UP AN EVERYDAY MENU

One way for the busy cook to keep menu planning simple but still produce interesting meals is to regularly prepare certain family favorites and seasonal standards like rice and other grains, lentils, potatoes, pasta, mixed steamed vegetables, hearty casseroles, and so forth all year round, but prepare different, flavorful sauces, condiments, dressings, and marinades that highlight the particular tastes and qualities you want. There are a basic few items to keep on hand all the time to serve in small dishes as condiments to accompany your daily meals. Some of these include:

Chopped Nuts:	plain walnut pieces, pecans or other nuts, or cashews and blanched slivered almonds fried in a little ghee
Coconut:	flaked or shredded, plain or lightly roasted in a heavy pan
Pickles:	sweet red peppers or sweet gherkins to stimulate the appetite
Citrus Fruits:	lemon, lime, and orange wedges
Fresh Ginger:	chopped or thinly peeled, served plain or mixed with lemon juice and salt

BALANCED MEALS FOR CHILDREN

When cooking for children the same Ayurvedic guidelines for balance apply. Give children more of what they should have and less of what causes imbalances. If children resist certain tastes and qualities or have not yet developed a liking for them, then include small amounts of that taste in something they enjoy. And do not force them to eat it or hold back the other foods they crave. There is a body of research showing children eat a balanced diet over time if they can choose for themselves. It is just as important to plan balanced menus for children as for adults; their recipes may require more clever adjustments. It is one of the age-old challenges of parenthood.

Parties and Celebrations

The menus in this section have an international flavor that for many of us signify a celebration. When entertaining people with varied dietary needs, serve these meals buffet style—there's something here for everyone to enjoy. The recipes in this chapter are designed to be included as part of a balanced meal for everyone, and the necessary tastes and qualities for healthful eating are well represented in each sample menu.

Whether simple or elaborate
every Ayurvedic meal is a celebration.

AN INDIAN FEAST

A complete meal of Indian-style food is easily balanced by tastes and qualities. Everything at the meal is offered in abundance and it is for each person to choose the appropriate amount of each dish according to the season and individual preference. In the following menu there are more recipes listed than you might usually cook at one meal. For an impressive feast the basic dahl, rice, bread, and vegetable dish can be enhanced by making many chutneys and condiments.

ōm
Saha nav avatu
Saha nau bhunaktu
Saha viryam karavavhai
Tejasvi nav adhitam astu
Ma vidvishavahai
shantih, shantih, shantih

—THE UPANISHADS

Let us be together
Let us eat together
Let us be vital together
Let us be radiating truth,
Radiating the light of life,
Never shall we denounce anyone
Never entertain negativity.

An Indian Menu

MASOOR DAHL AND RICE
(Astringent, Sweet, Dry, Cold)

SPICY VEGETABLE CURRY
(Pungent, Sour, Sweet, Slightly Bitter, Astringent, Salty, Hot)
OR
SWEET SUMMER CURRY WITH SAFFRON RICE
(Sweet, Salty, Astringent)

RAITAS
(Sour, Cold, Salty)

CHUTNEYS AND OTHER CONDIMENTS

PURIS OR CHAPATIS
(Sweet, Heavy)

CASHEW NUT BALLS
(Sweet, Oily, Slightly Heavy)

FRAGRANTLY SPICED LASSI
(Sour, Sweet, Cold)

ABOUT THE INDIAN MENU

MASOOR DAHL AND RICE

Dahl, a rich lentil soup, is best for all of your guests when it is made in a very liquid consistency. Eating dahl is good for people of all body types. For more information about other lentils used in making dahl, see Chapter 3, Something for Everyone. The Masoor Dahl on this menu, made from thin, coral-colored lentils, cooks faster than other lentils.

Although dahl can be made with various spice combinations, an easy and most delicious way is by using the Maharishi Ayur-Ved Product Vata Churna. This combination of spices never fails to produce a rich and authentically Indian dahl.

SPICY VEGETABLE CURRY

The secret of this mixed vegetable curry with its many subtle flavors is to prepare the ingredients in two separate pans with different spice combinations, then mix everything together at the end for rich and varied flavors that are delightfully discovered while eating. To receive the full benefit of a certain taste, it is necessary to experience it as clearly as possible. That's why Ayurveda recommends preparing differing taste and quality combinations separately, then putting them together before serving. All the ingredients are washed, peeled, chopped, ground, and so forth before beginning to cook. A labor-saving tip is to use Kapha Churna, a special blend of herbs and spices that helps balance Kapha dosha and adds a reasonable amount of spiciness at the same time. Otherwise a blend of sweet and pungent spices works well.

Select fresh, seasonally available vegetables. If you omit any vegetables that are listed in this recipe, be sure to substitute others in the correct quantity to make up the total amount called for. Although fresh vegetables are always the best choice, buying good-quality fresh tomatoes, peas, and other summer favorites might not be practical in other seasons. The occasional use—once every week or two—of canned or frozen ingredients is all right as long as they make up a small part of the recipe.

Spicy Vegetable Curry decreases Kapha and Vata and increases Pitta somewhat. It makes a good side dish for Pitta when served as part of a meal with other Pitta-reducing selections. In this meal Pitta would take less of the spicy curry and much more of the sweet curry. The predominant tastes are pungent, sour, sweet, slightly bitter, and astringent with hot and oily qualities. This combination makes it a good main dish anytime for those following a Kapha-reducing diet.

If any curry is left after the meal, save it until evening and heat it by frying in hot oil. Then stuff it in folded chapatis, tortillas, or pita bread. Serve these with a tossed salad for a light meal.

SWEET SUMMER CURRY

Curries are sometimes thought of as fiery dishes that must be followed by lots of cool drinks and yogurt. Not this one. It is sweet and unctuous, astringent, warm, heavy, and a little salty. This is a good main dish for Pitta and Vata. Kapha can eat very moderately of this curry.

The more pungent-tasting dishes suit Kapha better. Increasing the spinach and decreasing the sweet raisins, grapes, and the heavy potatoes makes this sweet curry a good side dish for Kapha types.

When you use sprouted lentils for frying to serve with mixed vegetables, soak them in warm water, cover, and allow them to sit overnight, or just long enough for the sprouts to begin coming out. The lentil has its greatest nutritional value at this point rather than when it is allowed to grow a long root. Wash the sprouted lentils well in cool water just before using.

Fried Spiced Potatoes, actually a recipe within the Sweet Summer Curry recipe, gives even greater richness and depth to the dish. It could also be prepared on its own for Vata or Pitta as a side dish or part of a light meal. Prepare the Fried Spiced Potatoes first, then cover them and let them steam while you cook the fruits and vegetables.

Rice is cold, sweet, and heavy. While it is an essential, nourishing grain for everyone to eat, it reduces Vata and Pitta and increases Kapha, so Kapha would eat much less rice at this meal. Because saffron is a heating herb it is good to prepare Kapha's rice with a little saffron (or ginger). Dry roasting or frying the rice in a little oil before boiling makes it less heavy. Vata types can use the heat of saffron also, but the rice does not need to be roasted or fried first to make it lighter in quality. Those with Pitta constitutions do not need to lighten the rice by frying either. Saffron can be eaten in moderation by Pitta types in cold months, if they care for the extra heat.

ABOUT RAITA

Raita is a yogurt-based side dish, like an Indian salad that serves as a sour, cold, refreshing foil to a spicy meal. It is traditionally served as part of a whole Indian meal. When eaten in small amounts, raita is good for everyone. In large quantities it increases Pitta and Kapha. Finely shredded carrots or radishes make a quick, colorful raita. Try thinly sliced bananas with honey and ginger for a Kapha raita. Almost any minced or shredded raw vegetable or spicy cooked vegetable mixed with twice as much yogurt qualifies as raita. Toasted, crushed cumin seeds are folded into a simple Vata-reducing raita. No matter what you mix with the yogurt to make raita the yogurt itself should be thick and freshly made from whole milk.

ABOUT CHUTNEYS AND OTHER CONDIMENTS

A feast in the Indian style includes quite an array of small dishes brimming with stewed fruits, nuts, pickles, and vegetables that offer a splendid selection of tastes and qualities. These chutneys and other Indian condiments, the jewels of the Indian cuisine, make any good meal even more interesting. A chutney may contain only one taste or all the tastes needed to balance the meal. And they can be served effectively at nearly any meal, not just Indian ones.

When included as part of a large meal, small amounts of these chutneys and other condiments can be eaten by anyone. Eating large amounts of one or two chutneys would imbalance the doshas.

Varied condiments give each person a chance to select and balance the different tastes according to his or her needs. Although there are several recipes for chutneys and condiments in this sample menu, only a few are actually served at each meal. For a simple dinner one or two chutneys are probably enough.

KINDS OF CHUTNEYS

There are three kinds of chutneys: fresh, cooked, and preserved. Preserved chutneys keep on the kitchen shelf for several months. Usually these are the imported kinds preserved in oil, which Ayurveda considers a healthful way of food preserving, although preserving in sugar and standard bottling and canning procedures are equally good.

Home-cooked chutneys keep well in the refrigerator for one or two months. They are made with large amounts of sugar, chilies, salt, oil, or vinegar, which all have preserving qualities.

Fresh chutneys are only used for one day. These "daily" chutneys are usually made in small amounts using chopped parsley, coriander, other finely minced vegetables, or fresh fruits. If any fresh chutney is left at the end of the noon meal, it can be fried in ghee or oil as the base for sautéed vegetables or soup at the next meal. Otherwise, discard it.

QUICK CONDIMENTS

When you look over the meal just before serving make a mental checklist of the tastes and qualities of all the food in the meal. The tastes most often missing in American cooking are bitter, astringent, and pungent. If these are missing Wilted Ginger Lettuce offers a quick, delicious fix. Simply sauté chopped lettuce or other bitter and astringent greens in olive oil or ghee with some freshly grated ginger, and your guests can serve themselves this appetizing little condiment.

If one or two tastes are underrepresented you can quickly put out a couple of condiments, depending on what's at hand, and you will give better balance to the whole meal. Spiced Cashew Nuts, Toasted Coconut, Lemon and Lime Wedges, and sweet gherkin pickles are a few easy condiments that add taste, texture, color, and more variety to any dinner. Small bowls and dishes of chutneys and condiments make a meal interesting to both the eye and the palate.

PURIS AND CHAPATIS

Typical Indian main dishes are served with fried unleavened breads used for "pushing" the food and sopping up the delectable juices. Puris and chapatis, the most frequently eaten of these breads, are good for everyone, although the sweet and heavy qualities can increase Kapha if too many are eaten. While the ingredients are identical, chapatis are fried on a hot griddle and puris, puffy breads, are deep-fried in oil. Like other wheat breads these reduce Vata and Pitta and increase Kapha if eaten in excess.

INDIAN DESSERT

Most Indian desserts are of the very sweet pastry or pudding variety. Laddu (Cashew Nut Balls) are ball-shaped sweets, something between cookies and candy. Like most Indian desserts they are very sweet and nourishing. This dessert is good for Vata and Pitta and all right for Kapha, too, in small amounts. They make a sweet, unctuous, slightly heavy, and satisfying end to an Indian meal.

After the meal is over sip small cups of Fragrantly Spiced Lassi or Plain Refreshing Lassi made by thinning yogurt with water. Lassi helps in the final digestion of the meal and brings an Indian feast to an appropriate close.

ABOUT THE FRENCH MENU

There is so much variety in French cooking that this menu can hardly represent it all. This is just a simple springtime dinner in the French style of cooking, the season when fresh peas are readily available for the Peas with Braised Lettuce, lots of green lettuces for the salad, tender new potatoes, and fresh asparagus stalks for the potato soup.

This French menu is an example of what you might typically encounter when you are eating out and the choices may not be clearly defined for your body type. It may seem at first glance that eating this dinner would aggravate Kapha dosha because of the sweetness of the menu, yet everyone can eat the food in this dinner since all six tastes are represented. Although the menu has a number of sweet-tasting dishes—good news for Vata and Pitta—thoughtful food selection will be necessary for Kapha. We'll look closely at the menu to give Kapha ideas of how to eat in a balanced way from a sweet-tasting menu.

A French Menu

POTAGE PRINTANIER
(Sweet, Salty, Slightly Astringent, Light)

PETIT POIS BRAISÉ LAITUE
(Sweet, Sour)

SIMPLE RICE PILAF
(Sweet, Salty, Light)

TOSSED GREEN SALAD
(Bitter, Astringent, Pungent)

FRENCH BREAD WITH SWEET BUTTER
(Sweet, Heavy)

PÊCHE CARDINAL
(Sweet, Heavy, Cold)

AN APPETIZING SOUP

Potage Printanier, a thin, savory potato soup, is a perfect appetizer for Vata and Pitta. It takes less than an hour to make, but it's so delicious your guests will think it took much longer. Within the context of the whole menu this soup is nourishing for everyone. A steaming bowl of Potage Printanier, a tossed green salad, and a slice of lightly buttered bread makes a good light supper for Kapha types. Tastes in this recipe are sweet, salty, and a little astringent. The soup could be modified for Kapha's benefit during cooking by using half the amount of ghee, substituting skim or low-fat milk for cream, and increasing the amount of ground pepper to increase the amount of pungency in the menu. If, while dining out, Kapha were served this soup and wanted to increase its digestibility, he or she should simply sprinkle on more black pepper. (If you are following a Kapha-reducing diet, think "Add pepper" whenever potatoes are served.)

PETIT POIS BRAISÉ LAITUE
The main sour taste in the menu comes from the entrée of small peas with braised lettuce. This dish is a delightful blend of sweet and sour tastes. It combines delicate textures with the refreshing lightness of spring vegetables, making a satisfying entrée when served with Simple Rice Pilaf or plain rice. There is just the right balance of sourness for Pitta and Kapha in this dish. Although this dish only increases Kapha slightly, if you're cooking for Kapha and those watching their weight, the sugar and butter could be reduced by half without changing the results too much.

SIMPLE RICE PILAF
There are probably as many kinds of pilafs as there are cooks who make them. While Indian pilaf can be pungent when served with curry, the Greek and Turkish ones are less spicy but full of local vegetables. This French one is not spicy but subtly tasty. The advantage of Pilaf is that it is a simple main dish to make using whatever is at hand. If the rice is dry roasted or sautéed first in a little ghee or oil before adding the liquid, it becomes lighter in quality and more digestible for Kapha. This recipe adds sweet and salty tastes to the meal. It is best served with steamed or sautéed vegetables. For those following a Pitta-reducing diet, omit the basil and increase the parsley to taste. Pilafs can also be made with other grains, such as barley for reducing Kapha and bulgur or cracked wheat for Pitta and Vata. Pilafs are a welcome change from pasta and potatoes.

TOSSED GREEN SALAD

The bitter and astringent tastes in the menu come from the Tossed Green Salad. Both Pitta and Kapha would eat freely of the salad with a dressing of choice, except perhaps blue cheese or similar sour, heavy kinds.

FRENCH BREAD

The taste and crunchy texture of this bread is authentically French. Like most plain wheat flour breads, this one is sweet-tasting, heavy, and good for increasing general nutrition. Eaten in moderation, it reduces Vata and Pitta, and when eaten moderately is neutral for Kapha. It's best always to eat bread spread with butter or ghee for ease of digestion. Vegetables and bread complement each other. They are most efficiently digested when eaten together during the same course of the meal.

PÊCHE CARDINAL (RED PEACHES)

The brilliant red and gold colors of this dessert announce an impressive conclusion to the French dinner. It has a combination of sweet tastes good for both Vata and Pitta. Kapha types should eliminate the Chantilly Cream and eat lightly of this dish.

SERVING YOURSELF

If you were dining out and wanted to know how much to eat of each dish, this chart may help you.

SELECTION	VATA	PITTA	KAPHA
Potage Printanier	Good appetizer. Eat fully.	Reduces Pitta. Eat fully.	As part of this menu or as part of a light meal. Add more pepper. Use skim milk and reduce butter.
Petit Pois Braisé Laitue	Eat moderately as part of a balanced menu.	Eat moderately as part of a balanced menu.	Slightly increases. Eat moderately.
Simple Rice Pilaf	Decreases Vata. Eat fully.	Neutral effect. Eat moderately or reduce basil.	Rice increases Kapha. Eat moderately.
Tossed Green Salad	Increases Vata. Eat small amount.	Eat fully.	Eat fully.
French Bread	Decreases Vata. Eat with butter.	Decreases Pitta. Eat with butter.	Eat moderately with a little butter.
Pêche Cardinal	Eat fully.	Eat fully.	Eat a small amount without the cream.

ABOUT THE ITALIAN MENU

This is a northern Italian–style menu. For some reason we Americans have come to believe that all Italian food is tomato and cheese-based, whether it is a plate of spaghetti with a thick tomato sauce or pizza covered with inches of melted (or nearly melted) cheese. In fact, care needs to be taken to avoid using a lot of sour tomatoes and hard-to-digest cheeses when cooking Italian food. Although peeled tomatoes are alright for Vata, excessive amounts of tomato and hard, sour cheese aggravates Pitta, Kapha, and Vata doshas. Eating a lot of hard cheese produces ama in the digestive system. Tomatoes are always considered a minor part of any meal for Pitta and Kapha. The pasta dish in this menu, Pasta and Green Sauce, is one that has a neutral effect on Pitta because there is no tomato sauce. It still increases Kapha because the wheat pasta is heavy and cold in quality.

Tomatoes do appear on the menu in the delicious, very well cooked Green Beans in Tomato Sauce recipe. When combined with all the other ingredients, the tomatoes have only a slightly sour effect.

This menu has a deep range of tastes and qualities that makes eating it very satisfying for everyone.

An Italian Menu

CHEESE CRACKERS AND ITALIAN CHEESES
(Salty, Sweet, Slightly Pungent, Sour, Oily)

PASTA AND GREEN SAUCE
(Sweet, Salty, Oily, Heavy)

GREEN BEANS IN TOMATO SAUCE
(FAGIOLONI IN UMIDO VOLPONI)
(Sweet, Salty, Slightly Sour)

SPINACH AND CHICORY SALAD
(Bitter, Astringent, Pungent, Light, Hot)

MACEDONIA DI FRUITA
(Sweet, Cold, Heavy)

ITALIAN HAZELNUT COOKIES
(Sweet, Bitter, Astringent, Dry)

THE APPETIZER

The meal begins with a modified antipasto tray that can include sweet pickled red peppers, Tuscan peppers or spicy pepperoncini, olives, sweet pickled cucumbers, and a selection of Italian cheeses, such as Gorgonzola, fontina, and mozzarella. Serve small dishes of dips and spreads for the crackers. The Cheese Crackers, more like soft little biscuits than crackers, are traditionally served warm. Pitta and Kapha should eat very lightly from the cheese tray. Whether eaten by themselves or with soup, these delightful little Cheese Crackers add a salty taste that is slightly pungent and sweet. Eating them reduces Vata, is neutral for Pitta, and increases Kapha.

PASTA AND GREEN SAUCE

The green herbs make this sauce a flavorful accompaniment to spaghetti or linguine. When served with pasta, this dish decreases Vata, is neutral for Pitta, and increases Kapha. Although it's not our idea of an Italian dish, Kapha could eat more of this as a main dish if cooked barley is substituted for the semolina wheat pasta. Parmesan cheese can be used by both Vata and Kapha in moderation. The combined qualities of this recipe are sweet, salty, oily, and heavy.

GREEN BEANS IN TOMATO SAUCE (FAGIOLONI IN UMIDO VOLPONI)

A delicious main dish, this has properly balanced tastes and qualities that reduce all doshas. It is pleasantly sweet and salty, and goes nicely with all kinds of pasta. Usually beans of all kinds increase Vata. This is the best way to cook green beans because they must be very well cooked to reduce Vata.

SPINACH AND CHICORY SALAD

The bitter, astringent, slightly pungent, light, hot, and dry properties of this salad are especially balancing in a Kapha diet. It is also a good salad to include in the menu for people with varied dietary needs. If the meal consists of several heavy or sweet dishes, then those following a Kapha diet can help themselves to a large amount of this healthy salad. Vata and Pitta types would eat smaller portions.

MACEDONIA DI FRUITA

For the culinary artist the fruits in this salad—apples, sweet oranges, cantaloupes, watermelon, honeydew and other melons, figs, grapes, dates, and other seasonally available fruits—are like colors on a palette waiting to be made into something spectacular. When prepared in a grand manner this dish can be used as an impressive centerpiece for a buffet dessert.

We spoke a little about this salad in Chapter 2, Cooking for Vata, Pitta, and Kapha. All the fruits in this salad are good for all the doshas when eaten as a part of a balanced meal, but fruit salad would not be good for Kapha to eat separately because it is sweet, cold, and heavy.

ITALIAN HAZELNUT COOKIES

These delicate cookies are sweet, bitter, astringent, dry, and good for all doshas. When made with both wheat and barley flour, they are best for Kapha. If you don't have barley flour on hand, use all white flour. The recipe calls for rolling the finished cookies in confectioners' sugar. This step could be eliminated for Kapha. The anise flavor develops best when they are stored in a sealed container for a day or two.

Serving Yourself

If you were dining out and wanted to know how much to eat from such a menu to be sure you've eaten a healthy, balanced meal, this chart may help you.

SELECTION	VATA	PITTA	KAPHA
Cheese Crackers Antipasto Tray	Eat several crackers with dips and spreads, but eat only a little cheese.	Go easy on the cheese. Eat a few crackers, pickles, and peppers.	Eat lightly of the crackers. Go easy on the cheese; enjoy the pungent peppers.
Pasta and Green Sauce	Eat fully as part of a balanced menu.	Eat moderately as part of a balanced menu.	Sweet, heavy, oily. Eat moderately. Increases Kapha.
Green Beans in Tomato Sauce	Decreases Vata. Eat fully.	Decreases Pitta. Eat fully.	Decreases Kapha. Eat fully.
Spinach and Chicory Salad	Increases Vata. Eat small amount.	Eat moderately. Neutral effect.	Eat fully. Good for Kapha.
Macedonia di Fruita	Decreases Vata. Eat fully.	Decreases Pitta. Eat fully.	Eat moderately as part of a balanced meal.
Italian Hazelnut Cookies	Eat fully.	Eat fully.	Eat moderately without the extra confectioners' sugar.

❖❖

ABOUT THE AMERICAN PICNIC MENU

A good picnic is easy to tote, eat, and clean up after and can happen at nearly any time or place. The beach, the roadside while traveling, or a city park all offer opportunities for a quick party. Your own backyard can be the setting for an elegant dinner or breakfast picnic that may feature scones, tea, coffee, and fresh fruit and juice, or thinly sliced bread spread with scented rose or parsley butter.

Many people wouldn't think of letting a patriotic holiday pass without an outdoor party with family and friends. The general fare always includes several salads, fruit, and for vegetarians ersatz burgers or franks. The Tofu Nut Burgers on our picnic menu are thoroughly nourishing, acting as a tonic on the body's tissues, and are a lot easier to digest and assimilate than meat burgers. When eaten with the usual selection of condiments—pickles, olives, mustard, catsup, and so forth —they are more digestible. Choose from condiments according to your taste. This body-building food decreases Vata, has a neutral effect on Pitta, and increases Kapha.

This menu could easily include more kinds of fruit and vegetable salads and casseroles of macaroni and cheese, or a baked vegetable loaf. It's the cook's choice.

Big, juicy red watermelons always show up at a picnic. In summer when the body needs to replenish liquids rapidly, watermelon is the fruit of choice for all constitutions. Although they are juicy, other melons such as cantaloupe, crenshaw, honeydew, and so forth are colder and heavier for Kapha and Vata to digest. Watermelon is good for balancing all doshas in summer.

OVEN-BAKED FRENCH FRIES

French fries, a very popular American food that nearly everyone loves, are so heavy, oily, and fat-increasing that Kapha should eat very little of them. However, they decrease Vata and are neutral for Pitta unless eaten excessively. This oven method of cooking results in "fried" potatoes that are easier to digest and much less oily. Also, the tofu burgers can be baked at the same time as the French fries.

American Picnic Menu

TOFU NUT BURGERS WITH CONDIMENTS
(Sweet, Heavy)

OVEN-BAKED FRENCH FRIES
(Sweet, Oily, Heavy)

CONFETTI RICE SALAD
(Sweet, Slightly Bitter, Pungent, Sour, Cold, Light)

TOSSED GREEN SALAD
(Bitter, Astringent, Pungent, Light)

WATERMELON
(Sweet, Cold)

SUPER CHOCOLATE BROWNIES
(Bitter, Sweet, Astringent, Slightly Salty)

AMERICAN APPLE PIE
(Sweet, Heavy)

WATERMELON-STRAWBERRY PUNCH
(Sweet, Cold)

CONFETTI RICE SALAD

This colorful, summertime party salad with light and cold qualities and sweet, bitter, pungent, and sour tastes is especially good for Vata and Pitta to eat. By adjusting the amount and kinds of fresh herbs you use, you can make this salad better for each of the different types. Both Kapha and Pitta appreciate such bitter- and astringent-tasting herbs as fennel, dill, summer or winter savory, celery, and coriander leaves. At the picnic Kapha would eat a small to moderate amount of this rice dish with a lot of green leafy salad or separately later on as a light meal. Just sauté leftover rice salad in hot oil with mixed vegetables.

SUPER CHOCOLATE BROWNIES

The particular combination of ingredients in this rich chocolate brownie is good for anyone who loves chocolate and makes a delicious, popular picnic dessert. They have just the right balance of dry and heavy qualities, bitter, astringent, slightly salty, and sweet tastes. Other brownies, like most Kapha-increasing desserts, are primarily heavy and sweet. What's noticeably different about these brownies is that they are also dry and astringent, making them more suitable for Kapha to eat. Making these brownies (and other baked goods) without eggs adds to their overall suitability for Pitta. Egg yolks increase Pitta. The only thing wrong with these brownies is that you have to wait until they are completely cool to cut them. For the best consistency, they are best made by hand, not with a food processor or electric mixer.

AMERICAN APPLE PIE

What would an American picnic be without apple pie? This is a pleasantly spicy pie that is sweet and heavy. It decreases Vata and Pitta and increases Kapha. You can make a perfectly delicious sugarless apple pie by using Golden Delicious apples (or other sweet apples) and some ground licorice root, and increasing the amount of cinnamon. Then Kapha types and those watching their weight who still want to eat a good slice of American apple pie can do so in moderation. The wheat flour crust adds to its Kapha-increasing properties, but not very much.

WATERMELON-STRAWBERRY PUNCH

This is a wonderfully refreshing fruit punch for a summer picnic or for cooling off on a hot afternoon. Many other fresh fruit combinations are great with watermelon juice, too. Add small amounts of bottled juices, if you like, but there is so much fresh fruit available in the summer it is easy to make delicious fresh drinks.

An attractive bowl for this punch is the hollowed-out watermelon itself, although any large bowl will do. Garnish the punch with fresh herbs and flowers, but be sure to use washed flowers or leaves that you know are edible. Blossoms from borage (blue shooting stars), nasturtium, pineapple sage, and sweet violets are a few of the more readily available ones.

Dining Well

AYURVEDIC DINING

An Ayurvedic meal is a time for enjoyment and celebration. When food is eaten at the right time, in a pleasant setting, with good company, and in the proper quantity, then eating becomes one of the best experiences in life. Ayurveda offers a few simple guidelines for good eating whether you are dining alone at home or eating out.

When dining out be aware of
what is best for you to eat,
what you feel like eating,
and order accordingly.

ATMOSPHERE

Meals should be enjoyed in a clean, calm setting. This is what enhances good digestion and allows for your full enjoyment of the meal. Allow yourself and others the proper setting and atmosphere to really pay attention to the food you are eating. Even the simplest dinner for two can be a celebration filled with laughter and good feelings, quiet music, or companionable silence. When dining alone, silence or some agreeable dinner music is the best accompaniment for good digestion. It's better to eat happily alone than with a disturbing crowd.

CONVERSATION

Table conversation should be light and entertaining for everyone. No unpleasant or weighty topics should be discussed. Mealtime is not the time to make deals and decisions. Discuss business or other important matters after eating. Positive decisions can be taken when everyone is feeling well satisfied by a good meal. Conversation includes listening to others and not talking and chewing food at the same time.

INTERRUPTIONS

Avoid visitors, telephone, television, loud music, reading, and other distractions while eating. The benefit of a good meal comes from eating with your full attention. Ask unexpected visitors to join you at your meal or make arrangements to meet with them after eating. Food should not be eaten while driving a car or during similar activities that require your full attention.

SIT COMFORTABLY

Sit down to eat . . . always. It is best for proper digestion. The stomach is in the best working position when there is a little pressure on it. Standing while eating or drinking gives the wrong message to the stomach, and because there is not enough pressure the food flows through too quickly. The stomach hasn't been given the message that it's time to go to work. The cook, or whoever is responsible for serving the meal, should have either already eaten or else have all the food conveniently located in the dining area so no one has to get up and down to help others during the meal. At the end of a meal everyone just sits for five or ten minutes and relaxes.

> *Praise the food served to you, never criticize it.*
> *Food is Brahman.*
> *Food is the Self.*
>
> —THE UPANISHADS

TIME

Eat when you are hungry, that is, after the previous meal is completely digested. This will prevent overburdening agni. Take the time to eat well, paying attention to the various tastes and qualities of the food. The age-old advice of taking your time to chew your food thoroughly still applies. Just before eating pause for a moment or two and sit in silence with the eyes closed to allow the doshas to settle; or use that silent time for a brief prayer.

BEST TIME FOR DINNER: MIDDAY

If you can, it's best to invite guests to a special dinner at the midday meal rather than at night. According to Ayurveda the noon meal is the most substantial one of the day. Everyone's digestive juices function best when the sun is at its peak. In the evening and after sunset heavy food is not digested or assimilated as well. Feast at noon and eat a light meal at night.

HOW TO EAT: LAYERS OF FOOD AND WATER

Eat only two-thirds to three-fourths of your capacity. Sip small amounts of water while eating. One-third of the meal should be water and one-third solid food. The final third of the stomach is left empty to leave room for the action of digestion. Eat just until you feel satisfied but not full. Eating too much food puts pressure on the heart and it can also cause heartburn or gas.

> *Diet is not for filling the stomach cavity.*
> *Offer food to others and take the rest for yourself.*
>
> —DR. H. S. KASTURE

SIGNS OF A GOOD AYURVEDIC MEAL

BEFORE AND DURING THE MEAL

- Food is well prepared with the cook's full attention.
- It is presented promptly with appetizing colors.
- It smells, feels, and tastes delicious.
- The setting is comfortable, clean, pleasant.
- Everyone eats with a good appetite.

AFTER THE MEAL

- Feel increased mental energy, comfort and strength, clarity of senses.
- Feeling of satisfaction and well-being.

❖❖

Chapter 6

SPECIAL DIETS: WEIGHT LOSS AND LIGHT MEALS, NEW MOTHERS AND THEIR BABIES

The two special diets—weight loss and light eating, and a diet for new mothers—described in this chapter are recommended for normally active, healthy people. If you think you might need a restricted diet for a particular health problem such as diabetes, high blood pressure, serious overweight or underweight, high cholesterol levels, and so forth, or if you are pregnant, consult your doctor or a Maharishi Ayur-Ved physician (listed at the back of the book). Following fads and radical diets as a basis for nutritional planning is foolish. If you want to completely eliminate or substantially increase anything in your diet, you should obtain qualified advice before upsetting the natural balance of your physiology. Complete programs for normal health maintenance, weight loss, and maternity care are available through the Maharishi Ayur-Ved Health Centers.

Eat correctly and live a normal human lifespan:
36,000 days and nights . . .
a hundred years.

—DR. H. S. KASTURE

Weight Loss

BALANCING WEIGHT—LOSING AND GAINING

Maintaining the body's weight at a reasonably healthy level seems to be quite a balancing act for many of us. But a comfortable weight

❖❖

contributes to enjoying a long, healthy life. We've seen that a person with a Kapha body type or some combination such as Pitta-Kapha or Kapha-Vata gains weight more easily than most people and loses it more slowly, and most Vata types find it hard to gain weight easily. For very thin people gaining weight is a lifelong goal that is just as important as losing weight is for overweight people. But today losing excess weight consumes much of America's interest, and that is what we'll talk about now.

For many people losing weight is simply a matter of balancing the doshas and carefully following certain practical rules for proper eating as they develop good lifelong dietary habits. The suggestions for losing weight in this chapter are also useful for balancing Kapha dosha all year long, whether the person is overweight or not.

For those people who want to gain weight most of these same guidelines apply, except they should eat small, frequent meals and follow a rich, nourishing, warm Vata-balancing diet (see Chapter 2).

DIETING

When you follow the good-eating practices we've just discussed, maintaining your normal weight becomes easier without the need for regular dieting. Because people with predominantly Vata or Pitta constitutions rarely need to lose a lot of weight, they should discuss their plans for dieting or changing to a light, Kapha-reducing diet with a physician before they make changes in their regular eating patterns. Very light eating allows the body to rest and the digestive fires to become strong again.

THE OVEREATING HABIT

Unless someone has a metabolic or hormonal problem, overweight is really an indication that some habits need to be changed. There are probably many habits that lead to overeating. Some people eat by the clock: "Oh, it's five o'clock and time to eat." Why? Because they've always eaten at that time, their mother always served dinner at 5:00 P.M., and so they eat, but not necessarily because they are hungry. Others eat in anticipation that when mealtime comes around they'll be too busy or traveling and won't be able to eat so they stock up in advance of feeling hungry. There are recreational eaters who regularly

GOOD EATING PRACTICES FOR WEIGHT LOSS
AND GOOD HEALTH

- Always sit down to eat. Sitting applies the right amount of pressure to the stomach for the most efficient digestion.
- Eat only when hungry. Don't feel pressured to eat.
- Wait at least four to six hours before eating again after a main meal to allow the food to be fully assimilated. Otherwise agni becomes overburdened and digestion grows increasingly less efficient.
- Allow enough time to eat well. Give the body time to register the fact that it is being fed.
- Eat your largest meal at lunch when your digestive fire is strongest.
- Never eat when you are upset or angry. Feeding emotional upheavals contributes to poor digestion.
- Pause in silence and close the eyes for a moment before eating to help balance the doshas, or say a brief prayer.
- Eat in a settled, serene atmosphere with pleasant table conversation, soft dinner music, or comfortable silence.
- Don't read, watch television, or drive a vehicle while eating. Pay attention to the tastes, textures, and qualities of your food and enjoy it.
- Don't talk on the telephone, listen to loud music, get up and down to receive visitors, or do business.
- Eat comfortable sizes of food and chew thoroughly. Don't talk while chewing.
- Sip a little warm water after every few bites of food to layer the food with the water.
- Drinking milk while eating any food increases weight.
- Eat very lightly in the evening and be finished before 8 P.M. so digestion can be finished before bedtime.
- Leave the table just satisfied but not full. If you are still feeling hungry, eat one or two more bites of food and see how you feel. Eat enough to fill two-thirds of the stomach—about what will fit in the two cupped hands.
- Don't eat or drink anything but water or warm tea between meals.
- Drinking water or anything for an hour after the meal increases Kapha and weight.
- Eat freshly prepared food.
- Eat balanced meals that include some of the six tastes and six qualities.
- At the end of the meal sit and relax quietly for 5 to 10 minutes. Let your digestion get on peacefully.

read or watch TV and mindlessly consume large quantities of food; others snack constantly and overeat in response to stress or anxiety.

Whatever the reason, the result of eating without feeling hungry and without paying full attention to enjoying the delicious tastes of the food is that you lose the essential ability to tell when your body is hungry and when to stop because you've had enough to eat. This combination contributes to developing habits of overeating. Many of the good eating practices we've just discussed have to do with how best to use your attention before, during, and after the meal. Just as the quality of the cook's attention during the preparation of the meal creates nourishing, sattvic food, the conscious attention you devote to eating is equally important for getting the most out of your meals. If you do not attend to what you eat you're not giving the correct signals to your body, telling it that it is being fed. Dissatisfaction naturally results.

Ayurveda is dedicated
to all those who want to become
good eaters.

—DR. H. S. KASTURE

STYLES OF OVEREATING

The problem of overeating and excessive weight gain is a complex one that we will only briefly look at here in terms of the different body types, because each of the three constitutions and their combinations when out of balance display their own styles or habits of overeating. There are, of course, many other components to consider, but each individual's nature is a good place to start.

It's not only those with the slower, heavier Kapha metabolism that gain extra weight, it's just that Kaphas and those with some combination of Kapha dosha do it easily. Those with Vata and Pitta imbalances who overeat may not only develop digestive disorders, but they gain weight in such specific areas of the body as the hips and thighs, the abdomen, or the upper arms and calves rather than uniformly all over.

VATA: HURRY UP AND STOP
Vata's poorest eating habits include eating when nervous or worried (emotional eating), eating too quickly and talking excessively during

the meal, and not paying attention to what's being eaten. The not-well-chewed food goes in quickly and just seems to sit there while the body is not even sure it's been fed. Someone who eats this way doesn't learn to recognize the feeling of satisfaction that says it's time to stop eating. Vata's variable digestive fire says that stopping at this point seems okay, rather than because a feeling of satisfaction is achieved. A Pitta-Vata type with strong agni may simply refill the plate and (over)eat again more slowly to have the experience and the extra food. In either case discomfort, indigestion, gas, and ama naturally result.

PITTA'S FIRES
Pitta's wonderful digestion, when fully fired up and ready to go, can feel as if it could devour Philadelphia. There seems to be no end to Pitta's consuming agni, which is good for healthy digestion, but it can easily lead to overeating because Pitta types—including Pitta-Vata and Pitta-Kapha—can easily overfill the stomach. If your appetite is so intense that you eat too quickly without taking time to savor the food and listen to the body's subtle cues that hunger is assuaged and it's time to stop eating, then you may go on eating and eating until either agni just shuts down, stalling the digestive process, or you leave the table feeling uncomfortably full. This is a particularly delicate issue for Pitta-Kapha (Kapha-Pitta) types. If agni is deranged or out of control, then Pitta's excessive feeding further imbalances Kapha. In some cases weight gain is swifter and more effortless for someone with a Kapha-Pitta imbalance than any others.

The most meaningful eating practice for Pitta to follow when changing the overeating habit is to eat regularly—do not skip meals, sit quietly for a few minutes before the meal, and then eat in a settled atmosphere slowly savoring a Pitta-balancing diet. Pitta types benefit most from a serene dining situation, including subdued colors and music, friendly company, and conversation that pleases, nourishes, and ultimately satisfies the senses.

EASYGOING KAPHA
Kapha types gain weight by eating a lot of sweet-tasting, heavy, slow-to-digest, cold food . . . and by simply not exercising enough. The Kapha-balancing diet and the suggested guidelines for good eating are specifically designed for Kapha types. In many cases strictly following them is all Kapha has to do to maintain healthy eating habits and

normal weight. If overeating or overweight is an ongoing problem, increasing the use of the pungent taste and heavily favoring weight-reducing foods helps.

A Light Vata-Reducing Diet

Some people with Vata imbalances find that they gain weight by eating too much of the heavy, oily foods in the regular Vata-balancing diet (page 45). Vata-types may not benefit from losing weight with a Kapha-reducing diet because the best foods for reducing Kapha are primarily light and dry ones, and the emphasis is on bitter, astringent-tasting salads and other green vegetables. All of these can aggravate Vata overtime.

Vata and Vata-Pitta types who gain weight easily might try following a light version of the Vata diet instead. The legume, vegetable, and fruit recommendations are about the same as those in the regular Vata diet; the main differences are in the oils, the kinds of grains, and the dairy products used.

If you want to lose weight on the Vata-reducing diet continue favoring wheat, oats, and rice, but in their lighter forms. For instance, eat crackers, biscuits, toasted sliced bread, tortillas, chapatis, and pita bread. Eat couscous instead of the heavier semolina pastas. Cream of wheat, cream of rice, and oatmeal are good breakfast and supper cereals if they are made with a lot of water. Dry roast basmati or other long-grain white rice before boiling it.

Drink and cook with low-fat milk or use fresh goat's milk if it is available. It is much lighter in quality and nutrition than cow's milk. Make Lassi by mixing equal parts of water and yogurt. But reduce all other cheese and rich dairy foods.

All oils including small amounts of ghee are acceptable, except coconut oil. People have reported that canola oil, an all-purpose oil that is pressed from rape seed and has become widely available, gives them indigestion. You may or may not want to use it.

Although almost all vegetables are fine to eat, the light Vata diet contains more cucumbers, celery, asparagus, artichokes, skinned tomatoes, peeled zucchini and eggplant, carrots, spinach, and daikon radishes fried in oil. Adding a pinch of hing to the vegetables while they are cooking increases their digestibility. Use more lemon juice in food preparation.

The best spices in a light Vata-reducing diet are cumin, ginger, fenugreek, hing, mustard seeds, small amounts of black pepper, cinnamon, cardamom, anise, fennel, cloves, and salt. Use other spices and herbs in proportionately smaller amounts.

The foods in this diet should be fresh, very well cooked, delicious, and satisfying. It is important to eat only when you feel hungry, and on a regular schedule. And follow the other recommended practices for good eating mentioned on page 259.

SPECIAL WEIGHT-REDUCING FOODS FOR KAPHA

Some foods are especially good for losing weight. Most of these are light and dry in quality. In a weight-loss program favor foods with astringent, bitter, and pungent tastes. These are some other ingredients that go into a good weight-reducing diet especially for Kapha.

GRAINS

When following a weight-loss program eat barley once every day or every other day. It is light and astringent. Simply boil half a cup of barley in 3 cups of lightly salted water until the barley is soft. By dry roasting or frying it (before boiling) in a little oil for 2 or 3 minutes, or until it is lightly brown, barley becomes even lighter. Barley water, a natural diuretic, can be made by increasing the water to 4 or 5 cups. Strain and drink the cloudy liquid; eat the soft barley with vegetables.

Other Kapha-reducing grains to include in a reducing diet are cornmeal, buckwheat, and rye flours. You can substitute barley flour for up to one-third of wheat flour in a bread recipe without changing the end product. Try to avoid eating very much wheat and rice, although it is all right to substitute a rice cake or some wheat crackers for a slice of bread, because the baking process makes crackers and rice cakes very light and dry.

SPICES, TEAS, AND COFFEE

Increase the use of ginger—freshly grated is best—black pepper, and turmeric in your cooking. A little honey or honey mixed with water just before eating reduces Kapha's appetite. During the day sip warm ginseng tea or other Kapha-reducing tea, such as Maharishi Ayur-Ved Kapha Tea. But the best drink of all is water that has been boiled for about 10 minutes and cooled to a comfortably warm drinking temperature.

SALADS AND FRESH VEGETABLES
Bitter, astringent, light leafy greens, as well as such bitter-tasting steamed vegetables as Swiss chard, celery leaves, broccoli, and un-peeled zucchini, are part of an everyday weight-loss diet. If the urge to snack comes up, have some celery sticks with their leaves attached handy. Their bitter taste satisfies nicely.

BALANCE AND WEIGHT LOSS

The proper balance of the six tastes and qualities is still important even when reducing weight. A healthy weight-loss program includes variety from many food groups. Ninety-five percent of a main meal for weight loss should include Kapha-decreasing foods with bitter, pungent, and astringent tastes, and dry, light, and hot qualities predominating. The rest of the meal should be sweet, salty, sour, cold, heavy, and only slightly oily. Eat no Kapha-increasing desserts. Except for small amounts of honey, the sweet taste should appear least in any weight-loss meal.

A TYPICAL MEAL

If the digestive fire is strong as much as one-half of the main meal can be a salad of lettuce, other leafy greens, and fresh herbs, with a dash of lemon or lime juice for dressing. Light, dry, pungent, bitter, and as-tringent salads have all the best qualities Kapha types and those reduc-ing weight want most. But it is important to eat warm food, even as a side dish, too. A bowl of dahl or other soup, some steamed vegetables and corn bread, barley, or other light grains, or a serving of spicy mixed vegetables and cooked grain is best. Too much cold food will leave a dieter dissatisfied and hungry.

REDUCE SNACKING

A key element in maintaining a strong agni and normal weight is to follow the healthy principle found in nature that alternates rest and activity. Allow your digestive system periods of rest. Do not eat in

between meals. At the beginning of a weight-loss diet, if you feel
ravenously hungry (this feeling should subside in a day or two), sit
down and enjoy a piece of fruit, some celery or carrot sticks, or nibble
on a rice cake just until you feel satisfied. Or slowly sip some unsweetened tea or a cup of warm water simmered with grated fresh ginger
(or ½ teaspoon powdered ginger). Drinking some warm water or tea
during the day is not considered snacking. And keep in mind that it is
more important that you feel comfortable when changing incorrect
dietary habits than rigidly following rules. The whole point of the
change is to become more in tune with your body's signals of when to
eat and when to stop eating. Reducing the habit of snacking is one of
these salutary changes.

RECIPES FOR LIGHT EATING AND WEIGHT LOSS

When eating lightly in the evening any of the following recipes from
Chapter 4 will make a nutritious light meal for you.

Perfect Lentil Soup and Rice
Savory Wild Rice Casserole
Light Corn Bread and Soup or Salad
Potage Printanier/French Potato Soup
Masoor Dahl and Rice
R&S Couscous
Roasted and Spiced Barley with Vegetables
Simple Rice Pilaf
Spinach and Chicory Salad
Tossed Green Salad with Dressing of Choice
Vegetable Whole Grain Sauté
Vegetable Soup with Fresh Herbs

New Mothers and Their Babies

These dietary recommendations represent only a part of the Maharishi Ayur-Ved Program for Mothers and Babies. For complete information regarding medical consultations and postdelivery treatments in the home, contact a Maharishi Ayur-Ved Health Center. We are grateful to the founding director of the program, Mrs. Clara Berno, for providing this information.

THE NEW MOTHER

The first six weeks after giving birth are important for the new mother and her child. Ayurveda treats it as a time for rejuvenation, an opportunity to reach perfection. In this six-week program a new mother can rejuvenate and balance her whole body. The birth process naturally results in fatigue and disturbance of Vata. From that point the new mother and baby program builds up the entire psychophysiology to a state of increased balance and strength. And, of course, the baby benefits greatly from the mother's increased well-being.

> *We just give a helping hand to Mother Nature.*
> *She set the whole thing up,*
> *we just help make it easy.*
>
> —CLARA BERNO

A new mother is in a physically and emotionally delicate state. After the delivery of a baby, the mother's digestive fire, agni, is often diminished; her digestive system is as delicate as her baby's. The new mother's diet should be specifically designed for her. She neither needs nor can she properly use heavy, sour, or rough foods. Her diet should consist of delicious, warm, nutritious, nourishing, and Vata-balancing recipes. Chicken, fish, and other meats are such heavily concentrated proteins they cannot be easily digested. If there is a desire for meat it can be taken as a broth or very thin soup.

A NEW MOTHER'S GUIDELINES FOR GOOD EATING

- Eat before nursing.
- Never nurse when hungry.
- Don't nurse and eat at the same time.
- Eat fresh, good-quality food.
- Eat when you are hungry.
- Enjoy your food.
- Eat in pleasant surroundings.
- Eat sitting down.
- Do not eat or cook when you are upset.
- Practice moderation in eating.
- Follow the body's wisdom for food selection.
- Balance the six tastes at every meal.
- Eat a suitable amount.
- Consider time of day and seasonal changes.
- Follow common sense, not rigid rules.

GOOD DIGESTION

How well a mother's food is digested and assimilated determines the quality of her milk. Following these guidelines for eating well and maintaining a strong digestive fire are necessary for the best assimilation of food. For instance, both good appetizers and beautiful presentation of the meal help to ignite agni. Even something as simple as a tablespoon of warm rice and ghee before eating works. Some new mothers, depending on their physical strength or strong Pitta nature, will maintain healthy appetites and lively agni right after the birth process. Many others notice that they are not as hungry or able to digest their meals as well as they did before delivery. Whatever the case, it is important to respect the level of digestion the new mother experiences and prepare meals accordingly.

Appetizers before a meal are like kindling for a fire.
To make a roaring blaze,
start with paper, sticks, and kindling.
Once it's going then throw in a log.

—CLARA BERNO

BALANCING VATA

The naturally occurring imbalance in Vata after delivery can best be corrected by following a modified Vata-balancing diet, consulting a physician trained in Maharishi Ayur-Ved for special instructions, and by scheduling special in-home treatments. Many mothers enjoy the benefits so much they continue on the new mothers' diet for many months after the six-week program is over. Enjoyment and comfort are the deciding factors.

LOSS OF WEIGHT

Carefully following the new mothers' Ayurvedic diet results in any weight gained during pregnancy naturally coming off. In fact, many mothers say that after childbirth they are able to maintain a more natural weight than they've had in years. This diet also gives her baby a comfortable, healthy start in life.

BABY'S DIET

Ayurveda recommends mother's milk as the best food for a new baby's nourishment and digestion. Breast milk is being developed at the same time the baby is developing. And considering all the factors of time, the environment, the weather, climate, and so forth, a mother's milk is specifically suitable for her own newborn.

A MOTHER'S DIET AND HER BABY

Because of its immature digestive system a newborn baby has an easier time digesting milk if its mother follows a Vata-balancing diet. Many of the dietary suggestions in this book for nursing mothers help to nourish their new babies, too. Whatever a mother eats directly affects her baby. By following an Ayurvedic diet, she will find that her baby

experiences less discomfort from intestinal gas. If a mother is up at
night with an uncomfortable, crying baby, the quality of her emotional
state as well as increasing fatigue will affect the quality of her milk and
the child care she provides.

The most suitable diet for mother and baby is a modified Vata-
reducing diet, one that is very simple, wholesome, and easily digested.
Items from each food group are simply prepared. Most of the menu is
made up of fruit, vegetables, milk, dahl and rice, or simple vegetable
soups.

THE NEW MOTHERS' DIET
Warm • Sweet • Oily • Liquid • Soothing

Sweet fruits and vegetables simply steamed until they are well done
are easy to make and comfortable to digest. Stir-fried or sautéed vegetables should be thoroughly cooked until very soft. Vegetables taste
especially good when they are served in a little seasoned vegetable
broth. Eat only sweet, thoroughly ripened fruits, such as peaches,
mangoes, berries, and cherries.

A new mother should drink at least two cups of warm milk a day
with a little ghee added. To warm milk properly, bring it to a boil and
then allow it to cool to a comfortable temperature before drinking. A
pleasant drink can be made by mixing a cup of warm milk, a teaspoon
of ghee, a little sugar, and ground cardamom to taste.

Very soupy dahl and basmati rice or another long-grain rice mixed
together make a soothing dish for new mothers. Boil rice in a little
extra water to make it plump rather than dry, and add a teaspoon of
ghee to the water. Mung dahl from split mung beans causes less gas
than other types. And it is easily digested. Dahl should be well cooked
until the beans completely disappear, and it should remain very liquid
after cooking. Four or five cups of water for each half cup of lentils is
a good proportion. Add salt, ghee, and Vata Churna, to taste, before
cooking.

WHAT TO AVOID

Of the many foods usually included in a standard Vata-balancing diet,
a few should be avoided by new mothers. These are: yeast-risen breads

and leavened baked goods—substitute chapatis or heated flour tortillas for leavened bread—cream sauces, chocolate, cheese, tomatoes, such stimulating drinks as coffee, tea, and alcohol, carbonated drinks, and sour and heavy foods.

In the early days a new mother
craves a simple diet.
After that meals should be
sumptuously full of variety.

—JAN THATCHER, NEW MOTHER AND BABY PROGRAM PARTICIPANT

RECIPES FOR NEW MOTHERS

New mothers in the Maharishi Ayur-Ved Mother and Baby Program often say they prefer eating warm vegetable soups or creamy breakfast cereals. Cream of Wheat or rice cereals with a few raisins and finely ground blanched almonds make a nourishing breakfast or supper. There are many possible variations that can be made from the basic vegetable soup recipe in this section.

These recipes, created by Jan Thatcher and other members of the New Mother and Baby Program in Fairfield, Iowa, are tried and tested favorites. Several of the recipes are baked at the same temperature and can be prepared together to save time.

The baby is the direct recipient of
the new mother's increased well-being,
health, and happiness.

—CLARA BERNO

VATA-BALANCING DIET FOR NEW MOTHERS

FAVOR

General: warm, oily, sweet, salty, liquid foods
Dairy: whole milk
Sweeteners: sugar, molasses, raw honey
Oils: ghee, sesame oil, olive oil
Grains: rice, wheat (with ghee), unleavened baked goods
Fruits: sweet apples, avocado, berries, cherries, coconut, grapes,
               mango, papaya, peaches, pineapple, plums
Vegetables: asparagus, beet, carrot, cucumber, eggplant, yellow squash,
               butternut, acorn squash, pumpkin, spinach
Lentils: mung dahl
Spices: black pepper (limited), brown mustard seeds, caraway,
               cardamom, cinnamon, cumin, fennel, fenugreek, salt,
               ginger, saffron
Nuts: blanched almonds, finely ground
Meat: none in first six weeks. Broth from chicken or turkey, if
               desired for non-vegetarians

REDUCE

General: cold, dry, very light or heavy, raw foods, bitter, pungent,
               astringent tastes
Dairy: cheese, sour cream, heavy cream
Grains: barley, oats, corn, millet, buckwheat, rye
Breads: leavened with yeast, baking soda, or baking powder
Fruits: sour apples, pomegranate, cranberries
Vegetables: peas, broccoli, cabbage, cauliflower, Brussels sprouts,
               potatoes, green leafy and raw vegetables
Beans: all except mung lentils
Spices: allspice, basil, cayenne, turmeric, oregano, paprika
Meat: all

Mother's Baked Lentil Soup

The idea of "baking" a soup could only originate with a very busy person. Jan Thatcher, who became a new mother when her toddler son seemed to need most of her time and attention, designed this one. This extraordinarily neat and easy method of making a delicious dahl is good for everyone, not only new mothers. It's an extremely soupy dahl—the best consistency for Vata and Kapha to digest. In a regular diet you might want to double the amount of lentils or follow the Perfect Lentil Soup recipe on page 164. Very new mothers would have only about a quarter of a cup of this soup served over rice, or to taste.

To save time, bake rice in a separate covered casserole in the oven with the soup. You might make Saffron Rice (page 190) or simply put a cup of washed basmati rice—or unwashed enriched rice—in a 1-quart casserole with 2 1/2 cups water, 1 tablespoon ghee, and salt, to taste. Cover and bake for 30 minutes. This can be done at the beginning or end of the Mother's Baked Lentil Soup cooking time.

Serves 3 to 4

> *⅓ cup mung lentils, washed and cleaned*
> *½ teaspoon salt*
> *1 teaspoon ghee*
> *½ teaspoon Vata Churna*
> *4 cups boiling water*
> *½ cup chopped spinach (optional)*
> *1 teaspoon ghee*
> *1 teaspoon brown mustard seeds*
> *1 teaspoon Vata Churna*

1. Preheat the oven to 325°F.
2. Place the lentils, the salt, the ghee, and ½ teaspoon Vata Churna in a 1½- or 2-quart casserole. Pour the water over, sprinkle with the spinach, cover tightly, and bake for at least 2 hours. Even after 3 or 4 hours of baking this soup is great. It will make a very thin lentil dahl.
3. To prepare the spices: Just before serving, heat the ghee in a small pan over a moderate flame. Add the mustard seeds and when they start to pop stir in the Churna. Stir the spices into the cooked dahl, mixing well to combine. Serve with rice.

Fresh Spinach Puree

Many recipes in the new mothers' diet are appropriate for any convalescent. This is one of them. It is very soothing and easy to digest.

Serves 1

½ pound fresh spinach, washed and destemmed
1 tablespoon ghee
Pinch of nutmeg
1 teaspoon sesame seeds

Pat the spinach dry with paper towels. Then place it in a small saucepan with the ghee and the nutmeg. Cover and heat it over a low flame for 7 to 8 minutes, or until it is limp. Stir occasionally to cook evenly. Puree the spinach in a blender or a food processor. Toss in the sesame seeds and serve immediately.

Variable Vegetable Soup

This soup is similar to the Vata Broth recipe in Chapter 4, but the vegetables are kept in the soup and served. Use any combination of Vata-reducing vegetables from the recommended diet for new mothers (page 271).

Serves 4 to 6

6 cups water
4 cups chopped mixed vegetables
1 teaspoon salt, or to taste
1 tablespoon ghee
1 teaspoon brown mustard seeds
½ teaspoon ground cumin
½ teaspoon ground fenugreek
1 teaspoon ground cardamom
Black pepper, to taste

Bring the water to a boil in a large pot. Add the vegetables and the salt. Cover and simmer for 30 minutes. Heat the ghee in a small frying pan over a medium flame. Add the mustard seeds. When they begin popping, add the remaining spices and stir for 30 seconds. Stir them into the soup and simmer for another hour.

OTHER RECIPES GOOD FOR NEW MOTHERS

Here are some other recipes found in Chapter 4 that are good for balancing Vata and appealing to new mothers.

Curried Squash Soup
Khichari
Vata Broth
Lightly Seasoned Vegetables
Quick Vegetable Medley
Simply Baked Carrots
Puris and Chapatis
Saffron Rice (made with extra water)
Couscous
R&S Couscous
Sweet Potato–Apple Pie
American Apple Pie with Vanilla Sauce
    (or use other sweet fruits in pies and turnovers)
Creamy Rice Pudding
Jam Diagonals
Mother's Laddu
Simple Shortbread
Date Shake

APPENDIXES

1

THE TWENTY APPROACHES OF MAHARISHI AYUR-VED TO CREATE PERFECT HEALTH

1. **Consciousness**—Development of higher states of consciousness through Maharishi's Transcendental Meditation, its advanced techniques, and the TM-Sidhi programme.

2. **Primordial Sound**—Use of the primordial sounds of the Samhita of the four aspects of the Ved and their Ved-Angas and Up-Angas to eliminate imbalances in the functioning of human nature as a whole.

3. **Intellect**—To correct the mistake of the intellect, Pragya-aparadha, so that the totality of the unified structure of life is perceived while one is perceiving the diversified structure. In this state of knowledge of the Self, disease cannot flourish because life is intimately connected with the source of natural law.

4. **Emotions**—Strengthening of the finest level of feeling to develop the emotions fully.

5. **Language**—Using Vedic principles of the structure of language to promote balance and integrity in the mind and body.

6. **Gandharva-Ved**—Traditional music therapy using sound and melody to restore harmony in the physiology and eliminate the imbalances responsible for disease.

7. **Senses**—Vedic procedures to enliven through all five senses, perfect balance in psychophysiology.

8. **Pulse Diagnosis**—Detecting any existing or forthcoming imbalance simply by feeling the pulse.

9. **Psycho-Physiological Integration**—Restoration of homeostatic balance and acceleration of neuromuscular coordination and balance in the physiology and psychology.

10. **Neuromuscular Integration**—Vedic exercises to restore mind-body coordination and the integrated functioning of all levels of life.

11. **Neuro-Respiratory Integration**—Vedic exercises pertaining to the physiology of breathing to restore integrated functioning to all levels of mind and body.

12. **Physiological Purification**—Sophisticated purification procedures applied at regular intervals to eliminate and prevent the accumulation of physiological impurities due to faulty dietary and behavioral patterns.

13. **Diet**—Appropriate dietary measures to support the restoration of physiological balance in the prevention and treatment of disease.

14. **Herbs and Minerals**—Use of medicine, flora, and minerals from every country to bring perfect balance to the functioning of mind and body.

15. **Rasayana**—Sophisticated herbal and mineral preparations formulated for the prevention and cure of disease and the promotion of longevity.

16. **Behavior**—Bringing behavior into accord with natural law through daily and seasonal routines.

17. **Jyotish**—Securing perfect health for the future; mathematical prediction of environmental influences on health.

18. **Yagya**—Vedic performances to restore environmental balance and promote individual and collective health.

19. **Environment**—Creating collective health through the Transcendental Meditation and TM-Sidhi programme so that society provides a nourishing and strengthening environment for the individual to rise to perfect health.

20. **World Health/World Peace**—Group performance by 7,000 experts in Maharishi's Transcendental Meditation and TM-Sidhi programme to create coherence in world consciousness, the basis of world peace and collective health on a global scale.

2

QUESTIONS AND ANSWERS ABOUT AYURVEDA

By Dr. Richard Averbach
and Dr. H. S. Kasture

Question: What can everybody eat in winter or in summer?

Answer: Some of the dietary principles are really the same for all the *prakritis* (your "nature" from birth—see Glossary). In cold, wet, or windy seasons heavier foods are best for everyone. In hot, humid seasons, lighter foods are best. From one point of view, it's not even the responsibility of the cook, but your own responsibility to know what you should be eating, because you are the one who actually chooses which foods to eat. So if you know that a certain type of food isn't so suitable for you at a particular time, then take less of that food.

Question: Do the six tastes—sweet, sour, pungent, bitter, salty, and astringent—have to be in each dish in the meal? Can they spread out in a whole meal or be taken over the whole day?

Answer: Each meal should have the six types of tastes. If you are taking two meals, one at lunch and one at dinner, both meals should have the six tastes. One dish may be sweet, another pungent or bitter, but all the dishes taken together should provide the full range.

Question: Some children refuse to try all six tastes. How can we encourage them to eat something other than bread, milk, and pickles?

Answer: One has to prepare the meal according to the tastes of the children. That means six tastes should be mixed during the preparation into the foods they like to eat. So make the foods they like best and mix in the six tastes. Eating habits can be changed gradually.

Question: I'm Vata prakriti, whereas my husband and children are other prakritis. How am I going to feed my whole family?

Answer: Balance is the theme of the entire dietary regimen. The principle of eating all six tastes and qualities at every meal will ensure a balanced diet for each family member. You can prepare balanced meals by following the guidelines in this book. Allow slight variations for different members of the family, but do not prepare separate meals for each. For example, one person shouldn't have much pungent taste, and if there's a pungent pickle, let's say, maybe that individual just tastes it but doesn't have much of it. Someone else shouldn't have a very rich dessert so they have a few bites of the dessert. They just taste it and don't have very much. The point is that you don't cook a separate meal for each prakriti. There should be enough variety at each meal for everyone to select what is appealing and be satisfied. You simply need to understand the principles involved for each family member, and then it's very simple to serve balanced meals.

Question: What should you not mix in milk?

Answer: Actually milk is sweet, and that is why sweet things can be added to it. For example, sweet fruits such as banana can be added to milk. But any ingredients that are not sweet-tasting (sour, salty, astringent, and bitter) are not compatible with milk.

Question: It's my understanding that basmati rice is lighter than other rice and can be eaten by Kapha types.

Answer: Basmati rice is good for Kapha in moderate amounts. All rice is included in a Kapha diet, but when we can choose one rice over others, we choose basmati. Rice is a staple of the diet and can be eaten by everybody, only Kapha shouldn't take so much of it. And Kapha should dry roast or fry the rice in a little ghee before boiling it in water. Rice, wheat, mung beans, and lentil dahls are perfect foods. They are the main grain foods that can be taken by all prakritis.

Question: How do we get enough protein and follow a sattvic diet?

Answer: Many think that protein means eating meat and eggs. We advise reducing meat and eggs. They are not the only source of protein. You can have a diet high enough in protein by eating dairy products, especially milk, as well as soups or dahls made from various lentils and served with rice. Urad gram, whether prepared as whole beans or lentils have an abundant quantity of digestible protein.

Question: Is it okay to eat hot foods like rice and dahl with cold foods, meaning cold-temperature foods like salads, at the same meal?

Answer: Cold food is okay with rice and dahl. Salad is cool, not ice cold.

Question: Is it all right to mix fruit and vegetables at the same meal?

Answer: According to Maharishi Ayur-Ved, it is all right to eat fruit and vegetables at the same meal.

Question: When food such as wheat is eaten in a dry form, like crackers, what influence will that have on the doshas?

Answer: Processing is an important point in Maharishi Ayur-Ved. Wheat is heavy. When made into crackers, it becomes dry and light in quality. Then it may be lighter to digest and better for Kapha types.

Question: Should almonds be eaten with the skin on, or blanched to remove the skin, so that they're white?

Answer: Although almonds can be eaten both ways, it is better to remove the skin from the almond. The almond skin is sour. Eating many unblanched almonds can give a little pain in the chest or heartburn. When we remove the skin, almonds add a sweet taste and are good for all doshas. Of course, in a large quantity even blanched almonds produce gas. But in moderation they are okay. Digestion of almonds is slow and heavy, so for Kapha small quantities are best.

Question: Should I boil water for drinking?

Answer: Boiling water makes it light. Once or twice a day you might drink very warm water that has been boiled. This is a healthy habit to develop that is very good for digestion. But that doesn't mean that all day long we are to drink only warm water or that we should never have any cool water. You may want to boil water and then cool it to room temperature to drink with meals and during the day.

❖❖

Question: I like pepper in soups, but I heard Pitta-dominant people aren't supposed to eat it. What can I do?

Answer: The properties of black pepper are pungent, hot, light, dry, and rough. These properties promote digestion, increase Pitta and Vata, and decrease Kapha. That doesn't mean if you are the body type that pepper increases, you should *never* have it. If black pepper is used excessively it will tend to exaggerate that particular dosha. If you're a Pitta type, black pepper and cayenne pepper certainly wouldn't be something you'd take in large quantities, especially in the summertime when Pitta is more predominant. And Vata types would avoid large amounts of black pepper in light and dry seasons.

Question: I have trouble waiting three to six hours before eating. Is it permissible to snack between meals if I am hungry?

Answer: When you are hungry, you should eat. This is a rule of Maharishi Ayur-Ved. Sometimes we are ruled by our own habits instead. That is not good. An occasional snack is not so bad. But always snacking will invite many types of digestive complications. If you eat to your satisfaction at mealtime, you won't have the habit of snacking.

Question: What is the best kind of milk to drink?

Answer: Although there are eight types of milk described in Maharishi Ayur-Ved, cow's milk is the best. Goat's milk is a little lighter than cow's milk and a little lighter to digest. But cow's milk is the most excellent for taste, appetite, and nutrition.

Question: Some people have this feeling that sugar isn't such a good thing to eat. Can sugar be eaten or should it never be eaten?

Answer: Eat either raw, brown, or white sugar in moderation. There is not some magical sugar from Vedic times. Because of its sweet, cold, heavy properties, eating too much sugar aggravates Kapha dosha. (For more detailed information about sugar, see pages 92–93.)

Question: What is the best way to drink milk?

Answer: It is best to heat milk before it's taken. It shouldn't generally be taken right out of the refrigerator and served. First, milk should be brought to a full boil, then cooled to a comfortably hot or warm temperature before drinking. If milk is not well-tolerated, try boiling skim milk to a full frothing boil with a little grated gingerroot.

Question: I have heard some foods described as "auspicious." What does it mean?

Answer: Sattvic foods or food that is especially life-promoting, such as milk or ghee, is auspicious. (See "The Three Categories of Diet," page 232.)

3

CHARTS OF INGREDIENTS

I = INCREASE, D = DECREASE, — = NEUTRAL

	VATA	PITTA	KAPHA	TASTE AND QUALITY
BEVERAGES				
Juices:				
Apple	—	D	—	Sweet, Dry
Apricot	D	—	I	Sweet, Slightly Sour
Carrot	—	I	—	Sweet, Astringent, Hot
Coconut	—	—	I	Sweet, Oily, Heavy
Cranberry	D	—	I	Sour, Sweet, Astringent
Grape	—	D	I	Sweet, Cold
Grapefruit	—	I	I	Sour, Sharp
Lemon	D	I	I	Sour, Sweet
Lime	D	D	I	Sour
Orange (sour)	D	I	D	Sweet, Sour, Heavy
Orange (sweet)	D	I	I	Sweet, Heavy, Hot
Papaya (ripe)	—	I	D	Sweet
Peach	D	D	I	Sweet, Slightly Sour
Pear (ripe)	—	—	I	Sweet, Sour
Pineapple	D	D	I	Sweet, Sour
Pomegranate	D	D	—	Sweet, Astringent, Sour
Prune	D	D	I	Sweet, Sour, Heavy
Tomato	D	I	I	Sour
Teas:				
Chamomile	I	—	D	Bitter, Astringent
Jasmine	—	D	D	Astringent, Bitter, Sweet
Orange Pekoe	I	—	D	Astringent, Bitter
Peppermint	—	D	D	Pungent, Sweet, Sharp

	VATA	PITTA	KAPHA	TASTE AND QUALITY
Rosehips	D	I	I	Sour, Astringent aftertaste
Spearmint	—	D	D	Pungent, Sweet, Astringent, Sparkling, Sharp
Herbal Blends:				
Almond Sunset	D	I	I	Slightly Sweet, Bitter, Astringent
Cinnamon Rose	D	I	I	Slightly Sour, Astringent
Emperor's Choice	D	—	D	Sweet, Astringent, Bitter
Mandarin Orange-Spice	D	—	D	Sour, Astringent
Mocha Spice	I	—	D	Astringent, Bitter
Morning Thunder	I	—	D	Astringent, Bitter
Raspberry	D	—	D	Sour, Astringent aftertaste
Red Zinger (cold)	D	I	I	Slightly Sour
Red Zinger (hot)	D	I	D	Slightly Sour
Coffees:				
Decaffeinated	I	D	D	Bitter
Iced coffee	I	D	I	Bitter
With caffeine	I	D	D	Bitter
Raja's Cup	D	D	I	Sweet, Heavy
DAIRY PRODUCTS				
Butter	D	D	I	Sweet, Sour, Oily, Soft
Buttermilk	D	I	I	Sour, Cold, Heavy
Cream	D	D	I	Sweet, Oily, Heavy, Cold
Cottage cheese	D	I	I	Sour, Cold
Ghee	D	D	I	Sweet, Light, Cold
Milk (cow's)	D	D	I	Sweet, Oily, Heavy, Cold
Panir, ricotta, and soft cheese	D	D	I	Slightly Sour, Oily, Cold
Semihard and hard cheese	D	I	I	Sour, Heavy, Cold
Skim milk	D	D	I	Sweet, Oily, Heavy, Cold
Sour cream	D	I	I	Sour, Cold, Heavy
Yogurt	D	I	I	Sour, Hot, Heavy, Oily

	VATA	PITTA	KAPHA	TASTE AND QUALITY
HERBS AND SPICES				
Allspice	I	I	D	Pungent, Astringent
Anise	—	D	D	Sweet, Bitter, Astringent
Asafoetida (hing)	D	I	D	Astringent, Hot
Basil	D	I	D	Pungent
Bay leaves	—	I	D	Bitter, Astringent
Caraway	D	—	I	Bitter, Astringent
Cardamom	—	D	I	Sweet, Bitter, Astringent, Hot
Cayenne	D	I	D	Pungent, Light, Dry
Celery Seed	I	—	D	Pungent, Bitter
Chili pepper	—	I	D	Pungent, Dry, Hot
Cilantro	D	—	D	Pungent, Astringent, Bitter, Cold
Cinnamon	D	—	D	Pungent, Sweet
Cloves	D	I	D	Pungent, Hot, Light
Coriander	I	D	D	Sweet, Slightly Pungent, Oily
Cumin	D	I	D	Sweet, Bitter, Pungent, Light
Dill	D	D	—	Bitter, Astringent
Fennel	—	D	D	Sweet, Bitter, Astringent
Fenugreek	D	I	D	Sweet, Bitter, Hot
Garlic	D	I	I	Sour, Sweet, Oily, Hot
Ginger	D	I	D	Pungent, Sweet, Light, Dry
Horseradish	I	I	D	Bitter, Light, Pungent
Lemon thyme	—	I	D	Pungent
Licorice root	D	D	D	Sweet, Light
Mace	I	D	D	Bitter, Sweet, Dry
Marjoram	I	I	D	Pungent, Slightly Astringent
Mustard—black or yellow seed	D	I	D	Pungent, Oily, Sharp, Hot
Nasturtium	D	I	D	Slightly Sweet, Pungent
Nutmeg	I	D	D	Bitter, Sweet, Dry
Oregano	I	I	D	Pungent, Slightly Astringent

	VATA	PITTA	KAPHA	TASTE AND QUALITY
Paprika	I	—	D	Sweet, Slightly Pungent
Parsley	—	—	D	Pungent, Astringent, Slightly Bitter
Pepper (black)	D	I	D	Pungent, Dry, Light, Hot
Poppy seeds	D	—	I	Bitter, Heavy
Rosemary	I	I	D	Astringent, Slightly Bitter, Sharp
Saffron	D	I	D	Sweet, Pungent, Stimulating, Hot, Dry
Sage	I	I	D	Pungent, Astringent, Bitter
Salt	D	I	I	Salty, Smooth, Heavy
Savory	—	—	D	Pungent
Sesame Seed	D	I	I	Sweet, Astringent, Bitter
Tarragon	—	—	D	Pungent, Bitter
Thyme	I	I	D	Pungent, Astringent, Slightly Bitter
Turmeric	I	—	D	Bitter, Astringent, Hot, Dry

CONDIMENTS

Black olives	D	I	I	Salty
Catsup	D	I	I	Sour, Sweet
Chocolate—semisweet	I	D	I	Bitter, Astringent, Sweet
Chocolate—unsweetened	I	D	D	Bitter, Astringent
Honey	D	I	D	Sweet, Bitter, Astringent, Hot, Dry
Molasses	D	—	I	Sweet, Heavy, Hot
Mustard	D	I	D	Pungent, Oily, Sharp
Pickles—dill	D	I	D	Sour, Astringent, Salty
Pickles—sweet gherkin	D	—	D	Sweet, Slightly Astringent, Sour, Salty
Sugar	D	D	I	Sweet, Heavy, Cold
Tamari	D	I	I	Sour, Salty
Vanilla	—	—	—	Sweet
Vinegar	I	I	D	Astringent, Sour, Light, Dry

	VATA	PITTA	KAPHA	TASTE AND QUALITY
LENTILS AND BEANS				
Mung and other lentils	I	D	D	Light, Dry, Cold, Astringent
Other beans	I	D	I	Astringent, Dry, Heavy
Tofu (soy products)	—	D	I	Sweet, Heavy, Cold
Urad lentils	D	D	I	Sweet, Heavy, Oily, Hot
NUT BUTTERS				
Almond (blanched)	D	D	I	Sweet, Heavy, Oily
Almond (unblanched)	D	I	I	Sweet, Astringent, Hot, Heavy, Oily
Peanut	D	I	I	Sweet, Sour, Heavy, Oily
Raw cashew	D	D	I	Sweet, Heavy, Oily
Sesame (tahini)	D	I	I	Sweet, Astringent, Oily
VEGETABLES				
Artichoke	D	D	I	Sweet, Heavy, Cold
Asparagus	D	—	I	Sweet, Oily, Heavy
Avocado	D	—	I	Sweet, Oily, Heavy
Bean sprouts	I	D	D	Sweet, Salty, Bitter, Light
Beet greens	—	—	—	Sweet
Beets	D	D	I	Sweet, Astringent, Heavy
Broccoli	I	D	D	Sweet, Astringent, Bitter, Dry
Brussels sprouts	I	D	D	Sweet, Salty, Bitter, Dry
Cabbage	I	D	D	Sweet, Salty, Bitter, Dry
Carrots	—	I	D	Sweet, Oily, Astringent, Hot
Cauliflower	I	D	—	Sweet, Salty, Astringent, Dry
Celery (cooked)	D	D	I	Sweet
Celery (raw)	I	D	D	Astringent, Dry, Light, Cold
Celery leaves	I	I	D	Bitter, Astringent, Pungent
Corn	D	I	D	Sweet, Light, Hot
Cucumbers	D	—	I	Sweet, Cold, Heavy
Eggplant	I	D	D	Sweet, Light, Dry

	VATA	PITTA	KAPHA	TASTE AND QUALITY
Green beans	—	D	D	Sweet (if well cooked)
Lettuce	I	D	D	Sweet, Bitter, Pungent, Astringent, Light
Okra	D	D	I	Sweet, Smooth, Oily
Parsnips	I	D	—	Astringent, Sweet, Dry, Heavy
Peas	I	—	D	Sweet, Astringent, Light
Peppers (hot)	—	I	D	Pungent, Astringent
Peppers (sweet)	D	—	I	Sweet, Sharp
Popcorn	I	I	D	Sweet, Light Hot, Dry
Potato	I	D	I	Sweet, Astringent, Heavy, Dry
Radish	D	—	D	Pungent, Cold
Spinach	—	I	D	Astringent, Light, Hot
Squash	—	D	—	Sweet, Astringent, Heavy
Swiss chard	I	D	D	Bitter
Tomato	D	I	I	Sweet, Sour, Light
Water chestnuts	D	D	I	Sweet, Heavy, Cold
Yam or sweet potato	—	D	I	Sweet, Astringent, Dry, Heavy
Zucchini	I	—	D	Bitter, Sweet, Astringent, Cold
Zucchini (peeled)	—	—	D	Sweet, Astringent, Cold
FRUITS				
Apples	I	D	—	Sweet, Astringent, Light, Cold
Apples, green	D	I	D	Sour, Sweet, Light, Cold
Apricots	D	—	I	Sweet, Slightly Sour
Banana	D	I	I	Sweet, Heavy, Smooth
Cantaloupe (other melons)	D	D	I	Sweet, Cold, Heavy
Cherries (sour)	D	I	I	Sour, Heavy
Cherries (sweet)	D	D	I	Sweet, Heavy
Coconut	D	D	I	Sweet, Very Oily, Heavy
Cranberries	D	—	I	Sweet, Sour, Astringent
Currants	D	D	I	Sweet

	VATA	PITTA	KAPHA	TASTE AND QUALITY
Dates	D	D	I	Sweet, Heavy
Figs	D	D	I	Sweet, Heavy
Grapefruit	—	I	I	Sour, Sharp
Grapes	D	D	I	Sweet, Cold
Kiwi	D	D	I	Sweet, Cold
Lemon	D	I	I	Sour
Lime	D	D	I	Sour
Mango	D	I	I	Sweet, Sour, Cold
Orange (sour)	D	I	I	Sour, Sharp, Heavy
Orange (sweet)	D	—	I	Sweet, Sour
Papaya	—	I	D	Sweet
Peaches	D	D	I	Sweet, Slightly Sour, Heavy
Pears, unripe	I	D	D	Sour, Slightly Sweet, Dry, Light
Pears (very ripe or dried)	D	D	I	Sweet, Slightly Sour, Heavy, Cold
Persimmon	—	I	D	Sweet, Astringent
Pineapple (dried)	D	D	I	Sweet, Heavy
Pineapple (fresh)	D	D	I	Sweet, Slightly Sour, Cold
Pomegranate	I	D	D	Astringent, Sweet, Sour
Prunes and plums	D	D	I	Sweet, Slightly Sour, Heavy
Raisins	D	D	I	Sweet
Raspberries	D	D	I	Sweet, Slightly Bitter
Strawberries	D	I	I	Sweet, Slightly Sour
Watermelon	D	D	—	Sweet, Light, Cold
GRAINS				
Barley	I	—	D	Sweet, Astringent, Dry, Light
Buckwheat (kasha)	D	D	—	Sweet, Cold, Light
Corn	—	I	D	Sweet, Astringent, Hot, Light
Millet	—	—	D	Sweet
Oats	D	—	I	Sweet, Oily, Heavy
Rice, brown and white	D	D	I	Sweet, Cold, Light, Oily

	VATA	PITTA	KAPHA	TASTE AND QUALITY
Rye	D	I	D	Sour, Heavy
Wheat	D	D	I	Sweet, Cold, Oily, Heavy
OILS				
Coconut	D	D	I	Sweet, Very Heavy, Oily
Corn	D	I	D	Sweet, Light, Hot
Ghee	D	D	I	Sweet, Light, Cold, Oily
Margarine	D	I	I	Sweet, Astringent, Cold, Oily
Olive oil	D	D	I	Sweet, Astringent, Oily
Sesame oil	D	I	I	Sweet, Bitter, Astringent, Oily, Hot
Sunflower/ safflower oil	D	D	I	Sweet, Light, Oily
NUTS AND SEEDS				
Almonds (blanched)	D	D	D	Sweet, Heavy, Oily
Almonds (unblanched)	D	I	I	Sweet, Astringent, Hot, Oily
Cashews	D	D	I	Sweet, Heavy
Peanuts	D	I	I	Sweet, Sour, Heavy
Pumpkin seeds (roasted)	D	D	—	Sweet, Astringent
Sesame seeds	D	I	I	Sweet, Bitter, Astringent
Sunflower (raw)	D	D	I	Sweet, Heavy
Sunflower (roasted)	D	D	—	Sweet, Light
Walnuts	I	D	D	Astringent, Bitter

4

MAHARISHI AYUR-VED HEALTH CENTERS FOR NORTH AMERICA

This is a partial listing of Maharishi Ayur-Ved Health Centers, medical doctors, and chiropractic physicians. You can also find a professional trained in Maharishi Ayur-Ved by calling your local Transcendental Meditation Center or call 1-800-843-8332

Maharishi Ayur-Ved Health Center
National Office: United States
P.O. Box 282
Fairfield, IA 52556
515-472-8477

Maharishi Ayur-Ved Health Center
Canadian National Office
190 Lees Avenue
Ottawa, Ontario K1S 5L5
613-235-0952

Canada: Maharishi Ayur-Ved Health Center
RR #2
Huntsville, Ontario POA 1KO
705-635-2234

Los Angeles: Maharishi Ayur-Ved Health Center
17308 Sunset Boulevard
Pacific Palisades, CA 90272
213-454-5531

Massachusetts: Maharishi Ayur-Ved Health Center
679 George Hill Road
Lancaster, MA 01523
508-365-4549

Maharishi Ayur-Ved Health Center
4910 Massachusetts, NW, Suite 503
Washington, D.C. 20016
202-785-2700

MAIL-ORDER SOURCES FOR INGREDIENTS

Maharishi Ayur-Ved Products International (MAPI)
P.O. Box 541
Lancaster, MA 01523
1-800-ALL-VEDA (800-255-8332)
Ships worldwide all Maharishi Ayur-Ved teas, churnas, Purity Farms ghee.

Bazaar of India
1810 University Avenue
Berkeley, CA 94703
510-548-4110
Indian legumes, rice, and spices

Muskan Fine Indian Grocery
956 Thayer Avenue
Silver Spring, MD 20920
301-588-0331
Legumes, rice, herbal teas, churnas, ghee, high-quality hing, and other spices.

Frontier Herb and Spice Collection
P.O. Box 118
Norway, IA 52318
Extensive selection of teas, tea blends, herbs, and spices.

J.L. Hudson, Seedsman
P.O. Box 1058
Redwood City, CA 94064
Mexican cocoa beans.

GLOSSARY

AGNI (UGH-nee)—Fiery, heating element in nature; the digestive fire necessary for good digestion.

AMA (AH-muh)—A product of poor digestion and metabolism; a sticky substance that is inappropriately assimilated and deposited in the body, causing disease.

APPETIZER—A good appetizer tastes pungent or warm, sweet, and unctuous, or a combination of these. The colors red and gold are appetizing.

AYURVEDA (ah-yr-VAY-d-uh)—From the Sanskrit *ayu*, "life," and *veda* "knowledge." Ayurveda includes all aspects of life: consciousness, physiology, behavior, and environment.

DOSHAS (DOH-shus)—A fundamental quality or metabolic principle in the physiology and in all of nature. According to Ayurveda, each person is naturally an identifiable constitutional type called Vata, Pitta, or Kapha, or sometimes a combination of two or all three. Vata is most like air and space, Pitta like water and fire, and Kapha like earth and water.

GUNAS (GOO-nahs) or food categories—The three categories making up nature are first, the pure, light, superior sattva; second, active, energetic rajas; and third, dull, sleepy tamas. All three gunas are found in living things.

KAPHA (KUHF or KUHF-uh)—One of three doshas or fundamental qualities that provide structure in the physiology. Its nature is moist, cold, heavy, smooth, and solid.

MAHARISHI AYUR-VEDA—Maharishi Mahesh Yogi, founder of the Transcendental Meditation program, working closely with leading scholars and physicians, has restored the ancient science of Ayurveda to completeness. This fully integrated science of health is called Maharishi Ayur-Ved.

PITTA (PIT or PIT-uh)—A light, dry, hot, and energetic dosha or fundamental quality that governs metabolism and transformation in the physiology.

PRAKRITI (PRUH-kri-tee)—One's constitution or nature from birth, i.e., Vata, Pitta, Kapha, or a combination of these.

RASAYANAS (rah-SAI-uh-nahz)—Foods or herbs that promote longevity. A rasayana contains all the nutrition needed for the development of every body tissue. "Rasa" denotes essence, the first extraction in the digestive process that provides for the growth of the entire physical system.

TRANSCENDENTAL MEDITATION TECHNIQUE (TM)—A simple, natural mental technique, as taught by Maharishi Mahesh Yogi, for gaining deep rest, happiness, improved health, and clear thinking. Especially useful in preparation for all activities, including cooking. It is the primary approach of Maharishi Ayur-Ved to creating perfect health.

VATA (VAHT or VAHT-uh)—From the Sanskrit *vayu*, it is most like air and space. One of three doshas or fundamental qualities, dry, cold, lightweight, windy, Vata governs movement in the physiology.

ACKNOWLEDGMENTS

I wish to thank all those who helped with this project, especially Dr. Haridas S. Kasture and Dr. Pramod D. Subhedar, experts in Ayurveda, for sharing their vast knowledge and helping me research Ayurveda and the American cuisine. I am particularly grateful to them for the many times they acted as cheerful subjects, in what can only be called food experiments, who tasted—in the name of Science—many unfamiliar Western foods. My thanks, too, to the invaluable doctors and staff of the Maharishi Ayur-Ved Association of America in Fairfield, Iowa. To Joel Silver, M.D., who originated this book, Richard Averbach, M.D., and Stuart Rothenberg, M.D., whose class, Ayurvedic Diet and Menu Planning, served as the basis for the text, and to the Department of Continuing Education at Maharishi International University for offering its unique series of courses in Maharishi Ayur-Ved Science. And thanks to dear Clara Berno, good friend of hundreds of mothers and babies.

I am very grateful to all my friends, fellow cooks, and recipe developers for their contributions: Pamela Volponi, Tim and Lisa Messenger, Deanna Freeberg, Joanne Madden, Ulricke Selleck, Alan Scherr, Rick Weller, Jan Thatcher, Teresa Mottet, Bruce Rash, Judie Hickey, Lois Ducombs, and especially Elaine Arnold, who was always willing to make (and sample) just one more test batch of brownies. A special debt of gratitude goes to Pat Hurst, lover of good food, who tested and retested recipes, cheerfully developed new ones at a moment's notice, and helped at every research session.

For clear words about writing and publishing, my thanks to Melanie Brown, Denise Denniston Gerace, and Bill Cates. Thanks to Claudia Petrick, precise of pen and cheerful always, to John Michel and Valerie Kuscenko this edition's editors, to publisher Peter Guzzardi—a man of true vision and tenacity—and to my wise and spendid agent, Muriel Nellis, who for some reason never loses her sense of humor.

To Jay Glaser, M.D., medical director of Maharishi Ayur-Ved Health Center in Lancaster, Massachusetts, for generously giving of his time to comment on the manuscript and offer suggestions.

Thanks to the foremost Ayurvedic physicians, Dr. B. D. Triguna, Dr. Balaraj, Dr. V. M. Dwivedi, and Dr. Har Sharma, M.D., for helping to enliven Maharishi Ayur-Ved in its full and complete value.

Most of all I want to thank Maharishi Mahesh Yogi the complete knowledge of Vedic science and Maharishi Ayur-Ved, on which this book is based.

Jai Guru Dev

❖•❖

INDEX

Cookies and crackers (*cont.*)
  Jam Diagonals, 206–7
  Lemony Date Bars, 207–8
  Mother's Laddu, 208–9
  oatmeal raisin, 62, 63, 209–10
  shortbread, 210–11
Cooking generally. *See also* Vata;
    Pitta; Kapha; Menus
  equipment and utensils, 37–38
  heating of foods, 34
  kitchen and cook. *See* Kitchen
  methods of, 34–35, 232
  mixed group, cooking for, 38–39
  pressure cookers, 35
  before serving, 39–40
  time savers, 35
  workplace meals, 38
Coriander, 103
Corn bread, 77, 80–81, 96, 153–54,
    265
Couscous, 177–78
  rich and satisfying, 228, 265
Crackers. *See* Cookies and crackers
Cravings, 27
Cream
  Chantilly, 227–28, 246, 247
  English, 215–16
  whipping cream, 89
Cream Tahini Sauce, 132–33
Creamy Rice Pudding, 48, 52, 222–23
Creamy Summer Garden Soup, 61,
    62, 64–65, 159–60
Cucumber and tomato raita, 143–44
Cumin, 103
Curds and whey, 91–92
Curries and curried dishes
  cheese dip, 115–16
  panir and vegetables, 170–72
  squash soup, 160
  sweet summer, 188–89, 239, 240–41
  vegetable, 185–87, 239, 240
Custard pie, chocolate, 48, 52

Dahl, 97–98
  Masoor Dahl, 163, 239, 265

Perfect Lentil Soup, 164, 265
  salads with rice and, 279
Dairy products, 89–92. *See also*
    specific types
  charts of ingredients, 284
  curds and whey, 91–92
  for Kapha, 73
  for Pitta, 59
  for Vata, 45
Dates
  Lemony Date Bars, 207–8
  shake, 108
Deanna's Vinaigrette, 128
Desserts
  Apple Dumplings with Vanilla
    Sauce, 196–98
  brownies, 211–12, 252–53
  cakes. *See* Cakes
  Cashew Nut Balls or Squares,
    203–4, 239, 243
  chocolate mousse, 219, 220, 229
  cookies. *See* Cookies and crackers
  Creamy Rice Pudding, 48, 52,
    222–23
  Jam Diagonals, 206–7
  Kaffa's Dream, 223–25
  for Kapha, 77, 81, 83
  laddus, 203–4, 208–9
  Lemon Scones, 226
  Lemony Date Bars, 207–8
  Macedonia di Frutta, 248, 249,
    250
  mocha mousse, 229
  Mother's Laddu, 208–9
  Pêche Cardinal, 227–28, 244, 246,
    247
  pies and pastries. *See* Pies and
    pastries
  Pineapple Ice, 62, 63, 225–26
  for Pitta, 62, 63, 68–69
  rice pudding, 48, 52, 222–23
  R&S Couscous, 228
  shortbread, 210–11
  shortcake, 213–14
  for Vata, 48, 52, 54–55
  White Figs à la Kapha, 77, 81, 229

Vinegar, 126–27
Vishesha, 10

Water, 85–86
  boiled, 86, 263–64, 279
  iced, 85, 86
  with meals, 86, 256
Watermelon-Strawberry Punch, 113–
  14, 252, 253
Weather. *See* Climate and season
Webb, Bill D., 94
Weight loss
  diet, 257–65
  for new mothers, 268
Wheat, 95–96, 105, 279
White Figs à la Kapha, 77, 81, 229

White Figs in Apricot Cream Sauce,
  230
Wild rice casserole, 169–70, 265
Wilted Ginger Lettuce, 144–45, 242–
  43
Workplace meals, 38

Yogurt
  lassi. *See* Lassi
  making of, 150–51
  raitas, 143–44, 239, 241
  Strawberry Yogurt Pie, 200–201

Zucchini and Tomato Fry, 48, 51–52,
  193–94